THE GRIM SLEEPER

THE GRIM SLEEPER

THE LOST WOMEN OF SOUTH CENTRAL

CHRISTINE PELISEK

COUNTERPOINT
BERKELEY, CALIFORNIA

This book is based on police reports, court documents, autopsy reports, and interviews with detectives, family members, and other sources.

The names of certain individuals in this book have been changed to protect their privacy, and the author has reconstructed dialogue to the best of her recollection.

First Counterpoint hardcover edition: June 2017

ISBN: 978-1-61902-724-4

The Library of Congress Cataloging-in-Publication Data is available.

Jacket design by Natalia Mosquera
Book design by Tabitha Lahr

COUNTERPOINT
2560 Ninth Street, Suite 318
Berkeley, CA 94710
www.counterpointpress.com

Printed in the United States of America
Distributed by Publishers Group West

10 9 8 7 6 5 4 3 2

To my parents, Mary and Joe Pelisek

and

To the women of South Central: Debra, Henrietta, Barbara, Bernita, Mary, Lachrica, Monique, Princess, Valerie, Janecia, Sharon, Georgia Mae, Inez, Rolenia, Laura, and Enietra

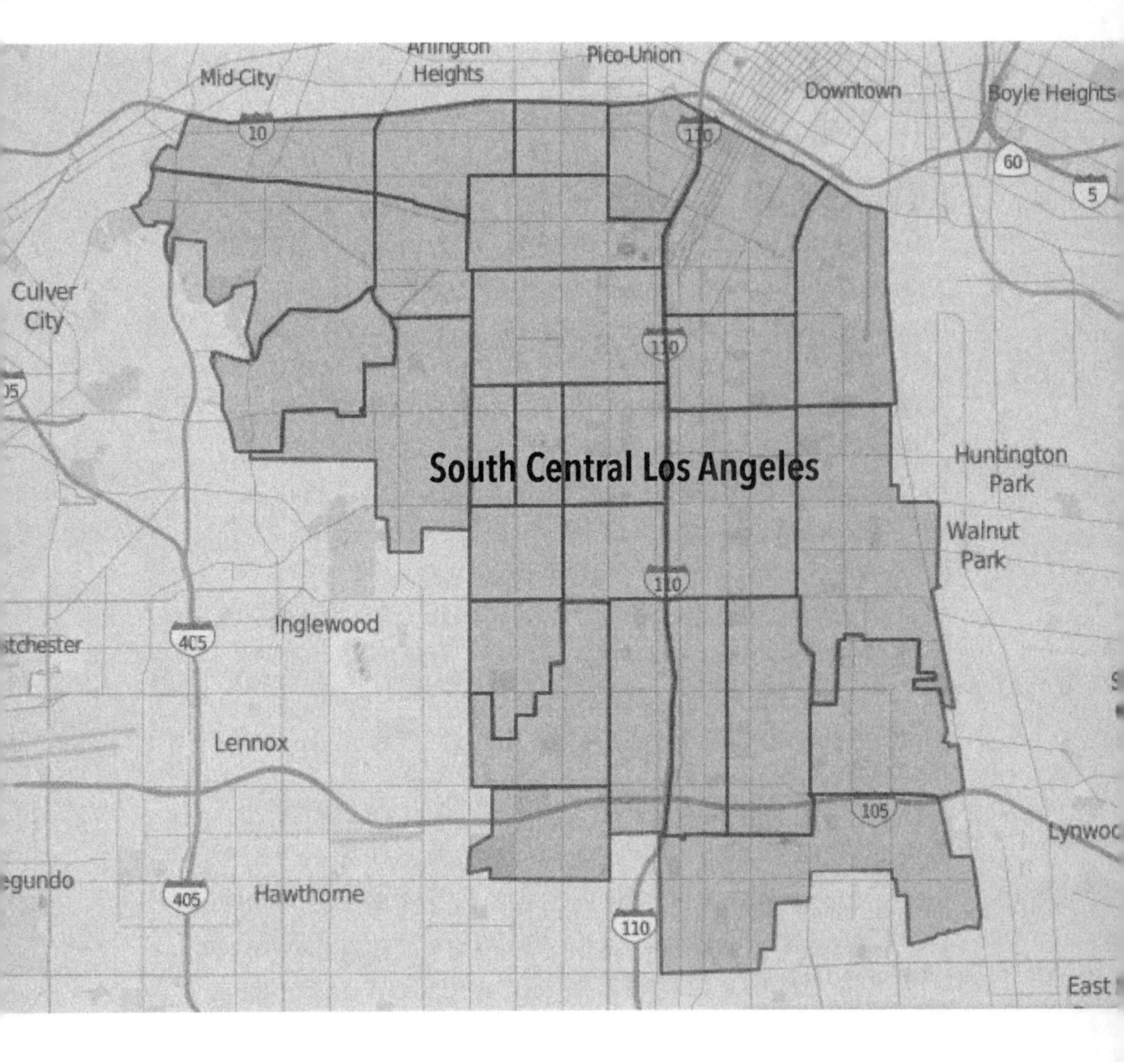
Mid-City
Heights
Pico-Union
Downtown
Boyle Heights
10
110
60
5
Culver
City
110
South Central Los Angeles
Huntington
Park
Walnut
Park
110
Inglewood
405
Lennox
105
405
Hawthorne
110
East

CONTENTS

Proximity of Crime Scenes Locations

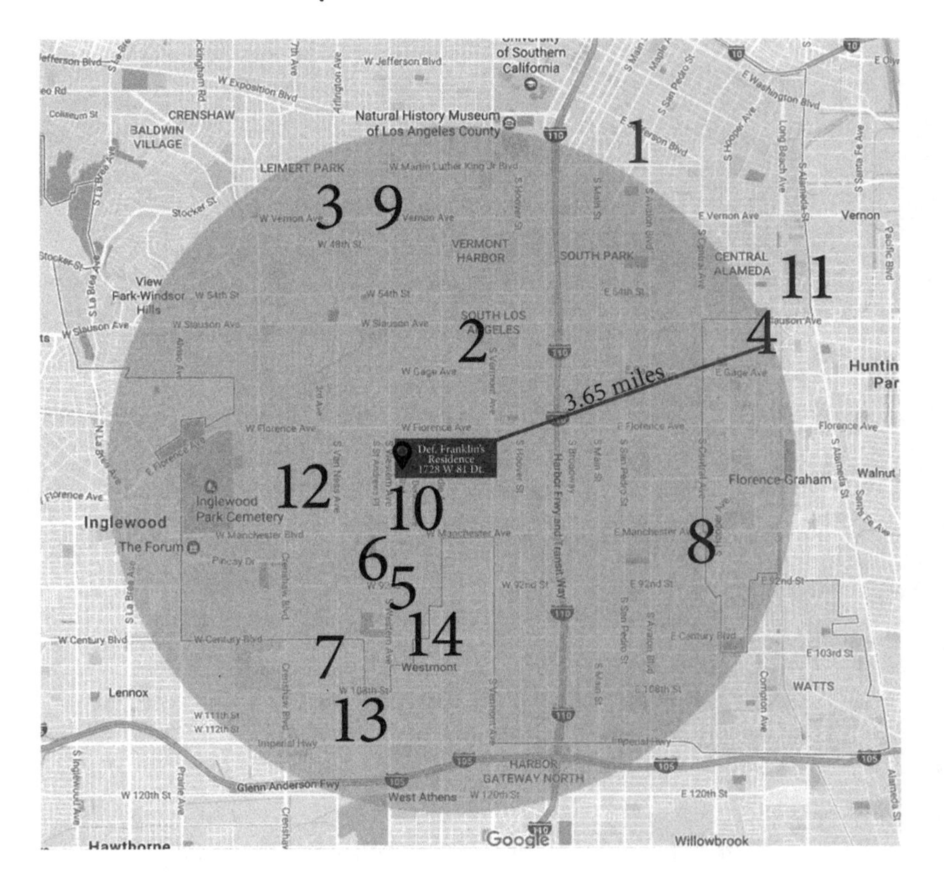

1. Sharon Dismuke
   January 15, 1984
   southwest corner:
   MLK Boulevard and
   San Predro Street

2. Debra Jackson
   August 10, 1985
   1017 W. Gage Avenue

3 Henrietta Wright
   August 12, 1986
   2514 W. Vernon Av-
   enue

4. Barbara Ware
   January 10, 1987
   1256 E. 56th Street

5. Bernita Sparks
   April 16, 1987
   9414 S. Western
   Avenue

6. Mary Lowe
   November 1, 1987
   8927 S. Hobart
   Boulevard

7. Lachrica Jefferson
   January 30, 1988
   2049 W. 102nd Place

8. Inez Warren
   August 15, 1988
   1137 E. 87th Street

9. Alicia Alexander
   September 11, 1988
   1720 W. 43rd Place

10. Enietra Washington
    November 20, 1988
    84th Street and
    Denker

11. Georgia Mae Thomas
    December 18, 2000
    1846 E. 57th Street

12. Princess Berthomieux
    March 19, 2002
    8121 S. Van Ness
    Boulevard

13. Valerie McCorvey
    July 11, 2003
    556 W. 108th Street

14. Janecia Peters
    January 1, 2007
    9508 S. Western
    Avenue

PROLOGUE
WINTER'S LIST

SO MANY CELEBRITIES HAVE PASSED through the Los Angeles County Department of Medical Examiner-Coroner, you'd think the city of stars would have located it in a better part of town. Instead the next-to-final resting place for the likes of John Belushi, Whitney Houston, and Michael Jackson is at the end of a rundown row of auto-body shops and cheap taco joints, two miles east of downtown.

On a cold morning in January of 2006, I parked Maude Jr., my beat-up red '94 Toyota Tercel, in the office lot and headed into the coroner's investigative division hoping for my next big headline. Once inside the wood-paneled lobby, I buzzed the reception desk.

"I'm here to see Assistant Chief Winter," I told the receptionist.

Five minutes later, she let me in.

I didn't need directions to the office of Ed Winter. As a crime reporter for the *L.A. Weekly*, an alternative paper modeled on New York's *Village Voice*, I had been there many times, following up on gang murders, robberies gone awry, organized crime hits, and the like. The unluckiest victims always wound up here. So did the bodies of departed Hollywood celebrities and has-beens. With more than fifty dead people a day passing through the busiest coroner's office in the U.S., there was usually a story to be told, if Winter was in the mood to tell it.

Winter, the coroner's media liaison, was a former cop who served in a Los Angeles suburb as a SWAT team member and undercover narcotics officer.

I started pestering him shortly after he was hired in 2003. He was brought in to help rehabilitate the coroner's office, which had been shaken by a series of scandals, including a rat infestation at the long-term storage crypt in which rodents had chewed into some of the body bags and gnawed on some of the corpses. Winter's experience and laid-back personality won him the position of official spokesman whenever a celebrity died. By the time I walked into his life with my chicken-scratch-filled reporter's notebook, he was a seasoned pro who had handled the hanging suicide of onetime child actor Jonathan Brandis; the strange death of Robert Pastorelli, who played portly painter Eldin Bernecky on *Murphy Brown*; and the death of "Super Freak" singer Rick James.

Winter's first day on the job catapulted him into one of the city's biggest murder mysteries: the death of 40-year-old Lana Clarkson, the B-list actress and House of Blues nightclub hostess found fatally shot in the Alhambra mansion of much-heralded but nonetheless oddball music producer Phil Spector. Winter learned quickly how important it was to choose his words carefully because they would appear the next day in print and could define a celebrity's life after death.

On this January day, he sat behind his scarred wooden desk and stared intently at his computer screen. His eyes shifted briefly to a mini replica of the Harley-Davidson he rode on the weekends. Then, he waved me to a seat.

"What brings you here today?" he asked. There was a hint of a smirk on his face as he rubbed his fingers over his salt-and-pepper goatee. It seemed something was up.

"Just checking in. Anything interesting going on?" I asked casually, gesturing to an autopsy report on his desk.

"No," he said flatly, and he slid the report into the top drawer. I smiled and reached across his desk to retrieve a butterscotch candy from a glass bowl. It was going to be one of those cat-and-mouse days.

As a crime reporter, I regularly popped by to see Winter. When I was on the hunt for an autopsy report or digging up information about a cause of death, he was the first person I called. Winter not only provided the information I was looking for, but when he was in the mood, he also gave me valuable investigative tips that only a veteran cop could know and understand as vital to doing a thorough job. And when he was in a really forthcoming mood, he would offer me a Starbucks iced coffee from his mini fridge.

It didn't appear that this day would be a Starbucks day.

"Did you have many deaths over the weekend?" I began, slowly.

Winter plucked a sheet of paper from his top desk drawer and gave me a quick rundown of the latest fatalities. He read them off like a high-school teacher calling out names on an attendance sheet. Two Hispanic families were killed in separate car accidents on the Interstate 5 Freeway near Norwalk, a suburban city seventeen miles southeast of downtown. An elderly black man had been found rotting on his couch in Northridge, an affluent neighborhood in the San Fernando Valley. His death went unnoticed for a month until the sickening sweet smell of decomposition reached the next-door neighbor, who called police.

There were at least six African American and Hispanic men, all under the age of 25, on the list. All shot in drive-bys, car-to-car gun battles, or street confrontations. In some of those cases, the last question the victim heard before being shot was, "Where are you from?" It wasn't a question about geography but about gang affiliation, and in Los Angeles in 2006, that simple question was synonymous with death. Although the murder rate in Los Angeles County was much lower than in the '80s and '90s, gang-related homicides were an ever-present danger.

"It's just another typical weekend in Los Angeles," Winter said sardonically as he tucked the list back inside his desk drawer. "As you can tell, we've been very, very busy."

"Anything else?" I asked, knowing full well gang-related deaths wouldn't electrify my editor, not in a city like Los Angeles where gang crime is as common as massage parlors and palm trees.

Winter put down his coffee cup and sent me a stern look. I wondered if I should make my way out.

"Actually, we've been looking at some female body-dump cases," he said. A body dump is a case in which the victim is killed in one location and then moved to another, often an alleyway or dumpster. Body dumps are notoriously difficult cases to solve.

He went on to tell me that many of the women were found in South Central. Other bodies were scattered around Los Angeles County, including the suburbs of Inglewood, Lynwood and Long Beach, and Hollywood, he said.

The coroner's investigators had told Winter six months earlier they'd noticed an alarming number of body dumps at routine death-scene locations. Winter's staff compiled a list of thirty-eight female victims who had died under suspicious circumstances in Los Angeles County since 2002. Winter launched a serial-killer task force of sorts a few weeks after his conversation with the coroner's investigators, suspecting that some of the cases might be linked. He didn't have the manpower to pull his crime-scene investigators from their day jobs, so when they had free time they were encouraged to look into the thirty-eight cases for similarities.

"Are any of the cases connected?" I asked.

"We don't know yet," he said testily. "They're suspicious. Some of them are similar. Some aren't. That's why we are looking at them."

"Have you made any progress?" I asked.

"No," he admitted. "We're always sidelined by new cases."

"Are the cops looking at the cases?" I asked.

With more than a hint of resentment in his voice, Winter said he reached out to the agencies handling the bulk of the cases, the Los Angeles Police Department and the Los Angeles County Sheriff's

Department, but was ignored. Homicide investigators do not like coroner officials—or journalists for that matter—poking around their cases.

"Let me have the list," I blurted out, not realizing the journey I was about to embark on. "I'll look into the cases."

"We are handling this," he said. "I don't need you poking your nose into this. I'll keep you posted. Keep this under wraps. Now, leave. I have work to do."

• • •

I left Winter's office wondering if there could be a serial killer responsible for the deaths of some of the women on the list. It seemed unlikely, but stranger things have occurred in Los Angeles County, which has a long history of producing and attracting twisted mad men.

Among them:

Skid Row Slasher Vaughn Greenwood, who terrorized transients in the Skid Row area of downtown Los Angeles and Hollywood in the '60s and '70s, cutting their throats as they slept.

Dating Game Killer Rodney Alcala, a *Los Angeles Times* typesetter, amateur photographer, and film student of Roman Polanski's, who photographed his victims before sexually assaulting, killing, and grotesquely posing them. Alcala's reign of terror began in 1968, one year before Charles Manson and his followers committed the terrifying and sensational Tate-LaBianca murders of seven people, including Polanski's wife, the pregnant actress Sharon Tate.

Hillside Strangler killers Angelo Buono and Kenneth Bianchi, who raped, tortured, and murdered girls and women between 1977 and 1978 and left their bodies on hillsides near downtown Los Angeles.

Freeway Killer William Bonin, an unemployed truck driver who confessed to raping, torturing, and killing twenty-one boys and men in Orange and Los Angeles counties in 1979 and 1980.

And Night Stalker Richard Ramirez, who in 1989 was convicted of thirteen horrific torture-murders during a 1985 killing spree.

• • •

Winter's list of dead women intrigued me. I had been fascinated with serial killers since I was a child growing up in the sleepy Canadian capital city of Ottawa. I devoured books about Ted Bundy and Killer Clown John Wayne Gacy and was fixated on shows like *Columbo* and *Murder, She Wrote*. I also read a lot of true-crime books, including *Helter Skelter*, which detailed the Manson murders.

When I moved to Los Angeles, I must admit I was hoping, however naïve I was or how dim my prospects were, to report on elusive criminal deviants. And, somehow, through my job at the *L.A. Weekly*, which I all but stumbled into, I was able to do just that. I spoke to a lot of retired detectives who had worked serial-killer cases, including the Night Stalker and Hillside Strangler. I was mesmerized by their investigative skills and intrigued by how they eventually caught the predators. I asked a lot of questions. And, for whatever reasons—maybe they liked the attention, maybe they saw my interest was serious, maybe both—they told me about their methods and all sorts of details about hours of legwork. I absorbed all that I could and learned much from their advice. All of which, I knew, would come into play and serve me well if I could get Winter to confirm what my budding gut instinct was telling me, that a serial killer was on the loose.

Like the detectives, I wanted to dig further. I liked doing the legwork, the research, all the fact-checking and cross-checking information. I needed to get a look at Winter's list.

It took two months of constant badgering and pestering before Winter finally handed it over. The day I got it, I rushed out of his office as fast as a burglar fleeing a tripped home-alarm system and hopped into Maude Jr., praying she'd start. She did, first try, and I sped out of the parking lot. I had visions of Winter having a change of heart and chasing me to the parking lot with his team of investigators in hot pursuit.

About two blocks from the coroner's office I pulled over at one of the many auto-repair shops on Mission Road and looked at the list of thirty-eight suspicious deaths. It was divided into two sections. The first section, titled "Current Coroner Cases Under Inquiry/Serial Homicide Team, Female Non-African American Supplement 2002–Present," listed the names and ages of twenty white, Asian, and Hispanic victims and the law-enforcement agencies and detectives handling the cases. The second section, "Current Coroner Cases Under Inquiry/Serial Homicide Team, Female African American Profile 2002–Present," had the same information about eighteen black women.

I was struck by the sheer number of dead women and pictured the tear-stained faces of those who grieved for them. I imagined their anger, fear, loss, and want for justice and revenge. I tried to put myself in their place and to imagine how they felt, knowing they would never see their loved ones again. I also thought about the detectives handling the deaths and wondered if they were making more headway tracking down their killers than the coroner's office was.

I put the pages down and my car in gear and was back at the *L.A. Weekly* office in fifteen minutes. The newspaper was in Hollywood on a sleazy stretch of Sunset Boulevard known for its cheap motels, fast-food joints, and crack-addicted prostitutes. During my first week on the job I was accosted by a john at 10 A.M. who asked if I wanted to party. He offered a six-pack of Budweiser as an incentive. The locale was shabby, but it was the perfect spot for the motley crew at the *L.A. Weekly*, the number one source for music, arts, film, theater, culture, and concerts in Los Angeles. Plenty of well-known writers had graced its pages, including Pulitzer Prize–winning food writer Jonathan Gold, *Los Angeles Times* reporter Gale Holland who writes about the homeless, *Los Angeles Times* arts and culture writer Deborah Vankin, award-winning journalist and writer Joe Donnelly, and Associated Press entertainment reporter and critic Sandy Cohen. It was also the one-time home of extreme performance artist Ron Athey and gender queen Dr. Vaginal Davis.

I made my way to news editor Alan Mittelstaedt's office waving the list I'd been given by Winter. Mittelstaedt was on his way out. He knew of my obsession with the list and my dogged pursuit of getting a copy.

"What's your game plan?" he asked.

To get a hold of the autopsy reports, which were vital to my investigation, I told him. These reports would give me the dates and circumstances of the deaths, including the locations. I was hoping the reports would provide me with some much-needed clues so I could find out if the cases were linked and whether or not a serial killer was on the loose. And if there was a serial killer, I hoped that the detectives handling the cases would confirm as much, if they even knew.

By the end of the month, I had, courtesy of Winter, a stack of autopsy reports as thick as a three-tiered birthday cake. I started calling the detectives in the reports and setting up appointments so I could learn more about the murders and find out if any had been solved. It took a few days for the detectives to start calling back, and when they did, I soon discovered that many of the cases on the list were not homicides at all. There were suicides, drug overdoses, and even natural deaths.

In one case, a prostitute was found dead in a car that had been set on fire. Police determined she died from a drug overdose. The car was set ablaze by a john after she overdosed because he didn't want his DNA evidence left behind. Another young woman on the list was found bloody and slumped in her bed. There were no signs of foul play or a break-in, and police eventually determined she had died of natural causes.

Still, there were plenty of homicide cases that hadn't yet been solved. Some of the cases involved random shootings, but the bulk of them were murdered prostitutes, the most invisible and vulnerable class of people. One truism I absorbed from my informal homicide schooling: Killers know it's easier to get away with murdering someone living on the fringes of society than a so-called mainstream citizen.

The Los Angeles County detectives were surprised by my interest in prostitute killings. They rarely got calls from reporters asking about dead, drug-addicted streetwalkers. It wasn't something the media usually focused on.

But where I grew up in Ottawa, Ontario, Canada, murder was never an everyday occurrence. In fact, my life had never been touched by murder. When I first moved to L.A. in the '90s, I was stunned by the level of gun violence. The daily bloodbaths in Los Angeles and the culture of guns and gangs were alien to me. I was particularly shocked at the sheer number of black prostitutes and drug-addicted women killed. These women, whose bodies appeared to litter the streets, seemed to be invisible in their own city. I wanted people to do something. I wanted grieving family members to get some acknowledgment of their loss, some salve for their pain. I felt as a reporter at a local paper it was my job to write about them, to tell their stories to the people in their city. I wanted to make them visible so the community had to face this sick and twisted problem and, somehow, do a better job of dealing with it.

In L.A., the death of a prostitute rarely made the nightly news, unless it involved a serial killer. The media tends to focus on mass killings or the disappearance of beautiful young students.

Murdered prostitutes made up nearly half of the thirty-eight women on Winter's list. Most of them were strangled, shot, or stabbed. Some were beaten so badly they were barely recognizable. Almost all of them were disposed of like trash in the dark alleyways of South Central[1] or tossed on the streets or in parks across Los Angeles County.

Each case was heart-wrenching. Ashley Veater was a 19-year-old

1. South Central, which later became known as South Los Angeles, is a region of Los Angeles County. It is fifty-one square miles and is divided into twenty-eight neighborhoods, including Watts, West Adams, and Exposition Park.

from Idaho who told her family she moved to Los Angeles to start a career in the fashion industry. She was found dead in a Hollywood alley on June 28, 2005. For the three days before she was killed, Ashley, who was thirteen weeks pregnant, strolled near the gas station on Sunset Boulevard and Fairfax Avenue. It was a good place to meet johns looking for a quickie in the middle of the afternoon. She was discrete, hanging out in alleyways next to the coffee shops and liquor stores a few blocks from the fabled Sunset Strip. It didn't take long for the striking blonde with a lovely smile to get a client. She worked from noon to 4 P.M., servicing men taking lunch breaks or on their way home from work. She was living at a sleazy Sunset Boulevard motel with her pimp boyfriend since returning to Los Angeles from a stay in Las Vegas. This was not her first foray into streetwalking; she had been arrested for prostitution in Hollywood the year before.

Ashley's feet and hands were bound with duct tape, and a black plastic trash bag covered her head. She had been strangled with a black-sock ligature, and part of her ear had been ripped off. The following day, an anonymous person placed candles where her body was found and painted a large heart around a patch of her dried blood. A message in red spray paint read: "I Love . . . with all MY HEART BYE BYE."

Police rarely get calls from loved ones when it comes to prostitutes, but Ashley's boyfriend alerted the police immediately when she didn't answer his calls or return to the motel. Police ruled him out as a suspect after checking his motel room code key and determining that he had not left their room all day. He told police he spoke to her minutes before she picked up her last client, and she seemed upbeat. The couple had arranged to meet at the gas station at 4 P.M.

The killer had left his human detritus behind, but the DNA didn't match any names in local, state, or federal felony databases, so there was little detectives could do with the information.

Another vicious murder on Winter's list was that of 38-year-old Leah Benjamin, a promising California State University, Stanislaus accounting student before she became a drug addict. Leah went in and out of drug treatment programs and sober-living homes but couldn't escape her addiction. She ended up among the black prostitutes with drug problems turning tricks on Figueroa Street, the infamous stretch in South Central known for its prostitution, liquor stores, used-car lots, and cheap motels. Her father, John Benjamin, had plans to meet his daughter at his insurance business the day she went missing. He wanted her to spend time with her daughter, the grandchild he and his wife were raising. But Leah never showed up.

Leah's body was discovered wrapped in a blanket in an alley in South Central on April 10, 2004. Her feet were bound with duct tape and her head was wrapped in a black plastic trash bag. She had numerous stab wounds to her head and face. Her dress was lifted up, exposing her genitals, and her nylons were pulled down around her ankles.[2]

As the months passed, I realized police suspected some of the cases on Winter's list could be linked, but without DNA confirmation they had no proof. By May of 2006 I had reviewed thirty-six cases on the coroner's list and was down to the last two: the March 9, 2002, strangulation murder of 15-year-old Princess Berthomieux, a foster-care runaway turned prostitute, in Inglewood, a city southwest of Los Angeles, and the July 11, 2003, strangulation murder of Valerie McCorvey, a 35-year-old black prostitute who had been working the streets of South Central on and off for years.

After numerous failed attempts to reach him, Inglewood Police Department Detective Jeffrey Steinhoff, the lead investigator in the Princess Berthomieux case, finally agreed to meet me in May. Standoffish at first, he wanted to know my interest in the case. When I told him about the list Winter had given me, he loosened up and became more forthcoming. He wanted to talk about Princess Berthomieux. He wanted her killer caught.

What he said next shocked me.

Princess was linked through DNA evidence to Valerie McCorvey, the last victim on Winter's list. And there was more. These two

2. In June of 2015, Hawthorne resident Jaqwun Turner was charged with the rape and murder of Leah Benjamin. He is awaiting trial. No one has been charged with Ashley Veater's killing.

cases were linked through DNA to a series of murders that began in August of 1985, when the crack epidemic in South Central was in a full-bore rage. All were tied by ballistics evidence to the same killer. These victims—Debra Jackson, Henrietta Wright, Barbara Ware, Bernita Sparks, Mary Lowe, Lachrica Jefferson, and Alicia "Monique" Alexander—were all young black women who lived in South Central and struggled with drug addiction. Their partially clothed bodies were all dumped in dirty neighborhood alleyways, left to rot under garbage and debris, near bustling Western Avenue. The seven women were shot at close range with a .25-caliber pistol. None were found with identification, but the killer left his mark—saliva on many of the victims' breasts. I later learned that there was one survivor, Enietra Washington, who was shot, sexually assaulted, and left for dead on the same mean streets.

I also discovered that back in the '80s, a task force of detectives with the Los Angeles County Sheriff's Department and the LAPD was set up to investigate serial murders plaguing the South Central neighborhood, including the seven murders Steinhoff had alerted me to.

Neither the police nor its Southside Slayer Task Force solved these seven murders, and the detectives moved on to other cases. But Steinhoff seemed to be focused on a man whom he thought might have escaped justice for more than two decades.

His name was Roger Hausmann. He was a white repo man and former pimp who went by the nickname Super Honky.

• • •

On Tuesday, August 3, 2005, Steinhoff received a phone call from J. J. Smith, a Fresno County District Attorney's office investigator who was assisting the Fresno Police Department in a kidnapping case involving Roger Hausmann and two black teenaged girls.

Smith told Steinhoff that when he interviewed the girls, they both mentioned that Hausmann admitted to murders in Los Angeles. And he said that he had rolled up the victims' bodies in rugs and blankets and tossed them in the river.

Hausmann, 65, had been the subject of a task-force investigation in the early '90s involving the death of twenty-five mostly young black female prostitutes between 18 and 30 years old, who were murdered between May 1977 and November 1990. They were shot, strangled, stabbed, or pummeled with a blunt object. Some of them had been bound and gagged. Their bodies were found in irrigation canals, vacant lots, fields, and abandoned houses in Fresno, about two hundred miles north of Los Angeles.

The Fresno Police Department considered Hausmann a suspect in the murders of the prostitutes after he was arrested in 1991 for allegedly beating a prostitute with a steam iron. According to a November 4, 1993, *Fresno Bee* article, the woman told police that Hausmann said, "You're harder to kill than the other ones." A man who allegedly witnessed the beating also heard Hausmann say, "This one is hard to kill."

Hausmann denied the allegations, pleaded no contest to assault with a deadly weapon and false imprisonment for the steam iron beating, spent twenty-nine months in jail, and got out in November 1993.

The task force disbanded but detectives still believed that Hausmann had something to do with some of the unsolved murders. In May 2006, Steinhoff filed a search warrant affidavit seeking a judge's permission to take Hausmann's DNA sample to see if he was responsible for the murders of Princess Berthomieux, Valerie McCorvey, and the seven related murders from the '80s. At the time, Hausmann was in jail in Fresno awaiting his trial for the kidnapping of the two teenagers.

"Based on my training and experience, I believe that Hausmann is a suspect in these homicides," Steinhoff wrote in the affidavit. "Hausmann admitted that he has killed people and wrapped them in carpets in the Los Angeles area. One victim was covered with a carpet, one covered with a blanket, one covered with a trash bag, and three were covered with debris."

Steinhoff also wrote that Hausmann was cited for a traffic offense in Inglewood three months before Princess's murder.

According to Steinhoff's affidavit, Hausmann had an extensive criminal history that dated back to 1959, with arrests in Los Angeles, Fresno, and Bakersfield for suspicion of lewd acts against a child, unlawful sexual intercourse, enticing a minor female for prostitution and pimping, carrying a loaded firearm, exhibiting a deadly weapon, and assault with a deadly weapon.

Steinhoff went to Hausmann's jail cell to obtain a saliva sample for a DNA test. While Steinhoff was waiting for Hausmann's DNA results, I drove to Fresno in Maude Jr. and met Hausmann's former boss at his repo job and asked him to arrange a jailhouse interview for me. I was surprised Hausmann was willing to talk. During our interview, the five-foot-seven convict with thinning blond hair and intense blue eyes told me he was innocent of the recent kidnapping charges.

"I was set up by the Fresno police," he said.

"Why would they set you up?" I asked.

"Because I'm a Christian Jew who loves black women," he told me. His last girlfriend, he said, was nicknamed peanut butter because she "spread so easy."

Charming.

Hausmann stared at me intently during our thirty-minute conversation. This was my first prison interview, and I found that slightly unnerving. I was reassured by the fact that I was speaking to him over the phone from behind a glass partition.

He denied murdering anyone in L.A. or Fresno, and he seemed to take his predicament in stride. His stories about police misconduct seemed far-fetched, exaggerated, and at times comical. He claimed he was a regular target of the Fresno police.

Police were after him, he said, because he refused to provide them with drugs.

"They called me a nigger lover and Jew boy slave," he told me, which I later detailed in an *L.A. Weekly* cover story.

"Were you ever a pimp or a drug dealer?" I asked.

"Yes," Hausmann replied with a slight grin, regaling me with tales of prostitution out of bars in Beverly Hills. He also sold cocaine in Fresno and Los Angeles. But all that changed, he said, when he became a Christian in 1995.

"I flushed down the toilet two kilos of cocaine, still in the Medellin Cartel wrappers," he said proudly.

When I asked him if he attacked the prostitute with a steam iron in 1991, Hausmann said he would never hit a lady unless she hit him first—then added that she smacked him over the head with a bronze ashtray. "The prostitute said that when you were attacking her, you told her, 'You're harder to kill than the other ones,'" I said.

"I never said that," he told me.

The real culprit, he said, was a buddy who he claimed whacked the woman he was referring to and had plans to roll her up in a carpet and toss her in a nearby lake. Hausmann said he attempted to save the woman's life.

I drove back to L.A. three days later. Hausmann, who was representing himself in the kidnapping case and therefore had access to the jail library and the phone, called me regularly. He assured me it was only a matter of time before he was found innocent of the L.A. murders.

He was right.

• • •

Hausmann was cleared of the .25-caliber killings two weeks after Steinhoff took his DNA. Steinhoff had hit a dead end, just like the detectives before him in the '80s. So the killer was still at large. He had eluded detectives for more than two decades and was still preying on young black women. He had defiled and degraded at least nine women, stripped them of their identification, and dumped their bodies in back alleys.

What added to the mystery was the block of time when the

serial killer seemed to have stopped murdering. He appeared to remain dormant for thirteen and a half years.

The LAPD, which was handling the bulk of the cases, was hampered by false leads, unreliable witnesses, and unsubstantiated suspects. Racial politics, fueled by a history of mistrust between police and black residents of South Central, also played its part.

Compounding the police investigation even further was the unfathomable: An unprecedented six serial killers were at work in the fifty-one-square-mile area. They were all hunting the same game: poor black women desperate to score a next hit of the highly addictive crack cocaine that was ravaging the working-class neighborhood, turning it into a gang-infested war zone. Police were focusing their resources on gang warfare and drug dealers, in a part of the city that often felt like a battlefield. And although the story I uncovered is one of grief and loss and justice and poverty and race and the plight of poor neighborhoods, at the heart of it are the lost women of South Central.

These women, society's most vulnerable, were the collateral damage, easy pickings for a serial killer.

This is their story.

PART ONE
THE MURDER BOOKS
1985–1988

CHAPTER 1
DEBRA, 1985

BEATRICE MASON WAS FED UP. Her wallet was missing and she was certain her girlfriend of fourteen months, a cocktail waitress named Debra Jackson, had taken it and blown her entire paycheck on cocaine. Beatrice, a 29-year-old former U.S. Army nurse, was tired of Debra's lying and denials about her fondness for drugs. It was time to end things, she decided.

It wasn't a decision Beatrice took lightly. Beatrice, a squat, heavy-set African American, was an introvert who exercised the discipline of a former soldier and expected loyalty and respect from friends. She was a diligent worker, held a steady job, and didn't do drugs. She didn't socialize much either, preferring to spend weekends at home watching sports on television.

Carefree, outgoing Debra was a cosmetology student when she met Beatrice on the steps of a Los Angeles beauty college. Debra was thin and pretty with a light complexion and an infectious grin. They had an immediate connection.

Debra had just returned from a drug rehab facility in South Central. She moved into Beatrice's two-bedroom apartment and got a job as a cocktail waitress at the Elegant Chateau Nightclub in Inglewood.

Debra was a bright light, always on, always ready for a party. Beatrice knew all along that Debra dabbled in drugs despite her stint in rehab, but it took her a while to realize the dabbling was an addiction.

They spent the first weekend of August 1985 in a bitter argument over the missing money. Beatrice was still raging Monday morning when she dropped Debra off at the house of Elizabeth Anderson—Debra's best friend—promising to pick her up at the end of her shift in nearby Culver City. Instead, Beatrice drove straight home after work.

At around 7 P.M. that Monday night, Debra telephoned. Beatrice told her she would leave a bag of her things with their neighbor, Donna. It wasn't until five days later that Beatrice got her first inkling something was amiss.

• • •

Debra Ronnette Jackson was born on March 2, 1956, and had her first child in Rhode Island when she was 14 years old. She named the girl Martha, after her mother. Two years later, on September 12, 1972, she named her first son Jermaine because of her crush on The Jackson 5 singer. Debra's youngest child, Anyata, was born in Springfield, Massachusetts, in 1975. Soon after, Debra, just 19, packed up the kids and moved to South Central to help take care of her maternal grandmother, who was in her 80s.

Debra was a devoted, strict parent. She took the kids to the beach and to Los Angeles's local theme parks but didn't hesitate to dish out punishment if they stepped out of line.

But as her addiction grew, Debra lost custody of her kids, who were placed in foster care twenty blocks from her home. Two weeks after they were taken from her, when their foster mother asked them to pick up bread at a local grocery store, Martha and Jermaine ran back home, where they found Debra crying over losing them. They were ecstatic to see her.

However, their reunion was short-lived. Debra told them they had to go back to their foster mother's home. "You have to do right by the law," she told Jermaine.

Jermaine was crushed. He and Martha cried as Debra drove them back to the grocery store. "We will be together soon," she told them. "When I get you back, we are going back to Big Ma's house," she said, referring to Debra's mother, still in Massachusetts.

It was not to be. When Jermaine was nine, he was placed at the Children's Baptist Home, a group home for at-risk boys, where he lived for three years. Anyata lived with another foster care family. Martha, Jermaine later recalled, was sent to MacLaren Hall, a home for abused and neglected children.

On Friday, August 9, 1985, four days after Beatrice ended her relationship with Debra, Anyata's foster mother called Beatrice looking for Debra. Anyata, now nine, regularly spoke to her mom on the phone, but Debra hadn't called for three days. Where was she?

• • •

The body of 29-year-old Debra Jackson was found on August 10, a warm Saturday morning. She was lying against a red wooden fence hidden under a discarded red carpet in a graffiti-strewn South Central alley off West Gage Avenue near Vermont Avenue. A single hand jutted out from under the carpet as if she were reaching out for help. A green nylon nightgown was draped over her stomach. She was dressed in blue jeans and a purple long-sleeve pullover sweater that was hiked up to her breasts. She wasn't wearing undergarments but had on a pair of white nylon tennis shoes. Her black hair hung loosely to her shoulders. Maggots crawled in and out of her eyes, nostrils, and ears. Her body was so puffy the detectives couldn't tell if it was bloated or if she had been beaten.

The killing, however, was eclipsed by another case. The day

before, police in Los Angeles County had held a press conference announcing they were searching for a killer in a series of gruesome murders, which included the recent shooting death of 34-year-old Dayle Okazaki and the wounding of her roommate, Maria Hernandez, at their condominium in the working-class Los Angeles suburb of Rosemead, about twenty miles from South Central.

Police said they were searching for the man responsible for twelve or thirteen slayings and more than fifteen rapes, beatings, and kidnappings, almost all of them in middle-to-upper class L.A. communities. The serial killer was given the nickname the Night Stalker because he crept into homes at night and attacked his victims as they slept. The FBI had prepared a psychological profile, and the police handed out composite sketches to the local media of a slim, curly-haired suspect with stained gapped teeth.

South Central L.A., where Debra's body was found, was a poor, mainly African American neighborhood where murders were as common as the stray dogs—sometimes called ghetto elk—that prowled the streets. Wars over turf played out street to street in a violent, escalating battle for control of the sale of highly addictive drugs. Innocent bystanders, including children and grandmothers, became victims. In the 1980s, L.A. was averaging close to eight hundred murders a year, more than half of them in South Central. Against that backdrop, Debra's murder, sadly, held no distinction.

The South Central L.A. homicide units were understaffed, and the detectives worked long hours juggling many cases, with one team of two detectives sometimes handling upward of three murders on any given weekend.

LAPD Seventy-seventh Division police station, the precinct where Debra's body was discovered, averaged around one hundred and thirty murders a year. There were only eight homicide detectives carrying the load of cases, and there was not a lot of support from police headquarters. It was their local problem.

"You were on your own," said one detective. "The guys took it, 'this is the way it is.' There was no whining. It wasn't uncommon for me to get calls from guys' wives who'd say, 'Don't put him on call this weekend; he can't handle it anymore.'"

The Night Stalker was captured on August 31, 1985.[3] Debra's killer would not be found for another two decades.

• • •

Two seasoned homicide detectives, Mark Arneson and Kenneth Crocker of the Seventy-seventh Division, were dispatched to investigate Debra Jackson's killing. Initially she was logged as "Jane Doe #59," being the fifty-ninth unidentified female corpse checked in by the Los Angeles County Department of Medical Examiner-Coroner in 1985. The autopsy report stated that the body on the cold slab was of a 135-pound, "well-built and well-nourished" female, young to middle-aged.

She had been shot three times in the chest with a .25-caliber pistol, known in police circles as a pocket pistol because it is small, lightweight, easy to conceal, and simple to fire. Her killer had shot downward and so close to her skin that deputy medical examiner Dr. Sara Reddy found gunshot residue in the wounds. The bullets penetrated the left side of her chest, hitting her heart and cutting her spinal cord in half, causing paralysis below the waist. Death would have occurred within two minutes.

The autopsy also revealed Debra had alcohol and a trace amount of cocaine in her system. Because of the advanced state of the decomposition of her body there was no way to determine if she had been sexually assaulted.

Detectives Arneson and Crocker found a black-and-white purse tucked underneath the victim's head, but it didn't contain any identification. LAPD latent fingerprint experts were able to get prints from the fingers on her left hand (the right hand was too badly decomposed), but they were not on file.

---

3. In 1989, Night Stalker Richard Ramirez was convicted of thirteen murders. He received the death penalty and was sent to California's death row. He died on June 7, 2013, at age 53 of complications from lymphoma.

However, in her purse were several scraps of paper with phone numbers scrawled on them. Detectives J. C. Johnson and Lionel Robert, who had taken over the investigation from Arneson and Crocker, started calling and reached Debra's sister, Michelle Jackson. Michelle told the detectives she had not been able to reach her sister over the past few days and gave them a physical description of Debra, which matched the body at the coroner's office.

Michelle told detectives that Debra had a roommate named Beatrice, but she didn't know her last name or where she worked. She did, however, give them Beatrice's address as well as the name of the nightclub where Debra worked.

The two investigators went to Beatrice's apartment on August 12. A neighbor, Henrietta Wood, told them she hadn't seen Debra in about a week. Beatrice, she added, followed a predictable schedule: she left for work at 7 A.M. and returned by 5:30 P.M.

• • •

The next day, the detectives interviewed Debra's coworkers at the Elegant Chateau Nightclub. Manager Mark Roland told detectives Debra had come to the nightclub the previous Wednesday, August 7, around 2 P.M. to pick up her paycheck. The checks were late, so Debra and two waitresses waited around at the bar. She left around 4 P.M. Roland suggested police talk to a regular customer, Robert Hunter.

Hunter said that he had given Debra a ride from the nightclub on Tuesday, August 6, around 9:30 P.M. He said Debra didn't want him to drop her off at her home. He suspected that she didn't want Beatrice to see her with a man, so he let her out a few blocks away. He wasn't sure exactly where, either by 79th Street or 73rd Street, off Figueroa Street.

He told detectives that during the ride Debra said she was looking for an apartment because Beatrice wanted her to move out and that she asked him for a loan. When he offered her his last ten dollars, she refused to take it, saying she would have some cash coming in soon. Debra, he said, appeared desperate and frightened.

Hunter saw Debra again the following afternoon. "Did you find an apartment?" he asked her.

"Yes," she said. "I'll tell you about it later." She walked out of the club. He never saw her again.

• • •

Beatrice had just arrived home from work at 4:45 P.M. on Tuesday, August 13, when she peered out her second-story window and saw two Los Angeles Police Department detectives looking up at her.

She got a bad feeling when she opened the door to let them in. They proceeded to ask Beatrice about Debra without mentioning her death. Beatrice admitted their relationship had seen better days. Their disputes, she told them, were usually about money and Debra's addiction to cocaine.

She told the detectives they had agreed to live apart during their last phone call. The detectives' line of questioning and demeanor gradually moved from one of concern to one of accusation, Beatrice later recalled. As they pushed her for more details, Beatrice started to get nervous and wondered why they were grilling her. She assumed Debra was the one in trouble.

She wasn't prepared for what came next.

One of the detectives reached into an envelope and pulled out a photograph of Debra's lifeless body taken in the alley. Beatrice was floored.

"He comes with the pictures of her dead," Beatrice later remembered, matter-of-factly. "I guess they wanted to see my expression."

Debra looked as though she'd been beaten up in the photograph. Beatrice asked if she'd been assaulted. The detective pressed her on that statement. "They asked me why I asked if she was beat up," she said. "She looked like it."

The detectives asked her point-blank if she killed Debra. Beatrice denied it. She told the detectives that she started worrying about Debra when she hadn't heard from her. In fact, she'd gone to the Elegant Chateau Nightclub on Friday, August 9, in search of Debra and was told she had not been seen since she picked up her paycheck two days earlier.

The detectives were skeptical. If Debra had plans to move out, why didn't she take her belongings with her? Beatrice, now agitated, reminded them that she and Debra agreed to break up on the phone.

By the end of the interview, the detectives "almost made me feel like I did it," Beatrice said.

On Wednesday, August 14, detectives Johnson and Robert interviewed Debra's best friend, Elizabeth Anderson, and her husband, Leo, at LAPD's Seventy-seventh Division Station. Leo told detectives that Beatrice owned a handgun. Elizabeth, whose statement contradicted what Hunter told police, told detectives Debra phoned her in the early evening of Tuesday, August 6, and said Beatrice had thrown her out of the apartment and asked Elizabeth to pick her up at a nearby corner. Elizabeth noticed that Debra's right eye was all but completely swollen shut.

Debra stayed at Elizabeth's place overnight.

The next day Elizabeth and Leo drove Debra to work to get her paycheck, then to a discount grocery store in the San Fernando Valley. Later that Wednesday evening, Debra told Elizabeth she was going to pick up some of her belongings at the home of her neighbor, Donna, where Beatrice had dropped off some of her stuff. She also owed Donna twenty dollars and wanted to pay her while she still had some money. Elizabeth watched Debra head down the street toward the bus. She never saw her again.

Debra never showed up at Donna's home. Everyone in Debra's small orbit was on edge. It just wasn't like her.

Beatrice was asked to drop by the Seventy-seventh Division Station for a follow-up interview. Police said they had information that she was abusive to Debra and that she owned a handgun. Beatrice was livid. She adamantly denied it all.

A polygraph test didn't go in Beatrice's favor. The polygraph examiner told detectives Johnson and Robert that Beatrice was "conclusively deceptive" on key questions regarding Debra's murder.

Confronted with the results, Beatrice again proclaimed her innocence. "They drilled me so long and heavy," Beatrice later recalled, "I was worried I was going to get arrested." She left the police station as the main suspect in Debra's murder. In the days that followed, the police took her fingerprints and samples from the bottoms of her shoes and searched her car.

But with scant evidence to prove Beatrice was involved, and with so many other murders to investigate, the case went stagnant. Debra's family was in shock over her death. Her mother, Martha, immediately made her way to Los Angeles to bury her daughter and bring Debra's children home with her to Massachusetts. Debra's other sister, Tanya Everett, who was 22 at the time, stayed home in Springfield to raise the money for the bus fare to bring the family home.

It was Debra's best friend Elizabeth Anderson who broke the news to Jermaine. His mother had been beaten up and shot, she told him. "They kept asking who did it, but there was nothing I knew," Elizabeth years later told the *Los Angeles Times*.

Jermaine was the one to break the news of their mother's murder to his sister Anyata. "It was the worst thing I ever did," he said. "I tried to console her the best I could."

Debra's funeral service was held at the Hyde Park Mortuary. Her burial followed, but Debra's children were not allowed to attend. Jermaine was never told why.

• • •

For close to a year after Debra Jackson's murder, LAPD detectives Robert and Johnson monitored all .25-caliber guns booked into evidence, hoping that the weapon used to kill Debra might turn up at another crime scene or during an arrest. The detectives would discover a year later that the same gun was used to kill another young black woman whose body was found in a different South Central alley on August 12, 1986.

These .25-caliber killings were not the only murders detectives were investigating. Another rash of murders by a serial killer dubbed the Southside Slayer haunted LAPD homicide. The murders in this spree were different than those of Debra and this new victim, as the killer's modus operandi was to stab and strangle his female victims.

CHAPTER 2
THE SOUTHSIDE SLAYER

JOHN ST. JOHN WAS ALREADY a legend among police officers in the LAPD when his elite Robbery-Homicide Division at Parker Center was called in to investigate the stabbing and strangulation murders of at least ten prostitutes, mostly African American. The string of horrors dated back to September of 1983.

The homicide detective had earned the nickname Jigsaw John early in his career after he solved a murder in which a man was found sliced up like a jigsaw puzzle in Griffith Park, in the high-end Los Feliz neighborhood of Los Angeles. His success at solving murders led *Los Angeles Times* writer Al Martinez to write a 1975 book about the detective titled *Jigsaw John*.

St. John was an eccentric heavy drinker with a gold front tooth. Chubby and short, he shuffled when he walked, and he dressed the part of a detective in a gray fedora and central-casting trench coat and carried a black briefcase. His business cards were made of metal. Of the approximately one thousand cases he worked, he solved two-thirds of them and never shot anyone. He was so consumed with detective work he was known to forget his uncashed paychecks for weeks at a time in his coat pocket.

In 1985, he was in his late 60s and had a reputation as a stellar detective with a soft spot for victims. He'd become one himself just one year into the job when a young prisoner attacked him from behind with an iron bar he'd ripped from a jail bunk. The attack blinded St. John in one eye.

The dead prostitutes and strawberries—the street term for women who exchanged sex for drugs—who St. John was now investigating had all plied their trade on the dimly lit streets of Western Avenue and Figueroa Street, next to crack houses and boarded-up storefronts. These were once thriving thoroughfares in a poor but respectable neighborhood. But the arrival of drugs, gang violence, and a high unemployment rate had turned the area by the 1980s into a hub of liquor stores, gambling parlors, cheap hotels, and prostitution strolls.

In early September of 1985 it appeared the famed detective had caught his first break in the Southside Slayer cases. Three African American prostitutes were attacked, in separate instances; all three survived, and two were talking. The other victim, 26, was in a coma after being strangled and stabbed. The two victims were able to give police a description of the suspect and car.

One of the women described her attacker as 30 to 35 years old, a dark-complexioned, medium-built black male with a small mustache and muscular arms, standing between five feet ten inches and six feet tall. In one attack, the suspect wore a FILA baseball cap and drove a 1984 or 1985 dark-colored Buick Regal with a baby seat in the back.

In the second assault, the woman described being picked up in a 1960 to 1969 gray Ford pickup.

At a September 24, 1985, press conference, the Los Angeles Police Department told reporters that the man who they believed attacked the three prostitutes was likely responsible for the stabbing and strangulation murders of ten other prostitutes since September 1983.

Seven of the dead women were found in South Central, two in nearby Inglewood, and one in neighboring Gardena. They had been dumped nude or partly clad in deserted parks, alleys, and schoolyards. The body of the last known victim, Gail Ficklin, was discovered on August 15, 1985, five days after Debra Jackson's body was found.

The police hoped their announcement would prompt Angelenos to come forward with tips. However, the plan backfired. The LAPD instead was criticized for taking so long to alert the community.

Margaret Prescod, a 37-year-old New York City transplant, led the charge. The black community activist and former teacher wanted to know why it took the police years to inform the community that there was an active serial killer in their midst.

On October 2, 1985, eight days after the press conference, Prescod and eleven other female activists picketed outside of LAPD's downtown headquarters. It would become the first of many weekly vigils. Standing next to a macabre prop—a plywood coffin draped with flowers—the Barbados-born community activist accused the police of not caring about the murdered women because they were mostly poor, black, drug-addicted prostitutes. "There seems to be selective protection to different groups and classes of our community," Prescod bellowed. "They are not giving this case the same kind of attention they did the Night Stalker."[4]

The Los Angeles Police Department balked at that insinuation. St. John's partner, Detective Fred Miller, told a *Los Angeles Times* reporter that the eight detectives assigned to the case, including him and St. John, were as devoted to the case as they were to the case of the Night Stalker, whose killing field was much more upscale than South Central. Miller reasoned that the department hadn't alerted the community sooner about the serial killer because "you have to know what you've got first." They had released a composite sketch of the suspect three weeks after they were able to cobble together a description from the surviving witnesses, he said.

4. Ron Harris, "Pickets Protest Police Handling of Prostitutes' Deaths," *Los Angeles Times*, October 3, 1985

Prescod's activism didn't win her any friends at the LAPD. Police Chief Daryl Gates even chimed in, calling Prescod and her cronies "asinine." "They're insensitive to the men who are working this case," he told the *Los Angeles Times*. "Those dummies should be applauding them instead of casting a negative light on the investigation. We care about human life. We don't care about what they are or who they are."

Despite the media attention and the police public-awareness campaign, the prostitute killings continued. By January of 1986 the death toll reached fifteen. (There were other prostitute murders during this time, but detectives did not believe they were linked to the same serial killer.) The LAPD beefed up the investigation, bringing a total of nineteen detectives, which also included detectives from the Los Angeles County Sheriff's Department, to what was now called the Southside Slayer Task Force.

"I know we're gonna catch this guy sooner or later," St. John, who had taken to referring to the killer as "this guy," told the *Los Angeles Times*, "but I don't know when and how. The how comes in the strangest ways sometimes." The prostitute murders, he said, were similar to other serial-killer cases he worked on in the past. "These guys all kill the same way you or me pick a banana off a tree," he said. "Whenever they get the urge, they go out and do it to get their sexual gratification or whatever. They'll keep doing it, too, until you stop them."

St. John and the other task-force detectives were working as many as fourteen hours a day investigating the slayings. During the day, St. John worked with the commander, Lt. John Zorn, formerly in internal affairs, assigning tips to detectives. But at night he and his partner walked the same darkened streets where the prostitutes had last been seen alive. The detectives were not alone. Prostitution along the Western Avenue and Figueroa Street was still thriving despite the knowledge that a serial killer was active in the area.

"We were involved in a program where we were warning women on the streets they were in danger, almost on an individual basis," remembered Zorn. "We had people go out every night and identify women working on the streets and walk up to them and ask them if they knew about the case and provide them with a composite sketch and do everything we could to deter them from working the streets. We felt we had an obligation to tell them."

In early March 1986, Prescod's newly formed coalition, Black Coalition Fighting Back Serial Murders, pressured the Los Angeles City Council to offer a $25,000 reward for information leading to the capture of the Southside Slayer, more than doubling the ten-thousand-dollar reward on the table since September from the Los Angeles County Board of Supervisors. Councilman Robert Farrell, whose district included South Central, introduced the motion at a press conference with Mayor Tom Bradley and Police Chief Gates.

At a candlelight vigil for the dead women on March 20, Prescod announced that her coalition would ask the FBI to step in. "If these murders had happened in Beverly Hills, we would have seen much more progress," Prescod told the press. "If police are having difficulty . . . it is past time to bring in other agencies."

In the streets, rumors were swirling that the women were being killed by people making snuff films. Some streetwalkers were sure police were involved in the murders. All of the women considered themselves street smart and capable of picking out a dangerous john.

"We thought that there was a law-enforcement connection," Prescod said. "If he wasn't a cop, then some of the cops knew something. A lot of people in the community felt that way."

Prescod shared the experience of a nameless woman who escaped after being dragged into a van by a man she was sure was the killer. "She wanted to come forward, but she was really scared. She was hiding out and wanted some protection. When we asked her about contacting the police, she said, 'I don't want to do that because I will end up in an alley with the rest of the girls.'"

Prescod became the go-to person between the community and the LAPD whenever a young black woman wound up dead.

"We were getting calls from people in the community letting us know that a body was found in a school yard or alley, and we would look to see if there was a report in the press, and we started thinking there were a lot more murders than the police were telling us about," she said.

The gruesome death of Debra Jackson seemed to prove their point.

Meanwhile, Prescod was getting crank calls and late-night hang-ups at her East L.A. home. Prescod suspected a police officer was following her, so coalition members started staying overnight to protect her. One night, she asked a television reporter who was interviewing her at her home to confront a man she believed had been parked outside her house for days. When the reporter approached the car, it drove off.

Prescod's coalition was also under pressure from the LAPD to ease up and call off the weekly vigils. The coalition refused to back down.

Prescod's attacks on the police drew mixed reactions in the black community. Church members had trouble supporting prostitutes. While they abhorred the murders, they saw the prostitutes as sinners and didn't want to be viewed as supporting that lifestyle. Mark Ridley-Thomas, the executive director of the Southern Christian Leadership Conference of Greater Los Angeles, said, "I respectfully choose not to comment," when asked about Prescod's activism by the *Los Angeles Times* in October 1986.

However, Councilman Farrell lauded her perseverance: "She's one of many persons in South Los Angeles to take the issue and generate the high visibility this issue deserves." But Farrell added that it was difficult to gauge how successful the coalition was "other than that they had clearly helped get out the message about the killer and helped get media attention."

Attorney Walter Gordon III was even more effusive in his praise. Prescod, he told the *Los Angeles Times*, "single-handedly built the coalition; she's brought people together of different races . . . Any time you have a black woman take a position and get noticed there's going to be a conflict. She's a powerful person with a charisma, so she gets called aggressive, pushy, confrontational. It's the same old hysterical female trip. So what? She gets things done."

By July 1986, police counted eighteen related unsolved murders of black prostitutes in South Central and neighboring communities. Los Angeles Mayor Tom Bradley held a press conference and again appealed for the public's help.

Councilman Farrell criticized the police response, suggesting that the "best and the brightest" detectives had not been assigned to the case and then passed out a press release to reporters that read: "There is an increasing perception among community groups in South Los Angeles and adjacent Los Angeles County areas that there is a lack of full commitment of city and county resources. We must take all actions available to us to alleviate these concerns and fears."

Los Angeles County Supervisor Kenneth Hahn, who was white but who represented the largely black South Central, told the press he had sent a telegram to FBI Director William H. Webster asking the bureau to enter the case. In the telegram, Hahn wrote that the Southside Slayer was responsible for a "record number of slayings of black women" in the "history of this, the largest county in America."

Hahn issued a statement in which he wrote that "although all of the victims of the Southside Slayer have been prostitutes, all their lives are precious in the eyes of God." They were "human beings, and the full protection of the government must be provided to them as it would be for our most prominent citizens."

"Furthermore," he continued, "we must keep in mind that the longer this criminal is at large, the more likely it becomes that some future victim might be a totally innocent woman waiting for a bus at night or lost in the streets."

Hahn's comments infuriated the Los Angeles Police Department. LAPD Captain Jerry Bova, the commanding officer of the Robbery-Homicide Division, which oversaw the task force, defended the department's handling of the case to reporters, dismissing any suggestion that the LAPD or the Los Angeles County Sheriff's Department needed any help from the FBI. He told reporters that the best homicide detectives were assigned to this case, "and they are very, very committed. I can't think of anything that the FBI can do that we are not already doing."

Chief Gates in a written statement called both Farrell and Hahn's comments "divisive, counterproductive, and demoralizing."

Gates's response was that he was "disturbed" that the public would think the police would do a less-thorough investigation based on the race or criminal records of the victims. "Color, descent, occupation, or sexual orientation have never affected our dedication and commitment to a murder investigation."

The investigators on this case, who he said were working "tirelessly," deserved the support of politicians, "not this kind of verbal haranguing."

Gates's final words of rebuttal were: "A human being is a human being, and a murderer is a murderer, and we do our very best in every case."

Nevertheless, on July 22, LAPD officials met with Mark Ridley-Thomas of the Southern Christian Leadership Conference of Greater Los Angeles to try to help improve community relations in South Central.

In early August, it was Councilman Farrell's turn to play nice toward the police of whom he'd been so critical. He sent out a statement saying that he now had a better understanding of the work the police were doing. "At a recent press conference, I put forth a community perception that queried the police department's staff deployment—whether the best and brightest were assigned to solve this heinous crime. LAPD Assistant Chief [Robert] Vernon and other police officers have now advised me of who is doing what on the case, and I am satisfied with what has been shared with me, both in open conversation and in confidence . . . I am confident that every effort is being made to bring this case to a speedy conclusion."

While police were fending off attacks by politicians and coalition members, they arrested 28-year-old Charles Edward Mosley for the July 25 murder of Canosha Griffin, considered a possible nineteenth victim of the Southside Slayer. Fearful the police might pin the many Southside Slayer murders on him, Mosley had showed up on his own at LAPD's Southwest Division Station and confessed to killing the 22-year-old Griffin, claiming self-defense. But that was it. He hadn't killed anyone else.[5] Griffin's body was found in a vegetable garden at Locke High School in South Central. Her throat had been slit.

Southside Slayer Task Force detectives believed Mosley's story. The five-foot-six, 145-pound Mosley didn't look like the composite sketch of the Southside Slayer, a much taller and heavier man. "At this time, after an investigation that is still very much going on, we have absolutely no specific information to indicate that Mr. Mosley is involved in any other crimes being investigated by this task force," LAPD Assistant Chief Vernon said at a press conference on August 12.

By this time police had already begun to suspect that their original theory—that one man was responsible for killing the eighteen prostitutes—was wrong.

Truth be told, the task-force detectives didn't know how many killers they were looking for, despite spending $1.4 million on the investigation and tracking down more than two thousand clues. It was possible there were at least four killers, maybe more. The detectives could not rule out that some of the women might have been killed by a john or a pimp and were not part of the series. Although many of the cases showed similarities, the detectives could not be certain it was the work of the same man.

As the summer of 1986 was waning, the body count was rising and the detectives pursuing the Southside Slayer were as lost as the women on the streets.

And now, there appeared to be another killer on the loose, with a different murderous methodology, a .25 caliber. This killer, it would turn out, had only just begun to haunt South Central and the LAPD.

5. John Crust, "Slayer May Have Struck for 18th Time," *Los Angeles Herald Examiner*, August 23, 1986.

CHAPTER 3
HENRIETTA, 1986

HENRIETTA "CODY" WRIGHT DIDN'T stay in one place for long. In the weeks since her stepfather kicked her out for using drugs, she alternated spending nights at fleabag hourly motels and crashing at her sister's place or friends' apartments. Every so often her younger sister, Theresa, would sneak her back home.

When the 34-year-old mother of five went missing, she, like so many of the women who were murdered in South Central at the time, disappeared in the middle of the night. Her body was found on Tuesday, August 12, 1986, at 11:20 A.M.—one week before her thirty-fifth birthday—in a litter-strewn alley, a known homeless hangout, to the rear of West Vernon Avenue. The rubble around her included two empty paint cans, an oversized brown pillow, and a pile of papers.

Again, the body was partially hidden, this time under a large mattress and a bright green blanket. Her left arm was extended out to the side and rested on top of a pair of brown double-knit men's pants. She was wearing a white cotton short-sleeved polo shirt and a pair of red-and-blue plaid shorts with a black belt. Her shorts were unzipped, and her shirt was pulled up to her breasts. She was missing her shoes, underwear, and identification. A portion of a men's long-sleeved shirt was stuffed inside her mouth, possibly as a gag, police surmised, to stop her from screaming.

There was blood across her mouth and cheeks, in her right ear and on her nose.

Henrietta had been shot twice at close range with .25-caliber bullets. A drug-and-alcohol test showed cocaine and a mix of morphine and codeine in her blood. Police found four .38-caliber slugs in the alleyway, but it was soon determined they had nothing to do with the murder. This appeared to be another body dump.

Detective John St. John and members of the Southside Slayer Task Force were called to the crime scene. But, because they were focusing on victims who had been strangled and stabbed, they passed on the case. Detectives Jay Collins and Don Hrycyk[6] from the LAPD's Seventy-seventh Division Station, the same precinct handling Debra Jackson's murder, picked it up.

Henrietta's fingerprints turned up immediately in a police database. That night, detectives Collins and Hrycyk arrived on Defiance Avenue in Watts in Southside Los Angeles to notify Ella Mae Hollingsworth of her sister's death. Their next stop was the East 46th Street home of Henrietta's younger sister Theresa, and Henrietta's stepfather, Oscar Dale. It was the last place Henrietta had been seen alive.

A distraught Theresa told detectives that Henrietta had been staying at two nearby motels, the Towns Motel and the Sand Piper Motel, but she had last seen her outside her bedroom window ear-

---

6. Hrycyk, a California State University, Long Beach criminology graduate who started with the LAPD in 1974, later became the head of the LAPD's art-theft detail after he left homicide. He handled dozens of capers, including the theft of a first-edition issue of the Superman comic book, Action Comics no. 1, from actor Nicolas Cage's house in 2000. The comic, which was released in 1938 and worth more than $1 million, was found eleven years later in a storage unit in Southern California. In 2009, Hrycyk's partner Stephanie Lazarus, then 49, was arrested by the Los Angeles Police Department for the jealousy-fueled 1986 killing of her ex-boyfriend's wife, Sherri Rae Rasmussen. In 2012, a Los Angeles jury found her guilty, and she was sentenced to twenty-seven years to life in prison, with the possibility of parole.

lier that morning, around 2 A.M. They made plans to meet up the next day for a birthday party. Theresa watched through her window as Henrietta chatted with someone who had just driven up. Theresa watched the car drive off toward Central Avenue. It looked as though Henrietta was following on foot.

Theresa told the police that Henrietta frequently hung out across the street, helping an older neighbor named Clarence with his grocery shopping. Sometimes she stayed the night, Theresa said.

After talking with Theresa, detectives stopped by the two motels looking for anyone who might have seen Henrietta or rented a room to her. No one admitted to renting to her, or even knowing her.

• • •

Henrietta Wright was born in Mississippi on August 18, 1951, one of eleven children of Luella McDonald and Robert Wright. When she was two, her family moved to Los Angeles in search of a better lifestyle and more job opportunities. Robert found work in construction, and Luella cleaned homes in Beverly Hills and Ladera Heights, a well-to-do community on L.A.'s west side. Growing up, all the kids were expected to help around the house.

The family didn't stay together for long. Robert left, and Luella and her children settled into Nickerson Gardens, a one-thousand-plus-unit public housing complex in Watts. The complex was built in the 1950s, intended as low-cost, safe, transitional housing. Its architect, Paul Revere Williams, also designed the homes of many celebrities, including Frank Sinatra, Lucille Ball and Desi Arnaz, and Lon Chaney. Nickerson Gardens later became one of the city's most dangerous housing projects.

Luella later had a relationship with Oscar Dale, and they had a daughter, Theresa, born in March of 1963. In 1966, at 36, Luella died of cervical cancer "from having all those babies," said Henrietta's sister Alice. "They opened her up for surgery and it spread and she died in her bed in the living room. She had no way to survive the cancer." Henrietta was only 15.

Luella didn't live long enough to see the birth of Henrietta's first child, a son, Irvin, born on June 5, 1967. Henrietta lived with an aunt before moving in with Willie Bush Sr. in a spacious, three-bedroom house on 78th Street and South Central Avenue. Willie Jr. soon followed, on January 28, 1969. Eight years later, Willie Sr.'s abuse drove them apart.

The newly single mother of two embraced her independence. She bought a gray Toyota Tercel and got a day job as a cafeteria worker with the Los Angeles Unified School District. She also worked nights as a cocktail waitress at the Melody Room. She took up shooting pool as a hobby and spent many weekends competing in tournaments around L.A., occasionally bringing home a trophy.

When she found out she was having a daughter, Henrietta was thrilled. Komisha was born in November of 1977. "Komisha was her love child," Henrietta's niece Irene said. "She always wanted a girl. She was still doing good when she had Komisha."

Henrietta's downward spiral can be traced back to a fire that ravaged the home she loved so much on 78th Street and Central Avenue. The house was destroyed, and so were her belongings. Henrietta and Komisha moved in with one of Henrietta's sisters, and her boys, Irvin and Willie Jr., went to live with their fathers and their families.

Henrietta began to abuse drugs and, in quick order, the drugs, not her children, became her main focus.

"It was a shock to see the decline," said Irene. "It happened rapidly in my eyes. One day everything was okay, and the next thing I knew she lost her house, lost her job, was on drugs, and then she was dead. There was a big difference in her appearance. Before, we couldn't go to the gas station without guys hitting on her and talking to her. We were all really close back then. We would do picnics and meet up at the beach. When the drugs came in, it all went out the window. It totally destroyed the family."

By the mid-1980s, Henrietta had become another casualty of the raging crack epidemic ripping through South Central.

"When crack came out, I was a teenager," Irene continued. "I could see the devastation in the community. People you knew were losing their houses and cars. You knew the girls were turning tricks to do drugs. I would see women late at night when I was working a graveyard shift and see girls hanging on the streets pulling down cars. I had classmates that got on the drugs. They think they can control it but it controls them."

Like many crack addicts before her, Henrietta soon began stealing for her next high. "She was a really nice person, but she got bad and started stealing from people," said Irene. "You don't want to be around people you can't trust."

Irene said Henrietta stole some of her husband's guns that were in boxes inside her apartment and sold them. "I forgave her, but who does that?" said Irene. "My husband was furious. She apologized, but he didn't want to hear it."

As Henrietta's life was spinning out of control, she found herself pregnant again. Rochell, another girl, was born in January of 1982. Henrietta's sister Ella Mae took over Rochell's parenting after Henrietta left the hospital without her. Baby Lucille came next, in January of 1986. This time, Henrietta gave her newborn daughter to a neighbor who lived across the street from her old home on 78th Street.

• • •

In many ways, Henrietta Wright never stood a chance. By the early '80s, crack cocaine, also known as rock, was flooding South Central and other largely black neighborhoods across the nation. It quickly became a scourge. The high was intense, short, and very addictive—and incredibly lucrative for drug dealers. Crack houses with fortified steel doors in the front and back popped up like weeds on South Central's busy streets and drew lines of zombielike men and women looking for their next high. Within five years, crack cocaine was embedded into the community and spawned a culture of viciousness.

One of the area's biggest dealers was a former high-school tennis player known on the streets as Freeway Rick Ross. The city's most violent black gangs were his most lucrative dealers. Gang shootings over turf became routine. Assault rifles and sawed-off shotguns were the weapons of choice in drive-by shootings. Addicts stole or solicited for their next high, while children of drug dealers were regularly kidnapped for ransom. Teenagers learned quickly they could make thousands of dollars a night selling on street corners. For many young people, there wasn't much of an incentive to go to school. Drug dealers addicted to crack became victims themselves. Many of them were killed for selling stones they claimed were crack cocaine.

The Los Angeles Police Department spent millions of dollars in an attempt to combat the gangs. Many African Americans in South Central, however, thought the police used the gang wars as an excuse to crack down on them. "For many in Black Los Angeles, gangs were seen as an excuse for police to brutalize blacks who weren't actually affiliated with gangs, and there was evidence to support this view," wrote Paul Robinson in his essay "Race, Space, and the Evolution of Black Los Angeles," a chapter in the anthology *Black Los Angeles: American Dreams and Racial Realities.*

The crack epidemic collided with Los Angeles's long history of racism. In 1920 there were around fifteen thousand blacks in Los Angeles. By 1930 the number grew to thirty-five thousand. Then, in the early 1940s, the black population soared with a huge influx of people from the South looking for work in the city's profitable manufacturing and defense industries. Most came from Mississippi, Alabama, Louisiana, and Tennessee.

"Between 1942 and 1945, two-hundred thousand African Americans, drawn by the demand for the half-million workers needed in the aviation, steel, rubber, and shipbuilding industries, would arrive in a city whose black population had barely topped sixty-two thousand in 1940," wrote historian Joe Domanick in his book *To Protect and to Serve: The LAPD's Century of War in the City of Dreams.* By the late '40s, when the U.S. Supreme Court ruled that restrictive covenants designed to enforce segregation in certain areas were unenforceable, blacks started to buy in the mostly white and middle-class neighborhood of South Central. Within a few years, the area changed into a thriving, blue-collar community with a large black homeownership.

Many white homeowners raged at the sight of blacks moving into the neighborhood and firebombed the homes and burned crosses on their lawns. The LAPD chief of police William H. Parker transformed the agency into a precision paramilitary operation. It was praised by some as the best in the nation. Others, however, saw it much differently.

The mostly white department faced mounting criticism for its aggressive and confrontational treatment of the city's African American and Hispanic populations. This era of conflict between the police and the communities became more divisive with the beginning of the modern civil-rights movement in the late '50s.

By the early 1960s, black gangs were springing up in South Central, and the area's low-income housing projects were becoming battlegrounds. The crime rate soared at the same time that South Central was experiencing devastating unemployment. "South Central and the surrounding black neighborhoods were places with wounds rubbed raw by rage, poverty, envy, and insanity. And by Bill Parker's police department," wrote Domanick. "In the two-year period from 1963 to 1965, sixty black Angelenos would be killed by the police, twenty-seven of whom were shot in the back."

The passage of Proposition 14 on the California ballot in November of 1964 overturned the Rumford Fair Housing Act, which called for an end to racial discrimination by property owners and landlords. The brewing racial unrest came to a head on August 11, 1965, in what became known as the Watts Riots.

Angered by the California Highway Patrol's arrest of a 21-year-old black man named Marquette Frye for allegedly driving drunk, a crowd of black protesters took their outrage to the streets. An explosion of mayhem, looting, and violence ensued, which took six days to extinguish. Thirty-four people, twenty-five of them black, died, and more than one thousand people were injured. Close to four thousand people, almost all of them black, were arrested, and there was more than $40 million in property damage.

The Watts riots spurred many of the well-to-do and middle-class black residents in South Central to move to safer suburbs and better schools. The white population also left, replaced by a large wave of immigrants from Mexico and Central America.

The riots crippled the South Central economy. Businesses closed, and widespread unemployment ensued. Liquor stores and cheap motels replaced mom-and-pop businesses. The shop owners who did remain installed metal bars over their windows.

As the 1960s turned into the 1970s, guns were almost as commonplace on the streets as sidewalks. By the early '80s, bulletproof glass became the norm, as did the lifeless bodies of young black women discarded in alleyways all across South Central.

• • •

It was late in the evening of August 12, 1986, when Henrietta's niece Irene—fresh off her shift as a cashier—turned on the nightly news. A dead woman had been found in an alley. Irene didn't think much of it. Living amidst violence had hardened her to the point of it hardly registering. It wasn't until her mother Ella Mae called and told her Henrietta was dead that she realized her aunt was the victim in the news report.

Detectives wanted Ella Mae to go to the coroner's office to identify the body. Irene and Henrietta's oldest son, Irvin, 19, went with her.

Irene couldn't help but think that Henrietta "had ripped someone off from drugs and they got her." Irvin, who had been living with his paternal grandparents, also believed drugs played a role in her death. Henrietta used to regularly attend his baseball games when he was growing up, but by the time he entered high school, he barely saw her. "I understood she was doing drugs," he recalled. "You see people on drugs every day. It wasn't something new to anybody."

Henrietta's other son, Willie Bush Jr., 17, was living in Fresno with his father when he heard the news.

"I got something to tell you," his father told him soon after he returned home from high-school football practice.

"What?" Willie asked.

"Your mom got killed," his father told him matter-of-factly.

Willie Jr. blacked out and fell to the floor.

• • •

On Friday, August 29, the case of Henrietta Wright took an unexpected turn. LAPD's Scientific Investigation Division notified Hrycyk that the bullets taken from Henrietta's chest were fired from the same .25-caliber gun used in the murder of cocktail waitress Debra Jackson.

Two months later, LAPD detectives Mark Arneson and Gary Lowder told Collins and Hrycyk they had been interviewing a female informant about another murder when she asked them if they were investigating "the lady" in the alley.

The informant, 20-year-old Shelly Brown, had been arrested in August for a gas station robbery. She told the detectives that on the evening of August 11—the night before Henrietta turned up dead—she was at the Stallion Motel on South Arlington Avenue with an unknown female and two male friends she knew as Pinky and Let Loose. The two men bought cocaine to smoke and two adjoining rooms.

Brown heard Let Loose and the unknown woman argue in the next room. The woman left the room and slammed the door. Brown and Pinky looked out the window and saw Let Loose chasing the woman westbound in the alley south of Vernon Avenue, toward 2nd Avenue. Pinky left the room and followed. By the time Brown made it to the alley, Pinky was holding the woman's arms behind her back while Let Loose punched her. Let Loose then pulled out a gun and shot the woman twice as she was lying on the ground. They took off the woman's panties and stuck them in her mouth. The two men dragged her body a short distance and covered her with a mattress. Once back at the motel, Let Loose started bragging about shoving the panties in the woman's mouth because she would not give him a blow job.

Brown was shown a picture of Henrietta Wright, and she identified her as the woman Pinky and Let Loose killed. Detectives identified Pinky as 27-year-old Dennis Pinkney and Let Loose as 19-year-old James Spencer.

Based on Brown's information, Spencer was arrested on November 11 for the murder of Henrietta Wright. Pinkney was picked up the following day. Police searched his home and found several pieces of stolen jewelry and two stolen guns under a mattress. However, neither gun was a .25 caliber.

Pinkney waived his rights and denied any knowledge of or participation in the murder of Henrietta.

Detectives interviewed Brown again on November 12. She knew where the murder occurred. She knew the killer had placed something in the victim's mouth, although it wasn't a pair of underwear. She also knew the number of times Henrietta had been shot and that Henrietta was a heavy abuser of cocaine.

Two days later, on November 14, the Los Angeles County District Attorney's office charged Pinkney with murder. He was sent to Los Angeles County jail to await trial. The district attorney's office rejected the case against Spencer, citing insufficient evidence.

But, ten days after the calendar turned to 1987, an anonymous caller reported a murder that would turn the .25-caliber investigation upside down.

CHAPTER 4
BARBARA, 1987

HE WOULDN'T LEAVE HIS NAME, but the tipster, calling from a phone booth, wanted to report "a murder or dead body or something."

It was nineteen minutes into Saturday, January 10, 1987.

"Where at?" asked the LAPD dispatcher.

"1346 East Fifty-sixth Street in the alley," the mystery caller said. "The guy that dropped her off was driving a white-and-blue Dodge van. 1PZP746."

"Did you get a look at him?" the operator asked.

"I didn't see him," said the caller.

"How long ago did this happen?" she asked.

"It happened about thirty minutes ago. I am down the street at the phone. He threw her out. He threw a gas tank on top of her. Only thing you can see out is her feet."

"What's your name?" the operator asked.

"Oh, I'm staying anonymous," the tipster said with what sounded like a chuckle. "I know too many people."

He then hung up.

The dispatcher immediately sent the message of a "possible 187," the California penal code for murder, to LAPD's Newton Division commander. When patrol officers Robert Diaz and Allan Seeget arrived in the graffiti-tagged alley, it was half past midnight. They turned on their flashlights but at first didn't see anything. They were heading back out when they spotted a body partially hidden under a pile of cardboard boxes, plastic bags, dried leaves, and weeds. The victim was facedown, and her head and half of her body were inside a black garbage bag. A gas tank from a car was on top of her, pinning her legs to the ground, just as the caller had said. Diaz and Seeget locked down the crime scene and put up yellow crime-scene tape.

The woman was wearing two-tone gray jeans with a thin pink belt and a white long-sleeved cardigan sweater that was covered in dirt. The shirt she wore underneath, a black halter top with KANGOL printed in white across the chest, had been pulled up, exposing her stomach. Once the bag was removed, officers could see that her mouth and nose were smeared in blood and her right eye was swollen shut. There were four plastic hair curlers, one yellow, two pink, and one green, hanging loosely in her curly black hair. There was no identification, and the body was tagged as a Jane Doe.

By this point, the Southside Slayer Task Force numbered fifty officers, both LAPD and Los Angeles County Sheriff's deputies, and detectives had a mandate to investigate every female body dump scene. Lt. John Zorn, the LAPD commander of the task force, and some of his detectives were called to the scene, as were Newton Division homicide detectives.

Police ran the license-plate number given by the anonymous tipster. The van was registered to the Cosmopolitan Church on South Normandie Avenue. The Pentecostal church had opened its doors six years earlier under the spiritual tutelage of Bishop F. P. Matthews and had amassed a dedicated following. The night that the body was found, the church was hosting a late-night service. Most of the parishioners had been shuttled to and from the church in its sixteen-seat blue-and-white van. Six church members stayed on for a planned sleepover.

When officers were dispatched to the Cosmopolitan Church to locate the van, they found the building's lights on, the front security gate open, and people inside the church. A 1976 Dodge van with the same license plate number reported by the anonymous caller was in the parking lot. One of the officers felt the van's hood. It was warm. A single green hair curler and a partially smoked filter cigarette lay on the ground nearby.

Church employee Ineal Poole and church secretary Marva Lawson were inside talking when a knock on the back door startled them. Poole peeked out a window and saw an LAPD cruiser in the parking lot.

"Oh, my God," she gasped, fearful of what might be going on.

When Poole didn't make a move for the door, her 18-year-old son Dwayne stepped up. "Don't open the door," she told him. "I'll do it." Poole opened the door, and two officers stepped inside.

"There's been a murder," one of the officers announced. He told all six members of the congregation who were sleeping over at the church that night that they needed to come to the police station for questioning as potential witnesses. They included Lawson, Poole, her son Dwayne and teenage daughter Audrey, and the children of church employee Yvonne Carter: 16-year-old Shawnece Carter and 22-year-old Arthur Wilson. All of them denied knowing anything about a murder.

During separate interviews, detectives asked each church member about the van and who drove it. The detectives quickly established that Poole had been the primary driver accompanied at different times by a variety of the other members of the congregation. The church members were locked in prayer during the three-hour service, which ended at 11:30 P.M. Poole couldn't say if the van was moved or not during that time.

The detectives asked where the keys were usually kept. Could the killer have come off the street and stolen them? Lawson said the keys were locked in her desk; Poole told detectives they were just left on Lawson's desk. The detectives wanted to know if Dwayne or Arthur had access to the keys. Poole told detectives that Dwayne did not.

"I was the one driving the van," she said. "They ride with me, keeping me from going by myself."

After interviewing Dwayne and Arthur, the detectives tested their hands for gunshot residue. When they came back clean, the two young men were allowed to leave.

Partial tire treads in the muddy alley where the body was found were compared to the church van's tires but didn't match. Investigators also examined the van for blood and came up empty. They lifted three prints from inside the van, one of which came from inside the front passenger window. The other two prints were pulled from the inside rear passenger window.

At this point, police began to ask themselves if the anonymous caller was playing games. Was he possibly seeking revenge on the church or a church member?

There were no lights in the alley where the body was discovered, so how could the caller have seen the license plate number? Also, a spare wheel on the back of the van partially obscured the plate. It would have been difficult to read it from a distance. The caller would have had to be standing within a few feet of the van to see it clearly.

Detectives had the caller's voice analyzed, and the determination was that the caller was a high-school educated black male with a West Coast accent.

• • •

Results from Jane Doe's fingerprints sent to the lab came back that morning positively identifying Barbara Bethune Ware. She had turned 23 two days earlier.

Barbara's father, Billy Ware, was known as the Mayor of Florence Avenue. A former naval officer from Wichita, Kansas, Billy owned Southwest Furniture on West Florence Avenue and was a popular fixture in the neighborhood. His many friends included furniture salesman Harry Hoffman (father of actor Dustin Hoffman) and Los Angeles County Supervisor Kenneth Hahn. When he wasn't in the store selling and fixing furniture, Billy attended estate sales in Beverly Hills (celebrities were always calling him to pick up their furniture, actor Redd Foxx among them) and was an avid car collector, with a '31 Plymouth, '56 Mercury, and a '31 Chevy among his fleet.

Barbara, called Beth by family members, was Billy's second child from his second marriage, to Barbara White, whom he met when the 17-year-old Texas beauty was visiting an uncle in L.A. It was love at first sight. Barbara White returned to Texas just long enough to let her family know that she was moving to be with Billy. Billy junior was born first. Barbara came along two years later, on January 8, 1964. But after a tumultuous few years that included a stint in drug rehab for the second Mrs. Ware, the couple divorced.

Then 35, the charismatic Billy Sr. didn't stay single long. In February of 1972, when Billy Jr. was 10 and Barbara was 8, he married 33-year-old Diana Frederick, a New Jersey native and divorced mother of a 12-year-old son and 17-year-old daughter. Meanwhile, Barbara White was now clean, engaged to be married, and working as a counselor at a rehab facility. She raised Billy Jr. and Barbara in a two-bedroom apartment. When Barbara was 12, her mother suffered a brain aneurysm, fell into a coma, and died a week later, changing the course of Barbara's life forever.

"Her mother's death devastated Barbara," said her stepmother, Diana Frederick Ware. "She was inconsolable at the funeral."

Barbara and her brother moved in with Billy Sr. and Diana in their three-bedroom home near Martin Luther King Jr. Boulevard. It wasn't long before Barbara started acting out. Billy Jr. and Barbara had a lot of independence growing up with their mother, while her father and Diana ran a strict Catholic household. Curfews were enforced. Church was a given. Barbara rebelled. She refused to do her chores or homework or go to Sunday services with the family. Her grades dropped and she started getting into fights at her middle school. Eventually, she was expelled. Diana and Billy enrolled her in another middle school, but in no time she was tossed out again for fighting. She later graduated from another middle school, but, clearly, she was having major trouble dealing with her mother's death. Her moods regularly turned dark. She would often butt heads with her father. She once called the police after he took a belt to her. The officers who showed up at the house told Billy that a belt wasn't the way to straighten out his daughter's behavior. "My child, my house, my rules," he told them.

"You take her," he added.

"No, Mr. Ware," one officer said. "Just don't leave any marks on her."

The next time the police dealt with Barbara, she was 13, and she wasn't the one who called. She'd started a fight with a girl at a roller rink, and it took two officers to hold her down. When police drove her home, they asked Diana and Billy how a five-foot-two-inch 105-pound teen had such strength.

"Is your daughter on drugs?" one of the officers asked.

Diana and Billy had no idea.

Diana and Billy thought spending more time with Barbara would help and her doctor prescribed antidepressants. It worked for a while, but she soon started acting out again.

Billy and Diana suggested that Barbara spend her high-school years with her maternal grandmother in Houston, Texas. They thought a change of environment might do her some good. Diana had watched South Central change before her eyes. Drugs and prostitution were rampant, as were gangs and drive-by shootings. They thought it best for Barbara to get as far away as possible from the dangers and temptations. They just hoped it wasn't too late.

Barbara was 14 when she moved to Texas. Her time there was momentous and short-lived. Within a year of starting high school, she announced she was pregnant, with no mention to Billy or Diana of who the baby's father might be. On January 2, 1981, at the age of 16, she gave birth to a girl, whom she named Naomi. Soon thereafter, Barbara told her parents she was tired of the Lone Star State and was moving back to L.A.

Billy and Diana hoped that baby Naomi would bring positive changes to Barbara's life. Billy moved his daughter and newborn granddaughter into an apartment in a building he owned behind the furniture store and encouraged her to go back to school.

Barbara didn't stay out of trouble for long. She started using drugs and was arrested for theft on September 15, 1982. Two months later, Barbara, then 18, was arrested for solicitation.

By her early 20s, Barbara's life had become a never-ending quest for drugs. She supported her habit by scrounging money off her father and friends. It was clear that Barbara was overwhelmed by the responsibility of raising Naomi. So Diana started taking care of the child on the weekends.

Barbara loved the anonymity of street life and regularly smoked sherm, a cigarette or joint dipped in PCP, a very potent combination. But that life came with much danger. On September 19, 1985, she called the police to report that she had been robbed of ten dollars and badly beaten at her apartment on Avalon Boulevard. She ended up in the hospital.

Barbara told Diana and Billy a different story. A gangbanger had mistaken her for someone else, she said. Billy and Diana didn't believe it. They suspected she was roughed up over a drug dispute. Billy knew his daughter was borrowing money from drug dealers and not paying them back. One had popped by the furniture store demanding that Billy pay him the $150 he said Barbara owed him. Fearing for his daughter's safety, Billy gave him the money.

Two days after she reported the robbery, Barbara took a handful of pills and turned on the gas stove. Police were called, and she was transported to the hospital again. Her suicide attempt triggered a call to child protective services. Naomi, then 4, was placed in foster care. Barbara was given a choice: go to rehab or lose your daughter to the foster-care system. Barbara agreed to rehab.

Six months later, Barbara appeared to be on the right track. She started taking classes to become a nurse's aide. She also got an evening job as a waitress at Hungry Al's, a local barbecue joint, and moved into a motel on 76th and Western Avenue. She began regular visits to Naomi, who was still in foster care. Billy and Diana were happy with the way Barbara's life seemed to be progressing.

But the pull of drugs once again proved too strong. Barbara would stop by her father's store every couple of months asking for money to pay rent. Billy suspected she was using the money to buy drugs. He offered her a job working with him at the furniture store, but she refused. He told her he wouldn't be giving her any more handouts. The last time most of Barbara's relatives saw her was on New Year's Eve 1986.

It was pouring rain, but Barbara was in good spirits. She and her half sister Treva Anderson, Billy's daughter from his first wife, had gone out to get Barbara cigarettes, and the two were giggling like little girls.

When they got back, Barbara informed Diana and Billy that she had been staying with a male friend on 74th Street. She had seen Naomi that morning at her foster-care mother's house, and, this time, she seemed confident that she was going to get her life back on track.

She never got the chance.

Only Barbara and her killer really knew what transpired on Saturday, January 10, 1987, but an autopsy the following day gave police some indication. Deputy Medical Examiner Dr. William Sherry concluded that the young black woman was shot in the chest with a .25-caliber bullet.

Distraught as he was, Billy immediately started searching for information about his daughter's murder. He thought she owed money to a drug dealer. The local drug dealers shopped at his store. On more than one occasion he watched as they pulled large bags of money out of their car trunks to pay for furniture. He gave them a good price, and they respected him for that. Word soon came back that Barbara didn't owe money to any of the local dealers. If it wasn't a drug dealer, who killed his daughter?

Barbara's funeral was held on Thursday, January 15. She was buried at Inglewood Park Cemetery, and plans were made for Naomi to be adopted by a cousin in Texas. On the same day Barbara was laid to rest, the LAPD's Scientific Investigation Division concluded that the gun that killed Barbara was used in the murders of Debra Jackson and Henrietta Wright.

• • •

By mid-January 1987, the Southside Slayer investigation had stalled, and there was talk in the LAPD about cutting back the manpower on the task force.

"At this point, there does not seem to be a single killer," LAPD task-force commander John Zorn told the *Los Angeles Herald Examiner.* Zorn planned to assess the task force and "make determinations if there should be alterations."

The department was spending around $95,000 a month in overtime costs on the task force, Zorn said. "[It] is a very large group of people, most of whom have been borrowed from other assignments. It's been a very expensive undertaking."[7] The reduction issue was brought up at a police commission meeting at the end of January. Both Los Angeles Police Commissioner Barbara L. Schlei and Police Chief Daryl Gates denied they were reducing manpower.

7. John Crust, "South Side Slayer Unit May Be Reduced," *Los Angeles Herald Examiner*, January 16, 1987.

Schlei said the police department was dedicated to the investigation. Forty-five detectives were working on the task force, and, over the year that the task force was up and running, they had looked into 4,326 clues and put in twenty-eight thousand hours of overtime, he said.[8]

Margaret Prescod, founder of the Black Coalition Fighting Back Serial Murders, was at the commission meeting. She voiced the community's concern. There was "a feeling among women that you don't care, that our lives don't count," she told the commission.

Gates denied that he planned to take officers off the task force. "There has been some [public] discussion about the sheriff's department . . . but I can't speak for the sheriff's department," he replied to Prescod's accusations, according to the *Los Angeles Times*. In fact, the Los Angeles County Sheriff's Department had already reassigned eight of its sixteen Southside Slayer Task Force investigators.

And now detectives had another murder on their hands. One month after Barbara Ware's death, the Southside Slayer Task Force took over her case as well as the murders of Henrietta Wright and Debra Jackson. LAPD detectives Rich Haro and Bill Gailey were named its chief investigators.

• • •

Bill Gailey was a seasoned detective with the LAPD's Robbery-Homicide Division. Rich Haro, his 39-year-old partner, joined the LAPD in 1969 following in the footsteps of his uncle, who was a sheriff in Cochise County, Arizona. Haro was a military man, a former U.S. Army officer who served in Panama and spent a year as a non-commissioned military police officer at West Point Military Academy. When he joined the LAPD, he was tapped to work undercover narcotics.

By early 1984, Haro, a married father of three girls, was work-

8. *Los Angeles Times*, "Vow Made to Keep Serial Killer Task Force at Existing Strength," January 28, 1987.

ing juvenile narcotics at LAPD's South Bureau. One morning during roll call, a supervisor asked three officers if one of them wanted to volunteer for a month in the LAPD's Robbery-Homicide Division. Haro was the only one to raise his hand. It was his dream to become a homicide detective with the exclusive unit. He joined and never left.

Haro's first case involved investigating one of his own. A prostitute claimed she had been picked up by a Los Angeles police officer, brought to his home, and raped. Haro discovered the car used in the case wasn't an LAPD squad car but a California Highway Patrol vehicle that had been sold at a car auction. The rapist only pretended to be a cop. The officer was exonerated.

Haro also began working serial cases, including the shooting of homeless men on Skid Row and the Night Stalker murders, two other infamous multi-murder cases that haunted Southern California. Haro would often arrive home with blood on his shoes. He would take them off and rinse them with the garden hose before he walked into the house.

After cracking open the files of the three South Central .25-caliber murder victims, Haro knew he had his work cut out for him.

• • •

Soon after Barbara Ware's murder, another killer linked to the Southside slayings was arrested.

Daniel Lee Siebert,[9] a white 32-year-old house painter in jail in Alabama awaiting trial for four murders, confessed to killing two prostitutes when he was living in Los Angeles a couple of years earlier.

Los Angeles County Sheriff Sherman Block doubted Siebert would be brought to trial in L.A. for the two murders because he was facing the death penalty in Alabama. Block also didn't believe Siebert was responsible for any more of the murders being investi-

9. In 2008, at the age of 53, Siebert died in prison in Alabama, apparently from complications from pancreatic cancer. He was never brought to L.A. to answer for the murders in court.

gated by the Southside Slayer Task Force. "He didn't admit to any others, and he wouldn't have any reason not to admit to them," he said in late March 1987, according to the *Los Angeles Times*.

Meanwhile, on March 29, 1987, after a preliminary hearing where police informant Shelly Brown was the main witness, Dennis Pinkney was ordered to stand trial for the murder of Henrietta Wright. A month later, another South Central woman was found dead, shot with a .25-caliber pistol.

CHAPTER 5
BERNITA, 1987

RIGOBERTO APARICIO AND JUSTAVO Padilla had just cut across the parking lot behind their employer, Chase's Appliances, on South Western Avenue on Thursday, April 16, 1987, when they made the gruesome discovery. In a back alley, Aparicio saw a white T-shirt wadded up on the ground about fifteen feet from the blue graffiti-covered dumpster. When he picked up the shirt, a Hanes brand, men's large, turned inside out, he saw a tear that ran from the collar to an angry, blood-soaked hole on the front. When he registered what he was holding, Aparicio dropped the shirt and peered inside the dumpster. A foot covered in a gray sock stuck up from a pile of plastic garbage bags. The men ran into the appliance store to call the police.

LAPD detectives Don Hrycyk and J. C. Johnson of the Seventy-seventh Division arrived forty minutes later. As in the case of Barbara Ware, this discarded female body also was covered with debris and garbage. Had Aparicio not looked inside the dumpster, there was a good chance that the body would have ended up in a landfill, and the woman would be forever a missing person.

An LAPD criminalist arrived and pulled aside the garbage and a piece of wood. It appeared the body of a black woman had been tossed headfirst into the dumpster. Still dressed in blue Levi's and a black buttoned-up shirt, the left side of her body was draped in a dirty gray blanket. There was a black tennis shoe on one foot.

Blood was smeared across her face, and some still oozed from her nose and mouth. Still, the detectives could see that she was young and pretty. A small yellow metal heart-shaped earring hung from her right ear lobe. Her jeans were unbuttoned, and the left front pocket of her pants was turned out, indicating to police that her killer probably dressed her after her murder. Several buttons on her shirt were undone, exposing her breasts and a bullet hole. There appeared to be a possible hand imprint on her lower back. A ligature mark ran along the right side of her neck. She wasn't wearing any undergarments. There was what looked like gunpowder residue on her shirt, suggesting to the detectives that she was shot at close range. No bullet casings were found at the scene.

Detectives noticed the word "Mom" tattooed on the front of her right hand. "Fred" and "Nee Nee" were inked on her right forearm.

The body had been dumped in an area known for illicit drug sales and run by the Westside 90th Street Gangsters. Gang tags covered the trash bins up and down the alley as well as the rear wall of Chase's Appliances. A rival gang, the Rolling 60s Crips, had tagged over some of the Westside 90th Street Gangsters' graffiti, a sign that a turf war was being waged.

Aparicio told detectives the garbage bin was empty when he closed the shop at 5:45 P.M. the day before but said it was common to find neighborhood garbage in the unlocked dumpster.

Relatively fresh tire tracks at the crime scene showed a vehicle had entered the parking lot eastbound from Western Avenue and turned sharply south in an arc, braking next to the T-shirt Aparicio had found. The tracks showed the vehicle backed up into the alley and drove off southbound. Photographs were taken of the tire marks as well as the footprints around the dumpster. A fingerprint expert was tasked with finding fingerprints along the surface of the dumpster.

The coroner's office labeled the body Jane Doe #25 on arrival at the morgue. The LAPD came up empty on fingerprints, but the Los Angeles County Sheriff's Department, which serves eighty-eight cities in L.A. County and has a larger fingerprint and forensic lab, was able to identify the dead woman as 26-year-old Bernita Roshell Sparks. She had two minor arrests in 1983, one for destroying evidence, the other for possession of a controlled substance.

Back on Western Avenue, detectives were knocking on doors looking for witnesses. Rosa Harris, who lived in a two-story apartment facing the alley, told detectives she woke up in the early hours of April 16 to the sounds of a woman screaming. She got out of bed and from her window saw a slim black man with a short Jheri curl, a yellow shirt, and light-colored pants leaving the alley. She estimated the man to be five feet eleven inches tall and about 140 pounds.

The LAPD's Hrycyk and Johnson were tasked with informing Bernita's mother, Eva Beard, of her death. Beard, a divorced nurse originally from Memphis, Tennessee, lived on nearby 69th Street with her sister Eunice, Eunice's son, and her own two sons and Bernita.

Eva told detectives she had last seen Bernita around 10:30 P.M. on Wednesday, April 15, the night before her body was found. Bernita was in the living room listening to music when Eva and Eunice went to bed. Bernita wished her mother a good night and said she was going to go to the liquor store half a block away. When Eva woke the next morning, the front door was unlocked.

When the detectives asked Eva if she knew anyone who wanted to harm her daughter, she responded adamantly, "No. Bernita was a good girl."

Bernita had a steady boyfriend, Fred, who she had known since high school. She had just been hired as a school monitor preparing lunches for kids at the 92nd Street Elementary School. Her first day would have been the following Monday.

After the detectives left, Eva Beard went to her room and quietly closed the door. Bernita's brother Alvin, who was four years older, went outside and punched a tree.

• • •

During the autopsy, deputy medical examiner Dr. Irwin Golden pulled a .25-caliber slug from the middle of Bernita's chest. She had suffered several blows to the head and was possibly strangled, as her eyes showed petechial hemorrhaging, the telltale sign of strangulation. Small spotty marks were visible under her arms, consistent with someone dragging her by the armpits. She tested positive for cocaine and alcohol.

The LAPD's Scientific Investigation Division matched the bullet with the .25-caliber slayings.

Detective John St. John notified Southside Slayer Task Force detectives Haro and Gailey that they had another homicide on their hands, the fourth, at least, by the same .25-caliber handgun. Hrycyk and Johnson, now off the case, briefed Haro and Gailey about a woman named Jane Cole, who witnessed a struggle near Chase's Appliances between a black woman and three black men in the early morning hours of April 16. She recognized one as a man called Bodine, who lived in the neighborhood. She saw two men on Bodine's orders drag the woman north on Hobart Boulevard from Century Boulevard. Cole said the woman looked familiar, but she didn't remember her name. Police believed the woman was Bernita.

Cole told detectives that Bodine lived in the Huts, low-income mini projects on Western Avenue, and drove a Chevrolet Blazer and a white Mercedes.

The Los Angeles County Sheriff's Department gang detail identified Bodine as 26-year-old Donald Ray Birdine. He was considered an intermediary to a major coke dealer in South Central and had a rap sheet dating back to when he was 15. There were two outstanding felony warrants for his arrest.

Detectives set up a sting, sending Undercover Narcotics Officer Howard Irvin to Birdine's single-family bungalow, fronted by a black wrought-iron door, to buy some cocaine. He asked for "three hun," street vernacular for $300 worth. Irvin, dressed in a blue jacket, white Oakland Raiders T-shirt, and black jeans, watched as Birdine got a scale and set it on a glass coffee table in the living room, pulled about eight rocks from a sandwich bag in his jacket pocket, and weighed them. Irvin told Birdine that he was going to be starting his own narcotics business in Perris, California, and the man he was purchasing it for wanted to check out the quality of the cocaine first. While they were talking, Irvin noticed the butt of a small-caliber pistol tucked into the left side of Birdine's waistband.

A week later, on May 5, a warrant was obtained to search the property. Irvin, this time wired, arrived around 7 P.M. and bought $400 worth of coke. Thirty minutes later, Birdine was pulled over in a 1975 Lincoln Continental on 87th Street and Western Avenue and taken into custody.

At about the same time, the SWAT team burst into Birdine's heavily fortified home. During the search, detectives found 6.1 grams of rock cocaine, 7.6 grams of marijuana, and, on a glass coffee table, a four-ounce bottle of Welch's grape juice filled with liquid PCP. Underneath a rug in the southeast bedroom, police discovered a Sterling .25-caliber pistol and forty-four live .25-caliber auto rounds. The pistol and bullets were tucked inside a video box for the horror movie *It's Alive.*

The gun, however, was not the .25-caliber weapon used to kill Bernita, Barbara, Debra, and Henrietta. Birdine's white Mercedes and brown Blazer were impounded, but no traces of blood were found in either vehicle.

After his May 5 arrest, Birdine waived his rights and agreed to speak to detectives. He denied knowing any of the murder victims or being involved in their deaths.

Cole, the witness who had fingered Birdine, was unable to identify him in a six-pack, police jargon for a photo lineup. Although

Birdine remained a suspect in the .25-caliber slayings; police didn't have enough evidence to arrest him.

They held him on $1 million bail on a charge of possession and sale of a controlled substance and possession of a firearm by a felon.

Birdine pleaded guilty to a drug charge and was sentenced on September [illegible] to four years in prison.

• • •

On July 6, 1987, the police informant Shelly Brown told Gailey that she had lied about Dennis "Pinky" Pinkney's and James "Let Loose" Spencer's involvement in Henrietta Wright's killing. She then told police that her boyfriend, Jimmy Lewis, was Henrietta's real killer. She had lied, she said, because Lewis threatened to kill her, her children, and her parents if she didn't point the finger at Let Loose and Pinky.

She said she saw Lewis shoot Wright twice in the chest with a small-caliber gun, drag her down the alley, shove a rag in her mouth, and then cover her up with a mattress.

Acting on Brown's information and intel that Birdine and Lewis were seen together in the area of 94th and Western before Bernita Sparks's murder, Haro and Gailey on July 11 ordered a surveillance team to follow Lewis. The street-savvy Lewis picked up on the tail almost immediately, and police took him to Parker Center for questioning. Lewis waived his rights to counsel and spoke to the detectives, denying he had anything to do with the .25-caliber killings.

While he was being questioned, search warrants were served on three homes he frequented, including that of his uncle and aunt and his own one-bedroom apartment. During that search, police found several shotguns and two handguns—a .45-caliber pistol traced to a burglary in Apple Valley, California, and a .357 Magnum, stolen from a sporting goods store in Texarkana, Texas.

Lewis insisted that he had an alibi. He was adamant a polygraph test would exonerate him, but the polygraph examiner told detectives that Lewis appeared deceptive on several key questions, including whether he owned a .25-caliber pistol.

Scared, Lewis copped to owning a .25 caliber. The California Highway Patrol had confiscated the weapon about a month before following the arrest of his friend for grand theft.

Detectives contacted the California Highway Patrol, and the gun was turned over to the Los Angeles Police Department for a ballistics check. The .25-caliber weapon was test-fired on July 14.

It wasn't a match to the bullets pulled out of the .25-caliber victims.

One day earlier, on July 13, Pinkney's case was dismissed by the Los Angeles County District Attorney's office, and he was released from jail.

"With the knowledge that [Shelly Brown] had committed perjury at the preliminary hearing as well as taking into account the rest of her prior inconsistent statements, it was apparent none of her testimony could be trusted—nor could any of it be honestly presented to a jury," Deputy District Attorney Dennis E. Ferris wrote in a memorandum to his boss on July 27.

The day after Pinkney's case was dismissed, Jimmy Lewis was charged with one count of receiving stolen property. Although the guns linked to Lewis and Birdine didn't match the .25-caliber weapon they were looking for, detectives still believed the two men had something to do with the murders. They were mistaken, it turned out.

• • •

At this point, the Southside Slayer Task Force was casting its net every which way it could. Even, in one case, at an especially suspicious-looking face in a crowd hanging around the scene of a strangulation murder. The body of Carolyn Barney, a 29-year-old black woman, was found on May 29, 1987, six weeks after Bernita Sparks's murder, in a vacant lot off of Grandee Avenue in Watts. The detectives noticed unemployed construction worker Louis Craine, 31 years old, at the scene, watching their every move.

They brought him in, and, after hours of intense questioning, Craine copped to Barney's murder and admitted he had killed two other prostitutes, later identified as Loretta Perry and Vivian Collins. Both women had been strangled to death.

Craine, who defense attorneys later said had a below-average IQ, confessed he picked up Barney on the street in his station wagon. He parked the car down the street from his parents' home, and they had oral sex. Craine told police he then sodomized Barney, she demanded extra cash, and they got into a fight. He said he pressed his forearm against her throat for about fifteen minutes and "thought she'd gone to sleep." He went inside his parents' home and took a nap. The next day, he tossed her body into a nearby abandoned lot.

Craine told detectives he and his brother, Roger, hired Vivian Collins for sex and took her to a vacant house. Craine said his brother began choking Collins while he sodomized her. They then swapped, with Craine doing the choking and Roger the sodomizing. Loretta Perry suffered the same fate.[10] Later, at his trial, Craine told a different story.

Roger Craine denied having anything to do with the murders and wasn't charged.

On January 15, 1988, while Louis Craine was in custody, the district attorney's office also charged him with the slayings of Sheila Burris and Gail Ficklin. The body of Burris was discovered in an alley, nude from the waist down, in November 1984. She had been strangled. Ficklin was found strangled to death in an alley on August 15, 1985.

His first trial ended in a mistrial, but Louis Craine was convicted in April of 1989 for the strangulation murders of Loretta Perry, Gail Ficklin, Vivian Collins, and Carolyn Barney and sentenced to die in the gas chamber at San Quentin. Craine, who was also convicted of sexually assaulting the victims, was acquitted of killing Sheila Burris.

Seven months after his sentencing, Craine died of AIDS in a hospital in San Rafael, California.

---

10. Robert W. Welkos and George Ramos, "2 Southside Killings Tied to Prisoner," *Los Angeles Times*, January 16, 1988.

CHAPTER 6
MARY, 1987

EUGENE "GINO" KING WASN'T the marrying kind. So, in the summer of 1977 when his Cuban lover of four months asked him to embrace her Catholic faith and marry her, he knew the relationship was over. Besides, Gino didn't want to mess things up with Jerry, his long-time girlfriend.

Bummed about the breakup, Gino was standing in front of the rum selection in a liquor store on Western Avenue in Hollywood when two pretty young women, a African American girl and her Caucasian friend, sidled up to him.

"Hi, mister, can you do me a favor?" asked the white girl, who introduced herself as Judy. "I'm 20 and can't buy a bottle. If we give you some money, can you buy us one?"

Gino's thoughts shifted from self-pity to opportunity. "Why don't you come back to my house and party with me?" he offered. "I'll buy the bottle."

"We have to go to the airport," Judy said. "We are taking a flight to San Francisco."

"I can drive you girls to the airport," he offered.

The women agreed, and Gino bought a bottle of black rum and a six-pack of cola. They piled into his Gremlin and headed to Gino's basement apartment on Crescent Heights Boulevard in West Hollywood, about one mile away.

It took a couple of drinks to get the black girl to open up, but when she did, she told Gino her name was Brenda, and that she was named after the comic-strip character Brenda Starr. Aptly, she was a big fan of comic strips. She loved Flash Gordon and Little Orphan Annie.

Partying with the two young women gave Gino the ego boost he needed. What man pushing 50 wouldn't want the company of hot young girls? They went for hamburgers before Gino drove them to the airport, as promised. He never expected to see them again.

But four days later Gino was happily surprised to find Brenda at his apartment door. She had left San Francisco abruptly after Judy introduced her to a pimp. "The bitch is trying to put me on the streets," Brenda griped. "I didn't like the son of a bitch, and I wouldn't have a pimp anyways." She told Gino she took a bus back to Los Angeles, but Gino suspected she'd hitchhiked. Once she'd cooled down, she was able to laugh about having to use two barf bags on the flight to San Francisco and swore she would never again drink and then get on a plane.

Gino liked Brenda's spunk. She didn't say much about her family or ambitions, and he appreciated that. All Gino knew was that she was from L.A. and just lived for the day. And that was fine with Gino. The less complicated, the better.

Brenda was a slim, stylish, pretty 20-year-old (at least, that's the age she told him; she was actually 16). She favored breezy summer dresses and high heels. Her shoulder-length black hair was always perfectly coiffed, and she had no qualms about spending the money to keep it either straightened or braided.

Brenda stayed with Gino for two nights. The third morning he woke up to find her gone. But she soon returned, and the two became lovers. Every two or three weeks Brenda would show up on Gino's doorstep. Sometimes she would stay a week, other times just overnight. Brenda was a free spirit. She did what she wanted. Gino suspected she turned tricks, but they never talked about it. Gino's basement apartment became a sanctuary of sorts for Brenda. He let her stay because he wanted to protect her.

Their unconventional relationship lasted ten years. One of Brenda's secrets came to light the day the car brakes failed on the Rambler that Gino had bought for her and she plowed into another car. Gino was negotiating a cash payment with the other driver when he learned Brenda's real name was Mary Lowe.

Soon after, Mary flew to Las Vegas. She didn't tell Gino the purpose of her trip, but when she returned a few days later, she had rolls of cash. Gino took her to East Los Angeles, and she spent $400 on a shoe-shopping spree. She bought so many pairs that Gino thought they wouldn't fit in his trunk.

Then, with no explanation, Mary Lowe just stopped coming by. Gino thought he'd seen the last of her. A year went by with no word, and then one day his phone rang. "Come and pick me up?" she asked, adding a warning. "You aren't going to recognize me."

An hour later Gino pulled up to the corner of Century Boulevard and Western Avenue. A heavyset girl was calling his name and waving at him from across the street. Gino couldn't believe his eyes. Mary, that slip of a girl, no more than one hundred pounds when he last saw her, was now carrying close to two hundred pounds on her five-foot-two-inch frame. She told him she had moved to the South to live with her grandmother. A couple of years later, he learned the truth. She accidentally let it slip when she was drunk that she had done time at Sybil Brand Institute, a women's jail in Los Angeles County. "I never want to get fat like I did at Sybil," he recalled her saying.

They soon slipped back into their old routine. Mary started to show up at Gino's every three weeks or so. Gino had no problems with that, most of the time. One morning, Gino was in bed with his girlfriend Sandra when Mary knocked on the door. It was 6 A.M., and Mary was wasted. She was wearing a dress but was without shoes or underwear.

"I was partying in Beverly Hills," she told Gino. He let her in, and she unrolled the sleeve of her dress and pulled out a wad of fifties and twenties. "Hold on to it," she said. "I need to get some sleep." Gino put the cash in his safe. Mary slept the entire day, and when she woke up she told Gino she was going out to buy something nice for her sister. A week later she came back for the money.

"She wanted crack," Gino later recounted.

It was, for Mary, the beginning of the end.

On October 29, 1987, Gino picked Mary up on Century Boulevard and Western Avenue. They ended up at a hotel in Harbor City, and they got into a fight.

Mary decided she wanted to see her mother. When they got there, her mother, Betty, told Mary she didn't look good and suggested she move in with Gino for a while. This infuriated Mary, who said, "I am going to live my own life," Gino recalled. "I don't care what you SOB's tell me, I am going to live and die on the street."

Mary lived just two more nights.

• • •

As the summer waned and 1987 turned toward fall, the Southside Slayer Task Force was working a disturbing case involving a teenager who stabbed two black prostitutes in South Central. The vicious assaults occurred on August 12 and September 8. The boy had bitten part of the tongue off of one of the women. He proclaimed he was on a satanic mission to kill streetwalkers.

On October 30, Southside Slayer Task Force member and LAPD detective Tom Lange, who later became the lead investigator in the O. J. Simpson case, played down the Satan-worshipping teen's potential involvement in some of the Southside Slayer murders, saying that there were plenty of other suspects being looked at.[11]

LAPD Lt. Dan Cooke took the comment one step further at an October 31 press conference when he stated the teen was not re-

11. United Press International, "Youth Accused of Attempt to Murder Two Women," *Los Angeles Times*, October 31, 1987.

sponsible for any of the Southside Slayer murders. "We have no reason to believe a satanic worshiper is doing it," Cooke said. "There is nothing in the homicides that would suggest an occult kind of killing."

• • •

Halloween 1987 was a treacherous night of torrential rain. There were more than one hundred traffic accidents in Los Angeles and power outages in two hundred homes in Watts. The rain also caused small rockslides near Palmdale.

In spite of the weather, Mary Lowe was celebrating a friend's birthday with Diane Robinson at a local Western Avenue haunt, the Love Trap Bar. She called Gino at 11:45 P.M., hoping to sweet-talk him into picking her up.

But Gino turned her down. Fifteen minutes later his stepmother called to say his father was in the hospital, dying. Gino forgot all about Mary and set out for Austin, Texas.

Diane Robinson last saw Mary at 1:15 A.M. with two black men she didn't know by name but remembered seeing at the club once or twice.

The following morning was overcast, and the streets were still wet. Around ten, a father and his 9-year-old son walking through the alley to the rear of 8927 South Hobart Boulevard came upon the body of a dead woman.

The twisted remains lay facedown between a huge cinder-block wall and a bush. The woman's left arm stuck straight out, and the palm of that hand faced the sky. Her other hand appeared to be resting on the top of her head. The front of her blue frilly blouse had been hoisted up over her waist. Blood soaked a small tear in her blouse made by a bullet. The victim was dressed in a brown-and-blue-checkered leather jacket and black mid-calf high-heel boots. Her beige pants, torn along the outer seams, were unbuttoned and only half-zipped up, the right knee soiled with dirt. She wasn't wearing underwear. A blue, single-snap leather purse containing a piece of a glass crack pipe was next to her right leg.

Police followed the leads and identified the victim as Mary Lowe. She'd been shot with a .25-caliber bullet at very close range.

A toxicology screen tested positive for cocaine and alcohol.

Homicide detectives Gary Lowder and Carlos Brizzolara at the 77th Street Division pieced together Mary's transient lifestyle, which included spurts of time at her parents' house, Gino's place, and squatting at a place known as the Barn or Young's #1 Game Room. The Barn was in the same building complex as the Love Trap, where Mary and her friends were regulars. The complex was owned by Angelo Daire, who at the time of Mary's murder was awaiting sentencing for selling cocaine.

During their investigation, police discovered Mary dropped out of George Washington High School after eleventh grade and held a variety of jobs, including a receptionist gig with First Class Answering Service in Inglewood. She often worked the streets on Western Avenue between Manchester Boulevard and Jesse Owens Park to pay for her drug habit. Mary had eight arrests on file, seven for prostitution and one for grand theft auto.

Several acquaintances provided leads for the detectives to pursue in the search for Mary's killer, all of which turned out to be false. There was "Lucky," a black man in his late 20s with a limp and a tattoo of a Playboy bunny on his back, who worked as a doorman at the Barn. He was overheard threatening to kill Mary at the Love Trap two to three days before her murder.

And there was Alfred Raymond Wright, the owner of Al's TV Shop on 89th Street and Western Avenue, near where her body was found, who was rumored to exchange drugs for sex with the local prostitutes. Both men were said to own guns.

On Wednesday, November 4, the link between Mary's murder and the other .25-caliber killings was confirmed, and Southside Slayer detectives Haro and Gailey took over the investigation.

The following day, Haro contacted the California Department

of Justice and asked for a prison check on all black males with the moniker Lucky. He also asked the LAPD firearms unit to run tests to see if bullets pulled from their victims had been fired by one of the .25-caliber pistols booked into custody at the Seventy-seventh Division Station as well as neighboring Southeast and Newton division stations. He asked the coroner's office to contact him if any cases involving a .25-caliber bullet turned up.

The detectives knocked on Gino's back door a few weeks later. "There was so much crap going on, I didn't know what they wanted to talk about," Gino recalled.

They were looking into his whereabouts the night of October 31, and he was easily able to give an alibi. "I was driving to Texas," Gino told them, and he presented a handful of gas receipts from San Diego, Albuquerque, New Mexico, Odessa, Abilene, and Austin. "I was using my credit card. They just looked at them and said okay. I guess you were there."

Detectives did a background check on the Love Trap Bar on November 12. Haro didn't think bar owner Angelo Daire had anything to do with Mary's murder, but he wasn't ruling out everyone at the bar.

Police interrogated Alfred Raymond Wright of Al's TV Shop on December 1. Wright denied all accusations against him. He said he never met Mary and didn't offer cocaine to prostitutes in exchange for sex. He suggested detectives speak to Marie, a restaurant owner on 89th Street and Western Avenue, about the details of Mary Lowe's murder. Wright allowed the detectives to search his shop for guns, and they found nothing to implicate him in the killing.

Marie's information pointed back to Lucky. A customer overheard Mary arguing with Lucky about drugs at a steakhouse on Western Avenue near Manchester Boulevard, she said. However, none of the steakhouse employees could recall a fight that Saturday night.

Another friend named Red told detectives on Monday, December 7, that Mary was probably killed because she ripped somebody off for money or cocaine. Red also told them that Lucky worked as a doorman at the Barn. "He's a space cadet," she added.

Haro interviewed a man known as McRonnie at the Seventy-seventh Division Station on December 8. McRonnie recalled a fight between Mary and Lucky that Saturday night in question at the Love Trap. Lucky had to be physically restrained by patrons inside the bar, McRonnie said, adding that he hadn't seen Lucky since Mary's murder. He told the detectives that a man named Chuckie might know his whereabouts. Chuckie was easy to find. He was locked up at the California Institution for Men in Chino.

On December 14, a shackled Chuckie told Haro that he was at the Love Trap the night of Mary's murder. He saw Mary there around 1 A.M. The last time he saw her, she was walking alone along Western Avenue. He did know Lucky, he told Haro, but he didn't associate with him.

Meanwhile, an undercover narcotics officer made a drug buy at the Love Trap, and detectives got a search warrant for the bar. Again, the detectives struck out. No weapons were recovered.

Detectives had hit a wall. LAPD's special operations unit known as CRASH (Community Resources Against Street Hoodlums) didn't have any intel on Lucky, nor did California's state prison system, which keeps tabs on gang monikers.

While Haro and Gailey focused their investigation on trying to find Lucky, the Los Angeles Police Department was cutting the number of detectives assigned to the Southside Slayer Task Force.

"The flow of clues is almost non-existent at this point," Lt. John Zorn, LAPD's task-force commander, told the *Los Angeles Times* in early December when he announced that thirty-three of the department's fifty officers would be reassigned.

The decision to cut staffing came in the wake of Pope John Paul II's visit to Los Angeles in September. Hundreds of police officers, including many task-force members, were temporarily assigned to the Pope security unit. A smaller task force operating during their absence was just as productive as the larger team.

"The investigation continues . . . but it's like a three-dimensional puzzle. We keep moving and turning the pieces to see if something fits together," Zorn said.

"This is a better way to use our resources," LAPD commander William Booth said.

That decision irked Margaret Prescod and the Black Coalition Fighting Back Serial Murders.

"If this was another community in which these murders had happened, you wouldn't have the lackadaisical attitude that you see on the part of the police," she said, defiantly. "We're not convinced that they've covered everything."

CHAPTER 7
LACHRICA, 1988

WITH A BIG PROMOTION AT WORK and a big Super Bowl coming up the next day, Karen Toshima and her boyfriend, Eddie Poon, were in a celebratory mood on Saturday night, January 30, 1988. They hit the shops along busy Broxton Avenue in the affluent West Los Angeles area of Westwood near the UCLA campus. In a violent flash, it turned out to be the wrong place at the wrong time.

Two rival black street gangs, the Rolling 60s Crips from South Central and the Mansfield Hustler Crips, had come face-to-face in a video arcade. The angry confrontation quickly spilled out onto the streets where Toshima and Poon were walking. Hustler member Tyrone Swain, certain the Rolling 60s were responsible for a recent drive-by attempt on his life, strode toward his rivals, snarling and taunting. Rolling 60s Crips gangster Durrell DeWitt "Baby Rock" Collins pulled a .38-caliber handgun out of his coat pocket. Two shots came blasting toward Swain.

Toshima and Poon were walking by. The bullets flew by Swain, and one of them struck Toshima in the temple. The 27-year-old graphic artist was rushed to UCLA Medical Center. She was declared dead at eleven the next morning.

Toshima's murder drew a quick and passionate response, not only in Los Angeles but also across the country. Local politicians were outraged that gang members had opened fire in the popular Westwood movie-and-restaurant district and killed an innocent bystander. Los Angeles Councilman Zev Yaroslavsky, whose district included Westwood, proposed the city offer a $25,000 reward for information leading to the suspect in the senseless shooting.

After Toshima's murder, police patrols in Westwood tripled, and more than thirty officers were assigned to catch her killer. Members of LAPD's CRASH brought in more than forty people for questioning. By the week's end, Baby Rock Collins was in custody.

Community activists in the black neighborhoods were outraged. Nothing was being done to help the victims of gang violence in South Central, but now that the violence had spilled into a wealthy white neighborhood, politicians were demanding action.

Of the 205 gang killings in Los Angeles in 1987, more than half occurred in South Central. Innocent bystanders accounted for approximately one-third of the gang-related homicide deaths. One of them was 9-year-old DeAndre Brown, who was playing in a sandbox when he was hit and killed by a stray bullet. Few of these killings got media attention.

"Unfortunately there is a perception that a life lost in South L.A. or East L.A. does not measure up to a life lost somewhere else," said Councilman Robert Farrell.

"We are tired, and we're not going to take it anymore," Maxine Waters, a member of the State Assembly, said at the time. "We are tired because our babies cannot play in the front yard because they might be shot."

Gang interventionist V. G. Guinses put it this way to the *New York Times*: "We sympathize with the young woman who got killed. But South Central has the highest homicide rate. There is nothing in the black and brown neighborhoods to keep kids from getting into gangs, no prevention. Nobody cares about blacks and browns. California is the land of opportunity only in Westwood and Sherman Oaks. In South Central, it is the land of crime."

Following the outrage over the Toshima shooting, the city allocated $6 million in emergency funds for anti-gang suppression programs. It also added 650 police officers to its roster, beefing up patrols in South Central where Police Chief Daryl Gates instituted Operation Hammer—a directive to stop and question gang members hanging out on the streets.

The goal, said Gates, was to "make life miserable for gang members" by apprehending them and their gang associates for petty crimes.

"For months, hundreds of officers swept through black neighborhoods on weekends. Every law was enforced. Every infraction became a cause for arrest," wrote reporter John Buntin in the *New York Times*. "Thousands of black Angelenos were arrested each Friday and Saturday for minor offenses and held in the city jail, their cars impounded (and not infrequently stripped of stereos and rims), then released on Monday. The approach was as desperate as it was alienating."

• • •

Hours before Karen Toshima was killed that Saturday evening of January 30 in Westwood, 22-year-old Lachrica Jefferson was shot to death and her body dumped in an alley in South Central. The media made no mention of it.

• • •

Lachrica's existence mostly centered on drugs. Her friends called her L.A. Crisha because she liked to party and go to clubs like Player's Choice and Total Experience.

Her lifestyle didn't sit well with her mother, Wanda Hutton, who had recurring dreams that her youngest daughter would end up dead.

"Keep your ass off the streets," Wanda would say whenever she discovered Lachrica getting into cars with men, like so many other girls addicted to crack.

"You can't tell me what to do," was always Lachrica's response. She lived as though she were invincible.

Lachrica was an outgoing kid who loved to roller skate, dance, sing, and go to the beach, and she had dreams of becoming a pediatrician. At one point, she moved to Kansas to live with her father, James Jefferson. Two years after her return to L.A., she was hooked on crack.

On January 29, Lachrica visited her mother with a man Wanda didn't know. Later she went to the home of her good friend La Tanya Williams on Florence Boulevard. She left for the apartment of another friend, Jody Gatewood, on 8100 South Western Avenue at around 9:30 P.M.

It was a familiar place for Lachrica. She had lived in the two-story apartment complex with her mother before moving to Crenshaw Boulevard, and her sister Romy and her husband, Al, and their four children and her aunt Yvonne Bell still lived in the building.

Narcotics officers also knew the building well. From the outside, it looked like any other apartment complex along bustling Western Avenue, but, inside, it was a veritable drug store for crack and marijuana.

Lachrica was also a semi-regular at the small white house right next door owned by Othus S. White, a widower who worked for Chrysler before he opened up a tire shop on the corner of 81st Street and Western Avenue. After he sold the shop, he maintained an open-door policy at home, and locals often stopped by for a beer and to watch White play dominoes with friends. Many of White's friends, including a woman named Brenda, showed up at the house around the first of the month when White received his retirement check. When White's grandson suspected he was being taken advantage of, he started picking up and safeguarding the checks. Many of the visitors disappeared. Others started stealing things, including guns, from the house.

Lachrica left Gatewood's apartment around 11:30 P.M., and more than an hour later Gatewood heard loud voices and looked out her kitchen window to see Lachrica in the passenger seat of a nearly new white four-door Mercedes with two racing stripes along its side arguing with a black man in the driver's seat. Lachrica shouted to her friend that the man, who Gatewood didn't recognize, wouldn't let her out of the car. "Get out of the car," she yelled at Lachrica. "Come upstairs."

Gatewood was relieved when Lachrica walked into her apartment a few minutes later. She sat down on the couch, and Gatewood offered her a beer. Lachrica rolled a joint and relayed a terrifying tale of her encounter with the man. Gatewood could tell she was already high.

"He grabbed my knife and held it up against my neck," Lachrica told her as she pounded back a beer and smoked her joint. The women talked until Lachrica passed out in a chair.

Gatewood's daughter's alarm rang at 5:10 the next morning, and Lachrica was gone twenty minutes later. She would be dead within four hours.

• • •

At 9:20 A.M., four miles away in Lennox, an unincorporated area in the South Bay, Randy Logins awoke to the shrill cries of his neighbor Bertha Johnson. Johnson had discovered a foot sticking out from underneath a dirty yellow mattress in the alley behind 2049 West 102nd Street. Groggy, Logins got up and headed to the alley, lifting the mattress to see what made Johnson scream—the body of a young black women. He dropped the mattress and five minutes later called the Los Angeles County Sheriff's Department's Lennox Station.

The victim was dressed in a green knit dress, a maroon coat with a hood, white stockings, and white sandals. She was lying on her back, and there was a red comb in her short brown hair. She was found near a cinder-block wall covered with gang graffiti. Paramedics pronounced her dead at 9:55 A.M.

Los Angeles County Coroner Investigator Deborah Kitchings

took charge of the body at 10:20 A.M. The woman was young, most likely in her early 20s, and was five foot four and weighed a mere ninety-nine pounds. Someone had placed a napkin with the word "AIDS" handwritten in pen on top of her nose and mouth.

Kitchings saw no obvious signs of trauma and told L.A. County Sheriff's Homicide Detective Stanley White that the victim most likely died of an overdose and was dumped in the alley. The woman was fully dressed but was wearing no underwear.

A crack pipe was in her coat pocket. When Kitchings removed her clothing at the coroner's office, she saw she was wrong. The woman had been shot twice in the left side of her chest.

As was so often the case, no identification was found on the body. However, a fingerprint search identified the dead woman as Lachrica Denise Jefferson, of 8100 Western Avenue.

The news that yet another young black woman had been found shot to death in an alley spread quickly in the LAPD. First thing on Monday morning, Haro called Los Angeles County Sheriff Department Sgt. Clinton Dillon. Lachrica's body was found in Lennox, which was under the jurisdiction of the sheriff's department. If Lachrica was killed with a .25-caliber pistol, a bullet would be made available for ballistic testing.

Fifteen minutes later, Dillon, who took over the investigation from White, watched Deputy Medical Examiner Dr. Susan Selser pull two .25-caliber slugs from Lachrica's body. Haro met Dillon at the sheriff's crime lab with the bullet removed from Barbara Ware. A bullet expert confirmed what the detectives already suspected: the bullets were fired from the same weapon. The task force had another victim of an unknown psycho who was killing women with a .25-caliber handgun.

Meanwhile, toxicology tests showed that Lachrica had been drinking and doing cocaine prior to her death.

Sgt. Dillon traced Lachrica's last hours starting with a visit to her mother, Wanda, to inform her that her daughter had been murdered.

La Tanya Williams later told Dillon that Lachrica was afraid of a local pimp, who had bailed her out of Sybil Brand Institute. The pimp wanted his money back. Lachrica did meet with him, but before any money changed hands, she gave him the slip.

• • •

On May 6, 1988, Jimmy Lewis, who was fingered by police informant Shelly Brown in the murder of Henrietta Wright, pleaded guilty to receiving stolen property—but not to killing anyone. While in jail, Lewis wrote a letter to the court asking for leniency.

"In 1987 there were rumors told to the Los Angeles Police Department that I was involved in several murders, which led the police to search in my house and two other relatives' homes, and a third person's house that I didn't know that well," he wrote. "From my home they took a lot of my property; they found a couple of guns, and a few blank money orders, and a few more items. The majority of things they found, like my jewelry and shotguns and other items, I had receipts for, but they took my box with all my papers and ID. They took me to jail and held me for seventy-two hours."[12]

In August, Lewis was sentenced to ninety days in county jail. Eventually he disappeared off the detective's radar as a suspect for any of the .25-caliber killings.

• • •

Nearly two years after the murder of Karen Toshima, a Los Angeles jury declared Baby Rock Collins guilty of first-degree murder and the attempted murder of rival gang member Tyrone Swain. During a November 1, 1989, interview with the *Los Angeles Times* after the verdict, Toshima's brother, Kevin, said, "I guess it sort of puts an end to the ordeal. It's like a final chapter to it all. I am ready to go on living my life, and my parents are, too."

Closure for Lachrica's sister, Romy, was still many years away.

---

12. Small spelling and grammatical errors were corrected.

CHAPTER 8
MONIQUE, 1988

ALICIA MONIQUE ALEXANDER BENT over the living room couch where her father was sleeping and gave his left shoulder a gentle nudge. "Dad," the 18-year-old whispered, "I'm going to A&A's. Do you want anything?" A&A's was a liquor store on Normandie Avenue and 67th Street, just two blocks away from the house where she grew up on a quaint tree-lined street in South Central.

Porter Alexander groggily shook his head. "No, I don't want anything, baby. All I want is for you to come back home," he said, peering at his youngest child, who the family called Monique. Porter, a supervisor with the U.S. Postal Service, grunted, rolled over, and was back asleep in seconds.

He woke an hour later to the sound of his wife, Mary, making dinner. "Where's Monique?" he asked.

"She hasn't come back yet," Mary said casually.

It was Tuesday, September 6, 1988. Porter Alexander would remember that date for the rest of his life. When Monique didn't return home the following day, Porter and Mary started to panic. Monique had left without telling her parents just once before, when she drove to Sacramento with a friend, but she returned the following day. This was out of character.

Mary called her 25-year-old son, Donnell. "Monique didn't come home last night," she told him in a panicked voice.

Donnell was not concerned. "She'll be home," he told his mother, adding that he would look around the neighborhood for her.

Monique had said she was just going to the store. Maybe she'd run into a friend, her parents reasoned. But they were worried. Monique had recently developed a drug habit, and that made her unpredictable.

Porter, who was born in Camden, Arkansas, in 1940 and raised in Stockton, California, was a firm parent but encouraged his children to spread their wings. He wanted them to become curious about the world outside the community, to have a well-rounded view of life, like he did. As a young man, he was stationed in Hawaii with the U.S. military. In the spring of 1962 he settled in Los Angeles, where he met Jasper, Texas, native Mary Deloris Limbrick, a 20-year-old single mother of two young children, Keevin and Anita.

Their first child together, Donnell, was born on August 27, 1963. Porter and Mary married two months later. Their second son, Darin, was born on August 16, 1964. In 1965, the young family bought their home on 69th Street. Monique arrived four years later on June 12, 1970. Her parents and older siblings doted on Monique, each forming a special bond. She was a chubby baby, and her family affectionately called her Moo or Moo Cow, a nickname that stuck.

As much as she was doted over, Monique loved taking care of people. She was in sync with her mother, a consummate nurturer. Monique invited friends to stay over in the room she shared with Shonnell, her brother Donnell's daughter, when they didn't want to go home.

Monique's half sister Anita, who was eight years older, had her own special bond with her younger sister. She potty-trained her and taught her how to walk when she was 8 months old.

Donnell would spend hours drawing with his baby sister at the foot of a picture window in their home. Monique drew horses and ballerinas, while Donnell, a high-school football star and avid sportsman, preferred cars, dragons, and scenes from *Rocky*. They also made skateboards, go-karts, and walking stilts from the scrap wood their father, who worked a side job in construction, kept in their backyard. The siblings spent hours racing through the neighborhood. They were like the Little Rascals, Donnell remembered.

When Porter wasn't working, he and Monique were inseparable. Porter called his daughter his road dog. Mary worked the dayshift at a company that made airplane parts, and Porter, who at that time worked the graveyard shift at the post office, would bring Monique everywhere. There were trips to the store and the local football games where he volunteered, and he got Monique and Anita involved in cheerleading. As Monique grew into a teen, it was clear she was a gifted student who loved ballet, hanging out at Santa Monica and Venice beaches, and going to movies—Spike Lee's 1988 comedy *School Daze* was a favorite. She went ice-skating in Lomita and was such a natural that Porter hired a trainer to teach her to jump.

Monique inherited her father's love for horses and would help him take care of his gray Arabian, Conquest, at a stable in Chino Hills in San Bernardino County.

Although the house was filled with love, Porter kept his children in line with military discipline. He removed their bedroom doors and assigned daily household chores. They were expected to be up each morning shortly after Porter, and they worked in the yard, weeding, mowing, and turning soil in the garden every Saturday.

But by October of 1987, nothing could keep the violence of the streets of South Central from infiltrating the shipshape Alexander home. One night, the family woke around 2 A.M. to the sounds of gunshots. The backyard building where Donnell and Darin slept was sprayed with bullets. Donnell was shot in the left leg but managed to jump the gunman. They grappled for the gun before the shooter ran off. Darin was not injured. Monique frantically called police as Donnell sat bleeding on the floor in the kitchen. An investigation into the shooting went nowhere.

• • •

The changes in Monique came gradually. She became unhappy at school and dropped out in the twelfth grade. She started staying out too late, and sometimes she would get up in the middle of the night and leave the house. Her family would wake up to her empty bed.

On July 5, 1988, one month after Monique's 18th birthday, the slight five-foot-four, 108-pound girl was arrested by the Los Angeles Police Department for possession of a controlled substance. In her mug shot, she is wearing a long-sleeved white shirt with green and blue dog designs. Her straightened hair is in a short ponytail. She looks as innocent as a child.

Monique was dating Ronnie Lewis, a 28-year-old married father of three, who she met at an African artifact store off of Hyde Park and West boulevards. Lewis was minding the store for the owner, a Trinidadian nicknamed Trini. Monique had stopped by to put a down payment on a $400 ceramic angel. Lewis liked that Monique didn't wear a lot of makeup and dressed conservatively.

"Why do you like that piece so much?" he asked her.

"I want to buy it for my mom," she told him.

From that day forward, Monique became a semi-regular at the shop and would sometimes help out, as did Lewis, who wired lights and speakers. Lewis asked for her number, and eventually she gave it to him. Lewis was still married, but he and his wife had separated, he told Monique. "That was a big loose end," he admitted. "I was smitten. If it [Monique's murder] didn't happen we probably would have been together."

The two became serious fast. Lewis idolized Monique's sense of family values, how she talked so affectionately about her parents and siblings. Her life seemed ideal. "For me she was living the perfect life as I wish mine had been," said Lewis. "She had both her mom and dad. Her brothers. They lived in a nice house. Porter worked hard."

In mid-August, Monique got into a fight with her older brother Donnell, who woke up to find his rental car gone. He thought the car had been stolen, until Monique pulled up in the driveway an hour later.

"When did you learn to drive?" he asked her as he dragged her out from behind the front seat.

"I'm good at it, too," she said with a grin. Donnell was still fuming when he drove off.

Just a few days before Donnell's birthday on August 27, Monique saw her brother at their cousin's house and wanted to bury the hatchet and wish him a happy birthday. "Hi, Donnell," she said warmly. The moment he saw his sister's sweet face, his anger melted. Monique had a way of doing that to him—to everybody. She had a way of making everyone forget they were mad at her.

But Donnell, like the rest of his family, couldn't help but worry about his sister. He asked her if she needed any money.

"No, thanks," she said.

"Take it," he said, handing her one hundred dollars and giving her a kiss.

• • •

Lewis and Monique went to Sizzler for dinner on Friday, September 2. That was the last time he saw her.

Two days after Monique vanished, Mary was at home worried sick about her daughter when Lewis pulled his yellow 1978 Ford Fiesta into the driveway. He was there to pick up Monique for a date.

"Monique is not here," said Mary, tears welling in her eyes. "She hasn't come back from the store. It's been two days."

"Have you checked the morgue?" he asked. The cold comment made Mary's heart sink. She wondered why he would say such a thing. Did he know something?

Lewis stuck around till 10 P.M., but Monique didn't show up. He could see the concern on Mary's face grow by the minute.

• • •

On the Sunday afternoon of September 11, six days after Monique went missing, four boys between the ages of 7 and 13 were walking a dog through an alley at the rear of 1720 West 43rd Place when the dog started digging near a large blue foam-rubber mattress that was pushed up against a garage. The rubber pad fell over, and the kids saw a foot. Horrified, they took off down the alley onto Vernon Avenue, where they ran into 32-year-old Douglas Booker.

"Show me," he told them. They took Booker to the spot in the alley. He lifted the foam pad with his cane, exposing a woman's nude decomposing body.

The young woman had been dead for several days, paramedics told the LAPD Southwest Division patrol officers when they arrived at the scene at 3:45 P.M. They noted that her body was lying up against the front side of a garage and her left shoulder was resting on a rimless rubber car tire. Her knees were slightly bent. A blue-and-white shirt had been twisted around her neck and knotted below her left ear. A gold earring lay on the ground, and the matching one was in her left ear. There appeared to be a small-caliber gunshot wound just under her left breast. No identification was found. Police noted that a bottle of Thunderbird wine lay nearby.

The body was in the advance stages of decomposition, so Coroner Investigator Lloyd Mahaney could only collect a partial sexual-assault kit on Jane Doe #59, so named because this murder victim would be the fifty-ninth unidentified female taken to the coroner in 1988.

The next day, a fingerprint was matched to an arrest record, and the dead girl was identified as Alicia "Monique" Alexander.

Her toxicology screen tested positive for cocaine and alcohol.

Southside Slayer Detective Rich Haro and L.A. County Sheriff's Department Sgt. Clinton Dillon, who was handling the Lachrica

Jefferson case, were present at the coroner's office for the autopsy. Monique was killed by a bullet to the chest fired from a .25-caliber pistol. She was another victim of the misery-making Southside murder rampage.

• • •

Monique's death was a devastating blow to the Alexanders. Why would someone kill Monique? Everyone loved her.

Donnell was angry. "How could they kill her on my watch?" he said.

In the back of Donnell's mind, he wondered if he had inadvertently set off a chain of events that led to Monique's death. Not long before she was murdered, he robbed someone during a drug deal. It haunted him that it might have led to his sister being killed. He told his father of his suspicions. "Dad said if it had to do with your sister, you need to talk to the police," Donnell remembered.

Donnell went to the police, and he was taken into custody on a bench warrant from a previous arrest and missed Monique's funeral. "For the longest time I thought I got my sister killed because of the way I conducted myself," Donnell said. "Part of me thought I was responsible. For a long time I lived with it. I lived with that possibility."

• • •

As the death toll mounted, it became clear to the detectives that the killer's signature stretched beyond the .25-caliber gun. He had an unwavering methodology. All seven victims were shot in the chest, in an almost-identical location. From the angle of the bullet entry points, it appeared the killer was sitting to the left of his victims when he fired. Haro figured that each of the victims was sitting in the passenger seat of a car when the shots were fired. In Monique's case, as with the other victims, it appeared the gun had been placed on or near her skin.

With Monique's death, Haro had a new significant clue to add to the mix. A witness had seen her get into a 1974 or 1975 Ford Pinto or Chevrolet Vega, dark brown or rust in color with a loud muffler, at 11 P.M. on September 6, on the southeast corner of 69th Street and Normandie Avenue. The car's side or rear windows were tinted or covered by a curtain. The witness noticed what appeared to be a spot on the right front fender, possibly due to a repair job, and an object hanging from the rearview mirror or lying on the dash. A bulletin as well as a sketch of the car was sent out to all vice and patrol units. But nothing came of it.

Then, just over two months later, police finally got their first big break: a live victim, and she described the suspect's car as an orange Ford Pinto.

CHAPTER 9
ENIETRA, 1988

ON SATURDAY, NOVEMBER 19, 1988, a 4.5-magnitude earthquake in the Pacific Ocean shook buildings and rattled the residents of Southern California from La Jolla in San Diego County to Ventura County, north of Los Angeles, and as far inland as Redlands. Enietra Washington had plans that night to go to a party with her friend, Lynda Hoover. Enietra had just returned from Louisiana and spent the day at her job doing housework for an elderly widower. After cleaning, doing chores, and shopping, she felt she deserved a night out. Working and raising two children—she had her first at 19—was rewarding but tiring. She needed to let off some steam. And a little rumbler wasn't going to change that. Her kids, now 5 and 11, were at a babysitter's house for the night, and she couldn't wait to paint the town.

Enietra stood in front of the hallway mirror, in her signature blue-and-cream peasant blouse and a tight Calvin Klein cream-denim miniskirt, and applied a final coat of ruby-red lipstick. After smoking a joint laced with cocaine, she was ready to go.

Her life was about to be shaken much harder than the earthquake had just shaken Southern California.

Enietra was tall—standing at five foot seven—handsome, and didn't have a problem attracting men. Her quick wit and gregarious personality made her a welcome guest at most house parties. Her Inglewood High School friends called her Chewy, an affectionate nickname given to her by her father because she ground her teeth at night. A life-long resident of South Central, there wasn't a street, alleyway, or intersection Enietra didn't know.

It was a cool autumn night by Los Angeles standards when Enietra finally stepped outside. The air felt good on her exposed arms and legs. Lynda's house was on 84th Street and Denker Avenue, a short walk away.

As she approached the D&S Market on 84th Place and Normandie Avenue, an orange Ford Pinto with a white racing stripe on the hood and down the driver's side caught her eye. Ford Pintos were a dime a dozen in the hood, but a racing stripe was a rarity. It looked like the miniature Hot Wheels car her children played with, she thought. A lot of the neighborhood boys were car junkies and had taught Enietra a few things growing up. She could change a tire and replace brake pads as well as any mechanic. She even helped her father install a new engine in his Chrysler LeBaron. She felt she knew cars as well as she knew men.

She took note of the Pinto, but she hadn't noticed the man who caught her looking at the car until she heard him say something to her. She paid him no heed and kept on walking. Seconds later, the same man, same car, came up alongside her. He rolled down the passenger window and offered her a ride. She turned to see a neatly dressed, stocky man with short-cropped hair. *Nerd* flashed in her mind. Despite his tidy appearance, she responded with her trademark sneer and told him, "Don't holler at me from a car. You have to get out and talk to me."

Enietra had come across her fair share of pushy men and shady characters, and she judged this guy to be as dangerous as a golden retriever. Still, he was a bit too dorky for her tastes, too timid and eager to please. When he got out of the car to talk to her, she noticed he was wearing khaki pants, a dark blue button-down shirt, and a tan jacket. He could be a gas-station attendant, she thought. He was about her age, 30, or slightly older, slightly taller—about five foot eight—soft-spoken, neat. But she didn't consider him attractive. She liked her men tall and muscular. Besides, she was still stinging from the breakup with her ex.

"Where are you headed?" he asked.

"I am going to a friend's house," she said.

She scanned the inside of his car. It was immaculate, no trash or traces of dust. "Can I take you?" he asked shyly. She gave him one of her well-rehearsed I-don't-think-so glares and started to walk away.

"What are you going to do with your friend?" he asked.

"We are going to a party," she responded.

"Let me take you over to your friend's," he persisted.

"No, that's okay," she told him. "I'm good."

"That's what's wrong with you black women," he said, pushing her buttons. "People can't be nice to you."

"Excuse me?" she bellowed, and then she caught herself chuckling when she saw the big grin on his own black face.

What the hell, she thought. He looked harmless. You couldn't knock a guy for trying to get some on the side. She knew she had a sharp tongue, and this guy seemed so dejected. She felt sorry for him. Because she was a taller woman, most short men who approached her had an attitude. Besides, he was only driving her a few blocks. What was the worst thing that could happen?

"Okay," she said. "I'll let you take me over to her house."

He smiled and told her to get in.

She noticed a lug-nut wrench lying on the floor next to a small green metal box socket set and some loose sockets. The dashboard was cracked in a spiderweb pattern on the passenger side. The seats were topped with light beige sheepskin covers.

She told him where she was going. He pulled away from the

curb, and when he got to Western and Denker avenues, he made a left turn instead of keeping straight.

"You are going the wrong way," she told him.

He said he had to make a quick stop at his uncle's house to get some money. It would only take a few minutes, he said. Soon enough he was on 81st Street, rolling up in front of a white stucco house next to an apartment complex and an auto-repair shop.

"I'll be right back," he said jovially. Enietra sunk into the seat and watched him amble up the driveway and around to the side of the house and then disappear inside. She lit a cigarette and decided she'd give him ten minutes. If he took longer, she would get out and walk.

He returned quickly, jumped into the car, drove down 81st Street, and then turned right on the next street, South Harvard Boulevard. He said something, but Enietra was listening to the radio and paid him no attention. In mere seconds his demeanor changed from easy-going smooth talker to vicious thug. And, for some reason, he called her Brenda.

Puzzled by his personality shift, Enietra thought he was confused and had mistaken her for a well-known local prostitute named Debbie, who called herself Brenda, who trolled for johns along Western Avenue.

"That's not my name," she said.

He said nothing but reached into the driver's-side door pocket, pulled out a small gun, pointed it at her chest, and pulled the trigger. It happened so quickly Enietra could barely compute what was happening.

She felt a sudden sting and then a searing pain. In a panic, she reached for the door handle.

"Don't touch that door, bitch," he said, gritting his teeth. "I'll shoot you again."

"Why did you shoot me?" she asked.

"You always dogging me out, Brenda," he said.

"I don't know you," she groaned, grabbing at her chest where the bullet entered.

Terror took hold. How could she have misjudged him so badly? He seemed so normal. Was she going to die? What would happen to her kids?

"I think you need to take me to the hospital," she pleaded.

"I can't do that," he said.

"If I die I am going to haunt you," she said. "You better take care of my kids."

Enietra was petrified, but she tried to stay calm. She knew that if she panicked she could go into shock. Keep your head straight, she told herself. But breathing was becoming difficult. She began gasping for air. She had a fleeting thought again of her children and wondered what they were doing while she was dying. All her energy leaked from her body, and she blacked out.

When she came to, the man was straddling her. She was still in the passenger seat of his car. Her skirt was jacked up past her waist. The seat had been tilted back, and she could barely breathe. She struggled to get out from under him, but she floated in and out of consciousness. She woke up to a flash of light and heard the distinctive zing of a Polaroid camera. Dazed and unable to move, Enietra finally felt a heavy weight ease from her body. She heard an engine start, and the car was moving.

The next thing she remembered was the driver pushing her out of the passenger side and hitting the ground like a stone. He left her crumpled and bleeding in the middle of the empty street. The pain was unbearable. Enietra remained still, eyes closed, waiting for the next shot or blow.

She didn't dare move until she heard the car start up. She opened her eyes to see the back of the Pinto disappear down the street, turning right one block away. Racked with pain on the cold roadway, it took her a few minutes to register that the sky had gone dark. She wondered how long she had been held by her attacker. She rolled to the curb and then dragged her battered frame off the road. Weak from blood loss, Enietra didn't scream or run to the nearest house for help. She knew any attempt would be futile—in 1988, few people in South Central answered their doors after dark. Shot, bleeding, and somehow shoeless, she hobbled toward what she thought was a main street. It was 84th Street. Her friend Lynda Hoover's house was just a few blocks away.

Enietra dragged herself onto the front porch of Lynda's house and cried out. "Help me. Open the door," she pleaded. And then she collapsed.

No one was home. Lynda and her husband had obviously grown tired of waiting for Enietra and had gone ahead to the party. Any neighbors who may have heard Enietra's woeful squeals drew their curtains or turned up their television sets.

When Lynda and her husband arrived home around 2 A.M. on November 20, they found Enietra curled in a fetal position and bleeding. Lynda noticed that her friend's underwear was ripped and hanging off her. She was still weakly knocking on their door.

"Don't let me die," Enietra implored, over and over again. "Don't let me die."

Enietra was clearly in shock. She was shaking, she seemed cold, but she was sweating. Lynda called an ambulance, and Enietra was rushed to the Harbor-UCLA Medical Center in Torrance, eleven miles away.

Her condition was dire. Her blood pressure had dropped so low that paramedics put her in a compression jacket. By the time she arrived at the hospital, she had lost 20 percent of the blood in her body.

Enietra could hear scattered bits of conversation between the doctors and nurses. She noticed that a surgeon standing over her looked like Superman, the old TV version played by actor George Reeves.

"Am I dying?" she asked.

Before the cardiothoracic surgeon could answer, Enietra passed out.

It would be four days before Enietra stabilized enough for the surgeon to remove the bullet from her chest. The .25-caliber slug had just missed her heart.

• • •

Around noon the day of Enietra's surgery, November 23, LAPD Detective Rich Haro knocked on Lynda Hoover's door. Since Enietra was shot under similar circumstances to the .25-caliber slayings they were investigating, Haro suspected her case was linked. If so, this was a huge break.

While Haro interviewed Lynda, the surgeon at Harbor-UCLA Medical Center removed the small-caliber slug from Enietra's left chest area and dropped it into a metal container. It was sent to the LAPD and booked into custody at the Seventy-seventh Division Station and was compared to the bullet removed from Barbara Ware's chest. The results were inconclusive. On Tuesday, November 29, Enietra's bullet was taken to the sheriff's firearms lab and compared to Lachrica Jefferson's bullet. The bullet pried out of Lachrica was in better condition than the bullet that felled Barbara Ware. The examiner concluded both bullets were fired from the same gun.

They had another .25-caliber victim, and this one was alive.

Later that day, Haro and a Los Angeles County Sheriff's Department composite artist interviewed Enietra at the hospital. She described her attacker as a dark-complexioned black man with pock marks on his face and short hair; he was of medium-build, around 145 to 155 pounds, about five foot eight, clean-shaven, and in his early 30s. He was calm and well-spoken.

In a follow-up interview, Enietra provided even more details. When she got into the car, a 1970s orange Ford Pinto with a hatchback, she noticed the man placed a black jacket and some books on the backseat. The car possibly had a roof rack and tinted windows, she recalled. The interior was green, and the seats had tan or brown sheepskin covers.

She told detectives the man stopped to pick up money while she waited in the car. Her attacker mentioned a relative, possibly a cousin or an uncle, that lived at the house. As well as the books, she recalled seeing some mechanical tools, possibly socket wrenches, on the backseat and floor of his car.

Enietra was released from the hospital, and five days later, on Wednesday, December 7, Haro and Gailey picked her up. They were going to try and follow the trail of her attacker. She led the detectives to the store and pointed out where she first met him, then directed the detectives to West 81st Street. A few minutes later, they were parked in front of 1742 West 81st Street, the house her attacker stopped at that night.

"That's the place," Enietra said.

The detectives noted the address and drove off. Back at police headquarters, they discovered 77-year-old Othus S. White owned the property. Haro and Gailey dropped by the next morning to speak to White. The house, like old-man White, was unkempt. The front lawn was overgrown and the paint on the exterior had chipped off and what remained had faded to a dull gray. Over the years, the house had slowly transformed from a family home into a drug den and hooker hangout.

The detectives noted that White was too old to fit Enietra's profile, but there were a lot of people going in and out of the house. White told the detectives he didn't recall any guests the night of Enietra's attack, nor did he recall seeing an orange Pinto. Undeterred, officers canvassed the neighborhood and beyond and set up surveillance for any signs of the car. They even left their card at the home of a friendly neighborhood man named Lonnie, but no one was home. The officers never returned to canvas the neighbor they missed, nor did Lonnie call them back.

On February 17, 1989, Haro and Gailey served White with a warrant to search his home. They found a Tanfoglio Giuseppe .25-caliber semiautomatic pistol and a magazine containing four live rounds underneath seat cushions in the living room. It was the same type of gun used in the attacks on Enietra and the seven other women. Two Polaroid cameras were also discovered. The .25-caliber gun and a shotgun were taken into evidence. It was later determined that the pistol, purchased by White on April 8, 1988, was not the weapon they were looking for.

• • •

In the meantime, the Southside Slayer Task Force was distracted by another killing spree in South L.A. in the fall of 1988. Three black prostitutes had been murdered in the area along the Harbor Freeway and Gage Avenue. The fatal shots all came from a 9mm pistol, not the .25-caliber gun used in the other killings.

The body of Judith Simpson, 27, was found shot on October 14 at 88th and San Pedro streets; Cynthia Walker, 35, was discovered dead November 18 at Flower and 46th streets; and Latanya Johnson, 24, was found murdered on December 11 on West 94th Street. Patrol officers in South Central were alerted to be extra vigilant.

At 1:30 A.M. on February 23, 1989, Seventy-seventh Division Officer Mike Acevedo and his partner, Ron "Snoopy" Smith, were on patrol in the area when they spotted a parked blue Ford Tempo with a couple sitting inside. As the officers walked toward the car, the driver peeled away. The officers sped off in pursuit, and, after they flashed their lights, the man pulled over.

The officers ordered the couple out of the car. The male driver, whose belt was unbuckled and pants were unbuttoned, was staggering and leaning on his car for support.

The driver identified himself as Rickey Ross, a Los Angeles County deputy sheriff. Ross, a 41-year-old African American veteran narcotics officer, was driving a county-leased unmarked car.

"What's the problem?" Ross said, incensed that the officers had pulled him over. "I wouldn't arrest you for drinking."

His passenger, Jimmie Joann McGhee, a prostitute who exchanged sexual favors for drugs, told the officers they were smoking marijuana but then changed her story and admitted it was cocaine.

Ross responded, "Man, she is lying. The only dope in that car is in a package. I have court tomorrow. You can search the whole car."

"The only thing I did with her was drink a Pepsi," he added. "I don't know if the bitch put anything in it."

Officer Smith opened the trunk and found a rusted loaded 9mm Baretta semiautomatic pistol and an evidence envelope containing cocaine.

Ross was arrested for driving under the influence and taken to the Seventy-seventh Division Station. McGhee was arrested on a traffic warrant.

At the station, Ross told a police sergeant that he "screwed up. I was out there trying to get a head job."

McGhee told the same sergeant that Ross picked her up around 12:30 A.M. near the Snooty Fox Motel on Western Avenue and asked her if she wanted to get high. She said Ross had a chip of rock cocaine, which they smoked through holes they punched in a Pepsi can. Ross tossed the can out the passenger window when he spotted the police.

At 3:15 A.M., Ross was turned over to a Los Angeles County Sheriff's Department lieutenant. Ross, who was part of a Drug Enforcement Agency task force at LAX, told the lieutenant he had been drinking earlier in the evening with a drug-enforcement officer from Minnesota in town for two weeks of training. Ross said he was driving through downtown L.A. on his way home when McGhee flagged him down. She was cute and he felt sorry for her and wanted to help her out, he said.

Ross said McGhee told him she was from Colorado, had no money, and was willing to do anything for cash. Ross said they drove around looking for a secluded spot so he could get "a little head."

On the way, he stopped at a store and bought McGhee a Pepsi. Ross said she suggested going to a motel, but he only had two dollars and was fearful she was going to set him up.

Ross said he was concerned when McGhee pulled out some cocaine but more concerned about "getting some head."

Ross's pants were down around his thighs when he saw a car pull up behind him with no headlights, and he drove off. When he realized the car tailing him was a police vehicle he pulled over.

After speaking to his attorney, Ross declined to speak anymore with the police and refused to provide a urine sample.

McGhee told a captain at the station that Ross had been throwing up a lot and had told her he had been mixing his drinks earlier in the evening and doing "tabs," street jargon for LSD.

Three hours and fifteen minutes after Ross was taken into custody, he was administered a Breathalyzer test. He passed.

About one hour later, a drug-recognition expert evaluated Ross and said that he didn't appear to be under the influence of any substance. However, an examination of his nasal cavity, pupil size, and pulse rate was consistent with cocaine usage.

Ross was released to the sheriff's lieutenant, who drove him to his home in Rialto, a city in nearby San Bernardino County. The confiscated pistol, which was badly rusted from rain, was sent for ballistics testing.

Ross's gun came back a ballistics match to the slugs dug out of the three prostitutes, and he was arrested at his home. The Pepsi can, which officers later went back to pick up, was subjected to a chemical and physical analysis and came back positive for cocaine. Police identified both McGhee's and Ross's fingerprints on the can.

Ross, the LAPD would discover, habitually did not follow proper procedure. The LAPD searched Ross's desk at the airport and found twelve balloons of heroin in a DEA evidence envelope, with the contents line left blank. The sheriff protocol mandated that officers put evidence envelopes in a secure locker and not in their desk.

Police conducted an audit on narcotics evidence Ross had handled and discovered he had written that fifteen grams of an unknown powder, fifteen grams of rock cocaine, and one marijuana cigarette were sent to the state for disposal. However, police were unable to locate a transmittal copy confirming the delivery.

They also discovered that Ross had not properly processed two handguns and $18,000 on November 1, 1988. The money was accounted for, but the handguns were found in Ross's desk instead of an evidence locker. Also, the cocaine found in Ross's car the night he picked up McGhee had not been properly checked out.

Police believed that Ross also owned a .25-caliber pistol and theorized that in addition to the three prostitute slayings, he was likely responsible for the attack on Enietra Washington and the seven .25-caliber killings between 1985 and 1988.

A search of his home failed to turn up any additional evidence. Still, based on the ballistics test on the 9mm gun they had found in his trunk, Ross was charged the following day with three counts of first-degree murder with special circumstances, making him eligible for the death penalty. Ross adamantly denied any involvement in the slayings of Simpson, Walker, and Johnson.

As Enietra watched Ross's arrest on the nightly news, she was glad the madman with a 9mm gun had finally been caught. But she never thought that the large man on the TV could ever be confused with the nerd who left her for dead.

Ross's colleagues were dumbfounded by his arrest. The detective, a born-again Christian and father of two who quoted Bible verses by heart, volunteered for more than eight years as a lay minister helping out inmates in county jail. He also belonged to a motorcycle club. In a recent employee evaluation, his supervisor described him as the airport's "ambassador of goodwill" because he regularly helped others.[13]

"He would help passengers when he could, he would give people directions," Sheriff's Captain Robert Wilber told the *Los Angeles Herald Examiner*. "I've never heard anything negative about him. I've met with his supervisors across the board, and people are unable to believe he would do something like this."

Coworkers called the six-foot-two, 220-pound hulking deputy "a gentle giant," "down to earth," and "happy-go-lucky." Ross had eighteen years on the force and an unblemished record. He was a heavy smoker and a poor eater, and he drank Jack Daniels with his fellow deputies, but he was never known to do drugs or fraternize with hookers.

But to some, Ross was going through a midlife change of sorts.

---

13. John Crust and Greg Krikorian, "Deputy Held as Suspect in Hooker Deaths," *Los Angeles Herald Examiner* February 25, 1989.

He and his family had upgraded from a rent-free apartment in Gardena to a more than $250,000 two-story, four-bedroom home in Rialto with a red-tile roof and pool and spectacular view of the golf course at El Rancho Verde Country Club. He had quit teaching his Bible-study class at the county jail and transferred to the drug task force. Police suspected he was on the take.

Ross's wife, Sylvia, was angered by the accusations. She and her husband, she explained, were able to put a down payment on the big house in Rialto because they had sold a previous home as well as some empty lots they owned. Before the purchase, they had lived rent-free above a car business where her husband moonlighted as nighttime security. Also, she noted, while Ross had given up his Bible-study class, he still taught it at the Gardena apartment.

"I don't know where people are getting all this stuff from that we didn't have any money," Sylvia said. "I was a flight attendant, I was making good money. My husband made good money . . . They went through all our bills. Trust me, they did all that . . . to try to insinuate that maybe drugs or something were the reason why we had our money or whatever. And none of that was found."

• • •

Two days after Ross's arrest, L.A. County Sheriff Sherman Block called a news conference to express his deep disappointment. "In law enforcement the most devastating thing that can happen to any organization is the death of one of its members. And close behind that is an incident where one of the agency's members goes over the line and is involved in serious criminal activity."

"This is a very sad day for the Los Angeles County Sheriff's Department," said Block.

At the same press conference, LAPD Chief Daryl Gates told the crowded room of reporters Ross spoke to investigators about his evening with McGhee but the chief would disclose only a portion of what was said.

"He was not able to explain all this, but he did talk freely to the officers . . . admitted that he picked up the young woman, but he did not believe she was a prostitute," Gates said. The area where Ross was stopped is known for prostitution, he said.

Also at the press conference, Los Angeles Deputy District Attorney Sterling E. Norris, alluding to the .25-caliber killings without explicitly saying so, said Ross was one of a number of possible suspects being looked at in a series of prostitution murders.

One week earlier, the LAPD had refused to supply victims' names or any other details for a KABC-TV report that noted that as many as twelve women over the previous three and a half years had been found shot to death with the same small-caliber handgun. The television reporter said that the first victim's body (later determined to be Debra Jackson) had been found in August 1985 in an alley off West Gage Avenue. The reporter also stated that the last body was found in September 1988, which turned out to be Monique Alexander.

The KABC-TV report alleged that the police kept the killings a secret because they were concerned about protests from residents of South Central. However, the LAPD denied the claims. "I can say without equivocation that our reluctance to publicize [the killings] has nothing to do with [a fear of] any major demonstrations," LAPD spokesman Fred Nixon told the *Los Angeles Times* on February 17.

On Tuesday, February 21, Margaret Prescod and other community activists voiced their frustration to the Los Angeles Police Commission that the LAPD was once again keeping the news of a serial killer a secret and in doing so was jeopardizing the safety of the girls on the street.

"We are outraged that you have made so deadly a calculation when so many lives were at risk, a deadly kind of calculation that would not have been made were it any other community at risk. Imagine twelve or thirteen or twenty-nine women killed in Westwood . . . Would it have been such a well-guarded secret?"

"There is too much of the 'us against them' mentality in the LAPD," said Mark Ridley-Thomas, the executive director of the Southern Christian Leadership Conference of Greater Los Angeles. "It just points to the fact that they have blinders on and they simply don't trust the community on how these things should be dealt with."[14]

Once again, Gates, LAPD's top cop, had to reassure South Central that race or occupation was not a factor in the police investigation. "We look to nothing except that the person is dead," he said. "We have to be very careful with what we say. Whether there will be a statement forthcoming, I can't say."

At this point, Ross was being held for his own protection in an isolated cell at Parker Center. His visitors included Encino attorney Richard A. Shinee, a young barrister known to represent Los Angeles County police officers in civil rights and officer-involved shooting cases, as well as lawyers from the firm of Los Angeles attorney Johnnie L. Cochran Jr.[15]

• • •

Despite the continuing murders, crack addiction soared and prostitution thrived along the seedy South Central streets.

Police were frustrated. They acknowledged they were not having much success solving the Southside Slayer murders or the murder of other prostitutes, but they lamented they weren't getting help from the community where the women were being attacked. "The obvious difficulty in working these cases is nobody cares," Seventy-seventh Division Homicide Supervisor Paul Mize told the *Los Angeles Times* in March of 1989. "The family of the women care, but the street community is hardly helping police or on the lookout for suspicious-looking drivers. There are rarely any eyewitnesses, and if there are, they make themselves invisible."

---

14. John Crust and Greg Krikorian, "Deputy Held as Suspect in Hooker Deaths," *Los Angeles Herald Examiner*, February 25, 1989.
15. Johnnie L. Cochran Jr. later became a member of the so-called Dream Team that successfully represented O. J. Simpson at trial, where Simpson was accused of killing his ex-wife Nicole Brown and her friend Ron Goldman.

Many of the murdered women were also invisible in a way. They were lost, near the point of hopelessness; in a haze of a drug addiction, they were already missing in the eyes of their relatives when they were found dead.

"A lot of them didn't have any contact with family members," Detective Rich Haro said later. "And when we did find next of kin, they were, like, it was just a matter of time. They knew it was coming sooner or later. Even if there were witnesses to the murders on the street, they didn't want to get involved with the police because they didn't trust us. For the most part we had to dig and try to get their confidence. It was a very difficult task."

In the upper-class mainly white neighborhoods where murders were rare, residents spoke out and witnesses willingly came forward. Everyone was eager to get a criminal off the street. The social norm was that citizens expected to feel safe. South Central was a different world. Residents feared sticking their noses into other people's business. They were afraid of being beat up or killed. Gangs ran the neighborhoods with big guns, and everyday citizens lived in fear.

• • •

Three weeks after Ross's arrest, a ballistics expert hired by Ross's attorney concluded that Ross's 9mm gun was not the weapon used to kill the three prostitutes, Walker, Johnson, and Simpson. In May, the district attorney's office agreed to have the gun examined by two independent experts in Northern California to resolve the conflicting test results. The first expert concluded that the gun wasn't a match. The second examination, conducted by the California Department of Justice, concluded that while Ross's gun could not be completely ruled out, the likelihood that the gun was used in the murders was minimal.

The murder case against Ross rapidly unraveled. Ross, who had put in a resignation letter citing personal reasons on April 27, the same day he was fired from the force, was soon to be a free man.

"Los Angeles Police Department's ballistics experts have reexamined their test results in view of the opinions of other experts and have changed their earlier opinion," Deputy District Attorney William Hodgman said in a written statement. "They cannot now say that it was the defendant's gun that was the murder weapon . . . Therefore, there is presently no convincing evidence that Rickey Ross committed these crimes."

However, the LAPD refused to concede the blunder. "The gun has not been ruled in with 100 percent certainty, and it hasn't been ruled out with any degree of certainty," Commander William Booth told the *Los Angeles Times.*

Booth did tell the *Times* that the department had started an internal administrative review to figure out why their ballistic examiners connected Ross's gun to the slayings when the outside experts did not.

"I have never killed anyone," Ross wrote in a public statement. "The gun found in the trunk of the car was a gun purchased by me, registered to me, and used in the performance of my duty as a deputy sheriff for over fifteen years. Is it logical that if I were killing people I would use a gun registered to me?"

After eighty-two days in jail, all charges against Ross were dropped, and he was set free. Hodgman said Ross still remained a suspect because he was "found in a kill zone with a strawberry," the *Los Angeles Times* reported. "Even now he's the only one [suspect], but it now becomes an open investigation."

However, Hodgman allowed, there was a chance that as the investigation continued it could "very well result that we can dismiss him as a suspect."

In late May, the *Los Angeles Times* interviewed Jimmie Joann McGhee at Sybil Brand Institute. McGhee said she lied to police about Ross giving her the cocaine because she was afraid she would end up in prison. Instead, she said, Ross gave her ten dollars to buy a rock of cocaine.

"I smoked a hit," she told the *Times*. "And he smoked a hit."

Ross's criminal defense lawyer, Jay Jaffe, disputed McGhee's claim, stating that "there was no use of drugs [by Ross] that night, and all the chemical tests confirm that," according to the *Times*.

In early August, the county civil service commission said Ross chose not to appeal his dismissal from the sheriff's department. Howard L. Weitzman,[16] who also represented Ross, told the *Los Angeles Times* that his client was "emotionally incapable of going back to law enforcement work."

A month later, Ross filed a federal lawsuit for $400 million against the LAPD and eleven officers alleging civil-rights violations, false arrest and imprisonment, unlawful search and seizure, and the filing of false police reports.

Ross claimed that his house was searched without a lawful warrant, and that an item of jewelry was missing after one of the searches, and that the LAPD held his wife a prisoner in their home for fourteen and a half hours. While in jail, Ross alleged he was in constant fear for his life and was racially discriminated against. He was, he concluded, a victim of malicious prosecution.[17]

"While incarcerated, Deputy Ross was forced to undergo the indignity of being nicknamed and referred to as the 'Strawberry Killer' and further being referred to as one of 'the double R's,' a reference to Richard Ramirez, the Night Stalker serial killer, who was in an isolation cell opposite Deputy Ross's isolation cell," the lawsuit stated.

Ross said he had been subjected daily to blood tests while in jail. "The LAPD drew three vials of blood from him, and conducted daily blood tests on him, to perform DNA testing to attempt to match Deputy Ross's blood with that of the [murderer's] found at the crime scene[s] of at least some of the murders for which he was suspect. When Deputy Ross asked whether he would be released

16. Weitzman is best known for representing high-profile-client automaker John Z. DeLorean, who was arrested for cocaine trafficking by the U.S. government and later acquitted in 1982.
17. In 1992, Ross was charged with conspiracy to possess cocaine for sale and with possession of monetary proceeds derived from the sale of narcotics. The case was tried in February of 1994 and resulted in a mistrial. Ross's federal civil-rights lawsuit finally went to court in March of 1997. After a two-week trial, a Los Angeles jury found Ross's lawsuit had no merit and ruled in favor of the city. Ross left the downtown courthouse dejected and bitter.

when the LAPD found no matchup, as Ross knew they would not because he was innocent, he was told he would not be released."

Ross also took aim at the LAPD's ballistic examiners, claiming that the three experts "falsified the results of ballistics tests performed upon the 9mm Smith and Wesson pistol" that was found in the trunk of his car.

• • •

Although Ross was a free man, police still believed he had something to do with the murders—little did they know the real killer was still out there, lying low, perhaps waiting for the heat to die down.

PART TWO
THE GRIM SLEEPER RETURNS
1989–2010

CHAPTER 10
WARMING THE COLD CASES

IN THE SPRING OF 1989, the Los Angeles County District Attorney had no choice but to drop all the charges against L.A. County Sheriff's Department Deputy Rickey Ross. Coincidentally the murders linked to the .25-caliber killer appeared to stop. Southside Slayer Task Force Detective Rich Haro moved on to new homicide cases and retired from the Robbery-Homicide Division in January of 2002. His partner, Bill Gailey, had already retired in 1991, after twenty-three years of service. John St. John, the legendary gumshoe who also worked the Southside Slayer murders, died in 1995, two years after retiring from a fifty-one-year stint with the LAPD.

Before disbanding in the late '80s, the Southside Slayer Task Force was able to close multiple murder investigations, including those of the serial killers Daniel Lee Siebert and Louis Craine.

Still, many of the Southside Slayer cases, some of which were later identified as the handiwork of at least six serial killers, remained unsolved—including the .25-caliber killings. Family members were coming to terms with the fact that the murder of their loved ones would remain a mystery.

In December of 1993, the police brought down another Southside monster when they picked up an African American named Michael Hubert Hughes. The former security guard and Navy machinist was arrested by Culver City police for the murders of four women between 1992 and 1993.

Like his serial-killer brethren, Hughes zeroed in on drug-addicted women, discarding their lifeless bodies in back alleys and parks. But his deadly pursuits stood out beyond even that. He had a penchant for positioning his victims in vulgar poses: often each was nude with her legs spread wide with one hand touching her vagina, as if she were masturbating.

He mainly targeted young black women but did stray from that profile.

Teresa Marie Ballard, 26, was discovered in Jesse Owens Park in South Central on September 23, 1992, nude from the waist down, legs splayed. Brenda Bradley, 38, was found on October 5, 1992, in nearby Culver City, also naked from the waist down but with her knees bent and two fingers from her right hand touching her pubic area. Terri Myles, 33, was discovered wrapped in a bed sheet curled in the fetal position in a Culver City alley on November 8, 1993. Jamie Harrington, a 29-year-old Caucasian woman, was found slouched in a shopping cart in Culver City by police on November 14, 1993. She weighed 320 pounds and was bound by floral-print sheet ligatures around her neck and ankles. A separate ligature tied one ankle to the bottom of the shopping cart. Pieces of the torn sheets used to bind her were found in Hughes's house.

Hughes, a native of Michigan, was convicted of the four slayings on December 16, 1998, and was sentenced to life in prison without the possibility of parole. Hughes was later connected through DNA evidence to four additional murders, including the May 1986 strangulation of 36-year-old African American prostitute Verna Patricia Williams, who was originally thought to be a victim of the Southside Slayer. Williams was found in an elementary school stairwell with a multicolored scarf tied tightly around her neck and her pants pulled down around one ankle, her legs spread. Williams's murder was investigated by John St. John and Bill Gailey as part of the Southside Slayer Task Force.

• • •

Despite the successful convictions and prison sentences for these serial killers, life in South Central in the early '90s did not improve. Crack was still ravaging the community. Lawlessness thrived as jobs dried up. Gangs and gang violence flourished, with the city murder rate rising to an all-time high. The Los Angeles Police Department was entering one of its toughest and most challenging decades, epitomized by the vicious beating of black motorist Rodney King by four white police officers on March 3, 1991, after a high-speed chase through Los Angeles County.

When King finally pulled over, the 25-year-old unemployed construction worker was pummeled with more than fifty baton strikes, leaving him with multiple broken bones, including a broken leg and a fracture at the base of his skull.

George Holliday recorded the beatdown from his apartment balcony. The nine-minute videotape, which he reportedly sold to KTLA-TV for $500, led to the indictment of LAPD Sergeant Stacey Koon and officers Laurence Michael Powell, Timothy Wind, and Theodore Briseno.

Two weeks later, on March 16, 1991, the racial unrest ignited by the King beating was compounded by the shooting of Latasha Harlins, a 15-year-old black girl, in a grocery store over a $1.79 bottle of orange juice. Soon Ja Du, the owner of the Korean American liquor and grocery mart, was charged with the killing and went on trial in October 1991. At the trial, prosecutors presented security-camera footage showing the confrontation and then the shot to the back of Harlins's head as she was leaving the store.

A jury found Soon guilty of voluntary manslaughter, which carried a maximum sentence of eleven years in prison. The judge sentenced Soon to probation, along with four hundred hours of community service and a $500 fine. The relative slap on Soon's wrist was perceived by the majority of L.A.'s black citizens as a slap in their collective face.

Six months later, on April 29, 1992, black Angelenos were enraged again by another seemingly racially blind judicial act, once more involving King. The four police officers were acquitted of the beating. This time, the outrage ensued with a violent chain reaction of protest. For six days, stores, including dozens of Korean-owned businesses, were looted and set on fire. Rioters attacked dozens of motorists, including white truck-driver Reginald Denny, whose brutal assault was also captured on videotape. More than fifty people died and as many as two thousand were injured. The anger-fueled mayhem became known as the Rodney King Riots.

The officers were tried months later in federal court on charges of violating King's civil rights. Koon and Powell were found guilty and eventually sentenced to two and a half years in prison. Briseno and Wind were acquitted.

But the social, racial, and media pressures squeezing the LAPD like a vise showed no signs of easing up. Two years later, police were still on edge and overworked when, on June 13, 1994, former pro football player O. J. Simpson's ex-wife Nicole Brown and her friend Ronald Goldman were found murdered in the affluent neighborhood of Brentwood. A few days later, Simpson was arrested for the murders.

The police handling of this case continued to shred the already-tattered reputation of the Los Angeles Police Department. Simpson's arrest and trial, which began in January of 1995, spotlighted sloppy forensic collection and a lackluster investigation by Robbery-Homicide and West L.A. Division Detective Mark Fuhrman, one of the first detectives on the scene. On October 3, 1995, the jury deliberated for less than four hours before they found Simpson not guilty. While the verdict was controversial, it at least kept peace in the streets. The anticipation of the violence that might have erupted if the appearance of racial injustice resulted in a conviction was real.

• • •

Another crisis, of a different sort, lay ahead for the LAPD. In 1999 it was hit with the worst corruption scandal in its history. Known as the Rampart Scandal, for the Rampart Police Station at its epicenter, it was triggered by charges of police misdoings by a corrupt anti-gang unit officer, Rafael Perez, who had been convicted of stealing cocaine that had been booked into evidence. Perez implicated numerous fellow officers in what had become commonplace corruption—making bogus arrests, writing false police reports, physically abusing suspects, tampering with evidence, and planting evidence on innocent civilians. The fallout was instantaneous and enormous, and public trust in the LAPD collapsed to an all-time low. The city paid out more than $75 million to settle civil lawsuits. Dozens of convictions were overturned, and the city was forced to accept federal oversight of LAPD operations.

The stench of the Rampart Scandal proved hard to escape, but, as the calendar ushered in the 2000s, a new era of advanced DNA testing jumpstarted the LAPD's resurrection. The department would soon become renowned worldwide for its skill in using DNA to solve crimes by taking biological samples—such as semen found on a blanket or saliva traces on a beer bottle—to create a profile of a suspect that could be compared against a database of felons. All this started with a $50 million grant from the California Department of Justice to pay for DNA testing to clear law enforcement's backlog of unsolved murders and sex crimes.

David Lambkin, a veteran sex-crime detective with the LAPD, had pushed the department for close to a decade to form a cold-case unit. Now, in late 2001, propelled by the prospects heralded by the new DNA capabilities, he got what he wanted and was put in charge. He ran the new cold-case unit from the LAPD's former library on the fifth floor of Parker Center.

The detectives picked for the new team were experts in their own right with decades of experience.

One of them, Tim Marcia, was a respected detective and had worked with Lambkin at LAPD's Hollywood Division. The same year Marcia joined the cold-case unit, he appeared in the documentary *James Ellroy's Feast of Death.* (James Ellroy, a true-crime writer, created the documentary because of his fascination with his mother's murder and the unsolved 1947 mutilation slaying of aspiring actress Elizabeth Short, the so-called Black Dahlia.) Rick Jackson, a smooth talker with a reputation as a methodical and hard-working Robbery-Homicide detective, was tapped to join the new unit, as was Richard Bengtson, who excelled in homicide investigations.

Also assigned to the cold-case team were Jose Ramirez, a seasoned gang-homicide detective known for his quick mind and respectable close rate; Vivian Flores, a gang investigator and one of the few female detectives in Robbery-Homicide; and Cliff Shepard, a homicide detective with LAPD's Central Division, with a reputation as a methodical investigator with a sharp memory for details.

The detectives were brought in to determine if any of the department's unsolved murder cases were potentially solvable—which meant finding out if there was still crime-scene evidence, such as blood, skin, or semen, available for DNA testing. If forensic evidence was available, the sample would be sent to labs for testing paid for by the state grant program. Once the evidence was tested, it was uploaded into the local, state, and federal felon databases to see if the DNA left at the crime scene was a genetic match to a profile already in the system.

Spending long hours poring through files looking for cases with evidence that could possibly be tested for DNA turned out to be frustrating work. Hundreds of pieces of evidence were destroyed in dozens of cases by previous detectives.

Detective Shepard was particularly peeved by the destruction of evidence. It galled him that dozens of murder cases would most likely never be solved and families would have to live their lives never knowing what happened to their loved ones. Even so, Shepard enjoyed the work. It was this kind of detail work—reading through murder books, the investigative reports detailing a homicide, looking for nuggets of information that could lead him to a killer—that attracted Shepard to the job.

Shepard grew up in a bucolic middle-class white neighborhood of St. Louis known as Clifton Heights. He was the middle son of a German-immigrant mother who met his father, then with the U.S. Army, at a club in Berlin in 1945.

The first inkling that he would choose a career in law enforcement came when he was 13 years old. He was buying candy at a neighborhood store when an older woman asked him if he would walk her one block to the bus stop. She was afraid to walk the street at night, and that bothered Shepard

Shepard set his sights on the Los Angeles Police Department after watching on live television the May 1974 shootout between LAPD SWAT officers and the Symbionese Liberation Army. The SLA, a band of urban guerrillas, had kidnapped Patty Hearst, the 19-year-old heiress and granddaughter of newspaper titan William Randolph Hearst. She was abducted from her apartment in Berkeley California, and after months as a captive she appeared to have joined her abductors. After tracking the group relentlessly, the LAPD, with guns at the ready, and TV news cameras also at the ready, surrounded the group, which was holed up in a home in South Central. Four SLA members died in the roaring fire that erupted when tear gas canisters ignited an ammunition cache inside the house. Two others were killed as they tried to run away from police, who unleashed a fusillade of over a thousand rounds of ammunition during the assault. Patty Hearst, it turned out, was not inside the house.

Shepard applied to the LAPD just a few months later, and, after a background check and psychological exam he was hired on January 20, 1975. After five months of training at the police academy in Elysian Park, Shepard was assigned to the foot beat at Central Division. One year later, he was transferred to the Communications Division at Parker Center, working as a dispatcher answering emergency calls.

In April of 1984, Shepard became a patrol-training officer at

Southeast Division in South Central at the height of the city's crack epidemic. For his last three years at Southeast he was assigned to detectives investigating property crimes, sex assaults, crimes against persons, and auto theft. On December 26, 1993, Shepard was promoted to Detective I and was transferred back to where he began, Central Division, where he worked burglaries. He was offered a detective position in homicide in 1996.

Two years later, he was assigned to investigate the murder of 41-year-old Paula Vance, a mentally ill transient who in early 1998 was lured to a walkway next to an office building in downtown L.A., where her killer knocked her to the ground and brutally raped her before strangling her. The chilling attack was caught on blurry black-and-white surveillance footage. Once the assault was over, a hulking black figure with a slight limp walked away. The blitz attack made Shepard think that the killer had murdered before.

When Shepard joined the cold-case squad in November of 2001, he took the Vance case with him. It fit the unit's mandate, and he sent off the suspect's DNA for testing.

On September 8, 2003, Shepard and his partner, Jose Ramirez, were at LAPD's Wilshire Division Station on an unrelated murder case when Ramirez's cell phone rang.

"You got a hit on one of your cold cases," Detective Vivian Flores told him.

It was the first one for Shepard and Ramirez since they joined the cold-case unit, and it felt like they hit the jackpot. Back at the office, Shepard realized the hit was related to the Vance case.

The same DNA found on Paula Vance matched the DNA found on Ramirez's cold-case murder of Mildred Beasley, a 45-year-old married mother with a bad drug habit. Beasley had been discovered at the side of the Harbor Freeway, south of Colden Avenue, on November 6, 1996. She was partially disrobed and appeared to have ligature marks around her neck.

Now they had a name attached to the genetic signature: Chester DeWayne Turner.

Turner, 37, was easy to track down. He was serving an eight-year sentence at the Sierra Conservation Center state prison in Jamestown, California, for the March 16, 2002, rape of Maria Martinez, a homeless woman who lived in a tent with her boyfriend on the streets of L.A.'s downtown Skid Row.

On the night of her attack, Martinez was walking to a twenty-four-hour hamburger joint on Los Angeles Street when Turner approached her and asked if she had a light. Martinez recognized him from the Midnight Mission, where he worked as a security guard.

When she handed Turner her lighter, he grabbed her hand, pulled her to him, and grabbed her by the throat. He dragged her to a parking lot and ordered her to pull her pants down. He pinned her to the ground, pressed her face into the grimy pavement, and sexually assaulted her for hours. After the brutal encounter, Turner told her he was on parole and that if she told the police, he would kill her.

They walked down the street together to 7th Street and Maple, where Martinez, in a state of shock, quickly walked away. She headed straight to the LAPD's Central Division station. Martinez went inside, but when she was told to wait to talk to an officer, she left. The following day, she told an administrator at a local mission what had happened and was urged to report the attack. She did.

Turner, who faced the possibility of more than twenty years in prison if convicted, pleaded guilty and was given eight years on September 17, 2002. As part of his guilty plea, Turner had to submit a DNA sample to authorities, which was then uploaded into the local, state, and felon DNA databanks.

Shepard and Ramirez examined Turner's extensive criminal history and became convinced that the Arkansas-born Turner, a high-school dropout who grew up in South Central during the crack and PCP epidemic of the '80s, had left more than Vance, Beasley, and the attack of Martinez in his wake.

Turner had registered as a sex offender in the early '90s after he was arrested for indecent exposure and later for lewd conduct for masturbating in front of a crossing guard.

On October 3, 2001, Turner attacked a woman who agreed to have sex with him for drugs. He made a tent out of cardboard and then bound the woman's arms together and stuffed strips of her shirt in her mouth. After repeatedly raping her, he threatened to kill her if she told anyone. She later did tell an officer about the attack by Turner, but when detectives arrived to interview her, she couldn't be found.

Turner's deviant past led Shepard and Ramirez to study what ended up being close to thirty unsolved cold cases from 1987 to 2002. All involved murders of women in South Central and downtown L.A. in which the victims were partially clothed and appeared to have been raped and in which the cause of death was strangulation.

The detectives knew most serial killers started young, and Turner, who had been nicknamed Chester the Molester by classmates, was no exception.

Turner's DNA was matched to eight more victims. The detectives were astounded. They knew Turner was a sexual sadist and killer, but they had no idea how prolific he had been.

With these findings, the detectives had unearthed another serial killer who stalked the Southside in the 1980s.

• • •

Ramirez and Shepard pieced together Turner's ruthless killing history. He took his first victim when he was a 20-year-old deliveryman for Domino's Pizza. On March 9, 1987, Diane Johnson was found nude from the waist down on a sidewalk alongside the 110 Freeway in South Central.

Louisiana-born Annette Ernest, 26, was next. She was found on October 29, 1987, facedown, her pants around her ankles and her blouse pulled up, exposing her breasts. Her body was just three blocks from where Johnson was discovered.

Anita Fishman, 31, disappeared fifteen months later, on January 20, 1989. Her partially nude, decomposing body was hidden behind a discarded door that was propped against a garage in an alley near the 9800 block of South Figueroa Street in South Central.

And nine months later, 27-year-old Regina Washington was six-and-a-half-months pregnant when her body was found, on September 23, 1989, with a coaxial cable wrapped around her neck inside the garage of a vacant home on South Figueroa Street, about ten blocks from where Fishman's body was found.

Turner appeared to take a killing break for a few years, but then he started again, killing five more women between April 1993 and April 1998, including Andrea Tripplett and Desarae Jones, both 29 years old, and Natalie Price, 31.

The Paula Vance murder, which tied Turner via DNA to all these other killings, was one of them but not the last. That was Brenda Bries, 39, who was found inside a portable toilet stall with ligature marks around her neck, and her pants and underwear around her knees, a block away from the Regal Hotel in downtown L.A., where Chester Turner sometimes lived.

As the detectives began investigating all the Turner slayings, they came across something that every detective dreads—a wrongful conviction. David Allen Jones, a part-time janitor with an IQ of 62, was in prison serving time for three of the murders that detectives now pinned to Turner.

Jones had been convicted even though there was no eyewitness or physical evidence tying him to the cases. None of the hair, blood, and semen samples collected at the crime scenes matched his O blood type. They did, however, match Turner's type A blood.

Jones's three alleged victims were Tammie Christmas, found dead on September 30, 1992, next to a portable classroom at an elementary school; Debra Williams, 32, discovered at the bottom of a stairwell at the same school almost two months later on November 16; and Mary Edwards, 41, whose body was found one month later in a carport at a rundown motel. All these death sites were within walking distance of the South Central home Turner at that point shared with his mother.

LAPD detectives interviewed Jones three times in early 1993 over a span of two days. At the time, Jones, then 33, was in jail. He had been arrested for the alleged rape of a woman in his backyard in December 1992.

During the interviews, Jones denied killing the women but admitted to having sex with Christmas, Williams, and Edwards and putting them in choke holds after they picked a fight with him. But, he insisted, all the women were still breathing when he left them. He was later convicted of the murder of Edwards and manslaughter in the deaths of Christmas and Williams.

Jones spent nine years in prison before he was exonerated in March 2004 after DNA evidence in the Edwards and Williams cases was matched to Turner. Jones was also cleared in the death of Christmas, although no DNA evidence in that case remained. It had been destroyed in 1998. Jones was given a $720,000 settlement by the city of Los Angeles.

• • •

Solving the Turner serial killings did a lot to abate the anxiety that gripped residents of Southside L.A. for nearly two decades. Victims' families, loved ones, and friends at long last had a measure of closure. The entire community, especially its population of young and often drug-weakened black women, was able to take a welcomed deep breath.

So, too, could the LAPD. Haunted by a rocky history with its black communities, it also enjoyed this respite.

CHAPTER 11
THE .25-CALIBER KILLER

THE LINKING OF THE COLD-CASE murders to Chester Turner was a big win for detectives Shepard and Ramirez, and supervisors acknowledged this.

Shepard was walking through the halls of Parker Center after Turner was charged when a member of the LAPD brass stopped him with a question.

"Are there any other serial murders you can solve?"

"Yes," Shepard said immediately. He was interested in one series of killings in particular: the Southside Slayer murders of the 1980s. Back in 1984, while Shepard was assigned to the Southeast Division, he worked overtime patrolling the alleyways and parks looking for victims of the Southside Slayer. He would often speak to the homicide detectives and ask them if they had a suspect he should be looking for. They always answered that they had no one because they were all stumped. And then the Southside Slayer Task Force disbanded, and the cases went cold.

Shepard got the go-ahead to reopen the Southside Slayer files. He dove into the archives and instantly grew frustrated. Although he knew about the Southside Slayer Task Force, he didn't know the names of the victims and had a hard time tracking down the murder books. As he slowly gathered the cases and read the files, he realized there was a separate task force within the Southside Slayer Task Force looking at a series of .25-caliber killings between 1985 and 1988. The victims—Debra Jackson, Henrietta Wright, Mary Lowe, Bernita Sparks, Barbara Ware, and Alicia "Monique" Alexander—were all fatally shot with the same .25-caliber handgun, and their bodies had all been dumped in dirty alleys off of Western Avenue. There was also an L.A. County Sheriff's Department case connection. That victim, Lachrica Jefferson, was linked to the other cases through ballistics testing.

Shepard asked for all the bullets to be analyzed again. The firearms examiner's conclusion was the same result as found in the '80s—all the bullets were fired from the same gun.

There were other notable similarities. All the victims were missing their panties or bra, or both. In some instances it looked as though they had been sloppily dressed, or, more likely, re-dressed after they were killed.

As Shepard reviewed the files, he came across a survivor, Enietra Washington.

In September of 2003, Shepard was combing through each of the murder books looking for vital crime-scene evidence. After months of review, Shepard submitted requests for DNA testing for the only three cases with available DNA evidence—those of Mary Lowe, Bernita Sparks, and Barbara Ware. The bodies of Debra Jackson and Monique Alexander were too badly decomposed to provide DNA, and the forensic evidence in the Henrietta Wright case had been destroyed.

Almost fifteen months later, on December 9, 2004, Shepard got a case-to-case DNA hit. The DNA found on 1987 murder victim Mary Lowe matched the DNA found on a new victim, Valerie Louise McCorvey, killed on July 11, 2003.

Shepard was shocked.

A school crossing guard notified police of the latest victim. Betty Walker had just arrived at her post at 108th Street near Denver Avenue at 6:35 A.M. on July 11 and was putting on her reflective vest when a car pulled up alongside her.

"You need to call the police," the man inside said matter-of-factly. "There's a body over there." He pointed toward the entrance of the alley off Denver.

Walker turned to look. "I don't see anything," she said.

"Well, it's there," he replied, and he drove off. The exchange was so unexpected that Walker didn't get a good look at the man or his car. All she remembered when she spoke to the police was that it was a light-colored midsized car.

Curious, she walked down the modest residential street toward the mouth of the alley. There it was: a woman's body, crumpled on the paved lane near a locked gated alley. Walker dialed 911.

The dead woman's clothes were askew. Her navy blue long-sleeved leotard was pulled down, exposing her breasts. Her brown pants were at her thighs, exposing her buttocks, and she wasn't wearing undergarments. And while she was wearing dirty socks, she didn't have shoes. A black-and-white wool knit sweater partially covered her head.

LAPD homicide supervisor Sal LaBarbera arrived on the scene and pulled a white screen from his car and put it around the body out of respect for the victim and passersby.

Behind the screen, Homicide Detective Roger Allen got to work. He saw the road rash on the top of the victim's left shoulder and arm and another abrasion on her left clavicle. He also noticed the petechial hemorrhaging in her eyes. Allen deduced this was a body dump.

Noting the dead woman was lying in a twisted position, with her left arm resting awkwardly under her head, Allen determined the road rash on her left shoulder and arm were consistent with being pushed out of the passenger side of a vehicle. It seemed to him that after she was shoved out, her body spun around and landed on the right hip. The bruises on the back of her right shoulder led Allen to believe that the woman could have lived for a few minutes after she was tossed out of the car.

Allen took note of the gang graffiti on the electrical pole near the dead woman, but he didn't believe this murder had anything directly to do with gangs.

Coroner Investigator Kay Fritz rolled the victim onto a plastic sheet on her back and collected trace evidence from the surface of her clothes. There was a suspicious mark on her left breast that looked like a bite. There were also signs of blunt-force trauma to her head.

A large, band-like ligature circled most of her neck, and Deputy Medical Examiner Dr. Darryl Garber, who performed an autopsy three days later, concluded that the young woman had been strangled. The white shell necklace hanging around her neck was the probable murder weapon. The necklace had strands of short black hair tangled in it. The victim might have clawed at her own neck to get at the ligature as she was being strangled. It would have taken about one to two minutes of constant pressure to kill her.

Her toxicology results revealed drugs and alcohol in her system.

She was swabbed for DNA, and samples were sent to the LAPD's Scientific Investigation Division for testing. A fingerprint search identified the victim as Valerie Louise McCorvey, 35, of South Central.

This murder didn't involve a .25-caliber bullet, but an exact DNA match to a murder committed sixteen years earlier could only mean one thing: the killer who haunted South Central throughout the 1980s was still at large and still murdering women.

Unfortunately for Shepard, the reawakened Southside killer wasn't in the county, state, or felon DNA databases. If he had been, there would have been a match, just as there had been in the Chester Turner case. So it would seem that the serial killer Shepard was after had never committed a crime that would have mandated a DNA swab.

CHAPTER 12

VALERIE, 2003

VALERIE MCCORVEY WAS A DRUG addict living on the streets with six prostitution arrests on her record when Robert Nobles, a convicted felon and pimp, took her under his wing.

His intentions were anything but noble. Valerie was just another one of his projects. He would get women clean so he could put them back on the street as prostitutes working for him.

But Valerie's drug addiction made her erratic and hard to pin down.

Nobles's daughter Lucinda recalled the day she met Valerie. "[Robert] knocked on my door at three in the morning, and he had her with him," she said.

"She looked like Pookie from *New Jack City*," she remembered, referring to Chris Rock's crack-addict character Benny "Pookie" Robinson.

They needed a place to stay, so Lucinda let them stay over that night, and Valerie became a fixture in Lucinda's life for the next few years.

Nobles got Valerie pregnant, twice. She had a daughter, Symphony, who was born with drugs in her system and was put into foster care. She then had a son, Matthew, who was born on October 22, 1999. She stayed clean for a while, lived in Section 8 housing, and even worked at a drug facility helping out other addicts, but sobriety ultimately eluded her.

When Matthew was 2 years old, Lucinda took custody of her half brother and eventually adopted him. Valerie would occasionally call and stop by to see her son. On one occasion when Valerie was clean, she stopped by and "cried because she wanted her baby," Lucinda recalled. "I told her, 'You don't have to worry about him, he is with his big sister. Just know your baby is fine until you can get it together.' I knew she loved him. So she sat there and cried and cried."

"When she was not on drugs, you could tell she could have been a lawyer or a teacher," Lucinda said. "I think she was very embarrassed when she came around me. She was a sweet person, and she wanted more, but she couldn't because the drugs had her."

As Valerie struggled to stay clean, she also struggled to end things with Nobles. "When Valerie wasn't on drugs, I believe she was a decent person, and I think she came to her senses and my dad probably wanted her to do things she didn't want to do," Lucinda said. "She disappeared on my father, and he wanted to find her so bad. He hated her so bad."

When Lucinda learned—from her father—that Valerie had been murdered, "I thought my father killed her," she said. "My father was a cold man. He told me that he would have put my mother on the streets if she hadn't got pregnant with me."[18]

Lucinda wouldn't find out for seven years that her father had nothing to do with Valerie's death.

• • •

18. Nobles was homeless and panhandling when he died of natural causes behind a Burbank liquor store in 2016.

As far as Shepard could tell, the killer's last target before Valerie McCorvey's 2003 murder was Enietra Washington in November of 1988, the only .25-caliber assault victim to survive. Shepard had all kinds of unanswered questions in his search for the murderer. Did he stop because he realized he left behind a living victim? Why had he resurfaced now? Had he been incarcerated during the '90s? Maybe he never stopped killing and police just hadn't found other victims. And what happened to the gun—the .25-caliber pistol that had killed so many women?

CHAPTER 13
PRINCESS, 2002

SIX DAYS LATER, ON DECEMBER 15, 2004, Shepard learned that the same unidentified killer was now linked through DNA to an Inglewood Police Department murder case. That victim was a 15-year-old foster-care runaway named Princess Berthomieux, who was murdered in Inglewood on March 9, 2002.

The brutal story of Princess's short life could be considered even more devastating than the sad lives and cruel deaths of the other Southside victims.

Princess Berthomieux never had a chance.

Her mother abandoned her when she was a toddler, leaving her with her father, Venus Berthomieux, a native of the Virgin Islands.

By the age of three, Princess was malnourished and covered in bruises. It was only after a call to police dispatch regarding an accidental poisoning at 2 A.M. on October 14, 1989, that Princess escaped her torturous childhood. But the damage had been done.

Paramedics arrived at the South Central apartment of Berthomieux and his girlfriend, Martha Germany, both 30, to find a battered little girl who couldn't walk or talk. They called the police.

While Berthomieux allegedly told the dispatchers she had accidentally swallowed rubbing alcohol, he told police she "might have been exposed to cocaine," according to the *Los Angeles Times*.

Princess had scars and bruises that indicated she had been beaten severely with a belt and a tree switch. Cigarette burns covered her buttocks and legs, and ligature marks scarred her wrists and ankles from being hog-tied with rope. She had also been forced to stay in a closet for days.

"She's pretty much a 3-year-old human punching bag," Sgt. Thomas Jones told the *Times*.

Berthomieux and Germany were arrested for child abuse and charged with eleven counts of felony child abuse and corporal injury to a child. Germany pleaded guilty to one count of child abuse and spent a year in Los Angeles County jail. Her probation conditions required her to complete a parenting class and not have contact with children under the age of 18 without supervision. She wasn't permitted to work with children. Berthomieux was sentenced to four years in prison on October 1, 1990.

After she was released from the hospital, Princess was put in the care of David Smart, an interior designer and former paratrooper, and his wife, Dolores, a former nurse, who spent years caring for the elderly.

The Smarts, who were black, lived in the mostly white well-to-do city of Claremont, on the eastern border of Los Angeles County in the foothills of the San Gabriel Mountains. They had a son, David, and a daughter, Samara, of their own, and foster parenting suited the warm and caring family. Dolores was known as the Kool-Aid mom on the block. A day wouldn't go by that she wasn't feeding someone in the neighborhood. Princess would become their second foster child.

Child protective services asked the Smarts to take in Princess, and the family welcomed the little girl with open arms.

"She had burns all over her body, especially on the buttocks; some of them were a little fresher than others," the Smarts' daughter,

Samara, later recalled. The cuts on her wrists and ankles were so deep they had to be stitched together.

Samara remembered that her mother "invested a lot of time and love to really reach her and let her know she was loved and she was safe."

Gradually, Princess's wounds faded, and, with the loving embrace of her foster family, she started to heal from the unspeakable acts of cruelty she had endured. But this stable environment could not completely erase the early years of abuse. Princess suffered from night terrors.

"She would wake up screaming, 'He is getting me. He is hurting me,'" recalled Samara.

And despite her lovely smile, she had a hard time relating to people. She was diagnosed with a learning disability and didn't have any friends at school. Princess was passive. Gullible. Easily picked on by other kids.

Princess had settled into her new home as well as could be expected when catastrophe struck. In February of 1997, Dolores, 55, died of congestive heart failure.

Just 10 years old, Princess would never recover from her death. She became reclusive and angry. She didn't care much about anything.

She didn't know how to cope, said Samara, and "I didn't understand what she was going through."

Meanwhile, David's health was deteriorating. He had already suffered a major heart attack and was having a difficult time taking care of the by now three foster children he was raising on his own.

By this time, Samara was 24 and had her own family. She offered to take care of Princess and the two younger foster sisters, and they moved into her Rancho Cucamonga home during the week while they were going to school.

But the arrangement didn't last. Samara, a full-time student taking care of six young kids, was overwhelmed. The younger foster sisters were taken in by family, but, after almost ten years with the Smarts, in the fall of 1998, Princess again became a ward of the county.

Leaving the only family she knew couldn't have been easy for 12-year-old Princess. She ran away from each foster home she was placed in and was reported missing to the Hawthorne Police Department on December 21, 2001, by her last foster mother, Ronnie Smith. Princess hooked up with a pimp and worked as a prostitute in Hawthorne, a city surrounded by the suburb communities of Inglewood, Gardena, and El Segundo.

• • •

On March 9, 2002, at 12:48 P.M., a man who identified himself as Mike to a 911 dispatcher said he saw a naked female body in an alley behind South Van Ness Boulevard in Inglewood. When the dispatcher asked for his phone number, he hung up.

An Inglewood Police Department patrol officer spotted the body lying on its right side in an overgrown patch of weeds.

The officer cordoned off the area with yellow crime tape, and Inglewood Police Department Homicide Detective Jeffrey Steinhoff and his partner arrived on the scene at 3 P.M. A glance around the area revealed a neighborhood of one- and two-story residential homes. The body lying in the alley revealed its dark underbelly. Steinhoff had walked past two feces-coated towels swarming with flies and stepped around the black ash and broken glass from a burned-out older-model Toyota to examine the body of a young black female with shoulder-length, braided hair pulled back behind her ears. There was a ligature-type mark on the back of her neck at the base of her hairline. She wasn't wearing jewelry, but a French-style manicure decorated the tips of her long thin fingers, and chipped red polish covered the nails on her toes. Her bare feet were dirty with green grass stains. Ants had left a trail of bites along her pubic hairline.

Forensic investigators took samples and bagged items from the scene to test for DNA evidence. Meanwhile, Coroner Investigator Debra Kowal told Steinhoff that the blood trailing from the victim's nose, the dark hemorrhages in the sclera of both eyes, as well as petechial hemorrhaging in both of her eyes, were signs of strangulation.

Medical Examiner Dr. Raffi Djabourian's March 12 autopsy revealed that Jane Doe #15 was five feet tall, one hundred pounds, between 14 and 21 years old, and sexually active. Her eyelids were swollen shut. She had old burn scars on her buttocks and the backs of both legs. This young girl had a short, hard life.

The victim had been sodomized—there were signs of trauma to her rectum and there was blood inside her anal cavity. The cause of death was confirmed to be asphyxia due to strangulation.

Steinhoff contacted the California Department of Justice and was sent a fax listing forty-nine missing females in the Los Angeles area who could match the description of his dead girl. He whittled it down by height and weight to seventeen possible matches and began calling the forty-two law-enforcement agencies around L.A. County to see if they had a missing girl that matched his Jane Doe.

On March 15, he gave a sketch artist photos of his victim. If he couldn't identify her soon, he would have to go to the media.

Ten days later, Steinhoff took the sexual-assault kit from the coroner's office to the lab for analysis. The following day, the Inglewood Police Department handed out the Jane Doe sketch at a press conference hoping media coverage would generate a lead. They didn't get one call.

On April 11, with no match for his Jane Doe in L.A. County, Steinhoff asked the California Department of Justice to expand the search for missing females to the surrounding counties of Orange, San Bernardino, and Riverside, but once again struck out.

On the same day, a Los Angeles County Sheriff's lab criminalist informed Steinhoff that Amylase, a pancreatic enzyme found in human saliva, was spotted in the swabs taken from the vagina, genitals, rectum, right knee, right ankle, left nipple, and right nipple of his Jane Doe. The criminalist would process the saliva for DNA evidence and upload it into the local, state, and federal DNA databank of felons.

Steinhoff had to wait five months before his Jane Doe was identified as Princess Berthomieux by the Hawthorne Police Department. On Thursday, September 5, Sgt. Chris Cognac received a coroner's alert about Jane Doe and noticed the similarities with a young prostitute named Princess Berthomieux. In April of 2001, a Hawthorne Police Department patrol officer caught a 35-year-old taxi driver having sex with Princess in his cab. Because Princess was underage, the man was charged with rape.

Cognac felt sorry for the pretty teen. "We realized she was very slow," Cognac said. "Not mentally disabled, but slow."

Princess disappeared just before the taxi driver was scheduled for trial. Cognac searched for her at local prostitution hangouts but never found her.

"She had been brought onto the earth to be abused and exploited," said Cognac, while all she wanted was "acceptance and love."

Cognac called Steinhoff and gave his Jane Doe a name: Princess Berthomieux. Last known address: Hawthorne.

The next day, Steinhoff arrived on foster-mother Ronnie Smith's doorstep with a photograph. Smith positively identified Princess.

• • •

By June of 2006, Roger Hausmann, the Fresno repo man known as Super Honky, had been ruled out as a suspect in the slayings of Princess Berthomieux, Valerie McCorvey, and the seven women in the '80s. This was shortly after my trip to visit Hausmann in Fresno jail.

Hausmann[19] had denied he had anything to do with the series of killings, and science verified that.

In the meantime, LAPD Cold-case Detective Cliff Shepard had been working on his own leads. Shepard discovered that the Southside Slayer Task Force detectives had looked at four possible suspects in the 1980s killings: Donald Ray Birdine, Dennis "Pinky" Pinkney, Jimmy Lewis, and former Los Angeles County Sheriff's Department Deputy Rickey Ross.

19. Roger Hausmann, 74, died in Fresno on April 13, 2015.

Birdine was crossed off the list of suspects immediately. He had been in prison custody since December 6, 1990, and was serving a 128-year sentence for forcible oral copulation, robbery, assault with a firearm, and false imprisonment by violence against three women. He could not have killed Valerie McCorvey or Princess Berthomieux. Also, his DNA profile was in the felon databanks as of April 9, 1997. Had he been the killer, his profile would have popped up.

Lewis, a suspect in the Henrietta Wright case in the '80s thanks to police informant Shelly Brown, was not in prison nor was his DNA in the database. Shepard asked the surveillance unit to follow him and get a DNA sample. An undercover officer picked a plastic spoon and paper napkin out of a trash bin that had been used by Lewis at Art's Famous Chili Dogs on Florence Avenue and transported them to Shepard.

Shepard later stopped by Lewis's house and was surprised when Lewis agreed to be interviewed. He told Shepard he had been wrongfully accused of killing Henrietta Wright and that one of his ex-girlfriends had tried to set him up. Shepard wanted a clean sample just in case the DNA picked up from the garbage can was contaminated. Lewis readily agreed. He was soon cleared of the killings.

After some digging, Shepard discovered that the two other suspects were dead. Pinkney, who was arrested for Henrietta Wright's murder in 1986 but whose charges were later dropped, was killed in July 1990 in downtown L.A. during a shootout with a Brink's truck driver he tried to rob. Ross died at 54 of natural causes on June 2, 2003, five weeks before the murder of Valerie McCorvey.

Shepard continued his investigation, following up on any lead that might hold promise. He was unwittingly unaware that the killer would claim his next victim within seven months.

CHAPTER 14
JANECIA, 2007

"I GOT A PLACE TO STAY!" Janecia Peters excitedly told her mother, Laverne, over the phone on that balmy late-December afternoon in 2006. "Do you still have my things?"

It was a Sunday, the last day of the year, and Janecia was referring to her old bedroom set and the suitcase of clothes Laverne had been keeping in the garage of her home in Fontana, a modest suburb about fifty miles east of Los Angeles.

For the last several months, Janecia—affectionately known as Necia to her mother and two sisters—had been in and out of seedy motels. Her life had started with so much promise, but a nasty drug problem had all but snuffed that out. But she was turning things around.

Janecia was a child with a mischievous streak. Affectionately called Baby Gaga, the little girl was born on December 15, 1981, and had a habit of slathering herself with Vaseline, crawling inside kitchen cabinets, and taking the labels off of the kitchen canned goods. Dinner was always a surprise at the Peters household.

Janecia loved to dance too and started a dance group called Ladies at Work when she was 8 years old with her older sister Jovanna.

However, the joys of childhood didn't last. By her late teens, three of Janecia's close friends were dead from gangbanging and drug deals gone badly. Others were serving lengthy prison sentences for everything from drug offenses to murder. Janecia couldn't escape a similar fate.

When she got pregnant at 19, she worried about what to do. Her mother assured her, "Necia, if you have a baby, I'm going to help you. Don't worry. I'm going to help you." And on February 4, 2002, her son Justin was born. Her sister Jovanna cut the umbilical cord.

Janecia was a good mother, and Laverne was right there to help out, reminding her daughter to add a little corn and string beans on top of the fried chicken she liked to serve.

Janecia graduated from Inglewood Adult School when Justin was about 1, and later she enrolled in computer classes at Southwest College in L.A. College was an expectation her mother laid on all her children. Laverne believed education was the way out of poverty. Janecia wanted to become a computer programmer or a teacher like her mother, but life wasn't unfolding as planned.

She developed a nasty coke addiction and, soon after, landed in jail on prostitution-related charges. Laverne took over the parenting of Justin.

Janecia's jail time couldn't scare her straight. As soon as she was released, she was back on the streets, turning tricks along Western Avenue.

However, on that last day in December 2006, she was on top of the world. Laverne suspected her daughter had found a man who was willing to take care of her, but Janecia didn't share any details, and Laverne didn't ask. During the phone conversation, Janecia talked about Justin and the possibility of living with her son again. Laverne made it clear that Justin was staying put in Fontana until Janecia got her act together, for real.

Before Janecia hung up, she told her mom: "Just tell Justin I love him."

• • •

At around 9 A.M. on New Year's Day 2007, Randy Hernandez, a homeless man with a bicycle, was scouring alleyways and garbage bins for recyclable bottles and cans to exchange for cash. He stopped beside the gray double-lidded dumpster at the end of the alleyway at 9508 South Western Avenue, parked his bike, and climbed inside.

Pushing aside broken-down cardboard boxes, a dried-up Christmas tree, and rotting produce, he came upon an enormous black plastic bag. He tried to yank it toward him, but it was too heavy, so he ripped it open, hoping to find a trove of recyclables inside. Instead, a human hand with painted red nails on all fingers except the middle one appeared to reach out to him.

Hernandez scrambled out of the dumpster and told the first person he saw to call 911. When that person walked away startled, he cycled to a pay phone and made the call himself. Then he returned to the scene and waited beside an abandoned four-door gray Cadillac for the police.

A Seventy-seventh Division patrol officer spoke to Hernandez and then approached the dumpster. The officer removed the tree and then used a discarded two-inch-by-six-inch piece of lumber to lift piles of garbage from the bin until he came to the large black trash bag.

It was fastened at the top with a white plastic zip tie, but when the officer peered through the hole Hernandez had made in the plastic, he definitely saw a human body inside. Homicide detectives Eric Crosson and David Craig took over at shortly after 2 P.M.

Crosson expanded the tear in the plastic with his pocketknife. He too saw the hand with red painted fingernails.

The dumpster was in the alley behind a two-story eight-unit apartment building. While the windows of the building faced north, overlooking the crime scene, the view was partially obscured by a black wrought-iron fence approximately six feet in height. Most likely no one saw the killer dump the body.

The dumpster and all its contents, including the young woman's body, was loaded onto a flatbed truck and taken to the Los Angeles County Department of Medical Examiner-Coroner for examination. The detectives didn't want to miss any DNA evidence.

At the coroner's office, the dumpster was placed on its side so the body wouldn't be damaged. A coroner's criminalist cut open the black plastic trash bag and removed the young woman from the dumpster.

Deputy Medical Examiner Dr. Lisa Scheinin opined at the January 3 autopsy that the victim had been shot in the lower back, injuring her spinal cord, which would have caused paralysis from the waist down. She would not have been able to run away or escape. Her left eye had signs of petechial hemorrhaging. Cause of death was a .25-caliber gunshot wound as well as possible asphyxia.

The victim spent several minutes gasping for breath as she died. Once dead, the body was folded into the fetal position, placed inside the trash bag, and sealed with a zip tie.

The coroner's report noted that the victim was wearing a gold necklace with a large heart pendant and a pair of white-and-black earrings as well as a yellow metal stud in one ear. A tattoo that read "Sexy" was inked over her right breast. A sexual-assault kit was performed, which included scraping under her nails, combing her pubic hair, and taking swabs from her breasts, vagina, and anus in search of potential DNA evidence. A toxicology report later determined she had cocaine in her system.

There were no bullet casings and there was no blood splatter at the scene that could provide further clues to what happened.

The day after the woman's body was found, she was identified as Janecia Lavette Peters. Vice cops knew her as Destiny. She hung out at the sleazy Fairlane Motel, which was just six blocks from the dumpster.

The motel janitor had seen Janecia in the parking lot around 8 P.M. on New Year's Eve, the night of her death. Her hair was in disarray and she was crying, and he asked her if anything was wrong.

She didn't answer him. They then smoked a rock together, and Janecia left to score some coke from a nearby dealer's apartment. The janitor saw her one more time that night, about 12:30 A.M. She was back at the Fairlane, getting into a dark-colored Jeep with a local pimp and a black woman.

Detectives passed Janecia's most recent mug shot around at the motel, and a prostitute recognized the woman in the photo as Destiny. She told the police that Destiny was a regular at the motel. She last saw her before midnight on New Year's Eve shooting the breeze with a couple of druggies and local girls behind the motel. She watched the soon-to-be dead girl walk away around 1 A.M.

The morning Janecia's body was found in the dumpster, Laverne Peters was celebrating the New Year with family members in nearby Inglewood. She heard a news report that a black teenager had been found dead along Western Avenue and could hear the helicopters flying overhead. It didn't cross her mind that the victim could be her daughter. She was hoping Janecia would stop by the family gathering. Justin, who would soon turn 5, had a belated Christmas present for his mother. It was a pair of sunglasses.

But Janecia didn't show up.

No one in the family was thinking the worst when two days later, on January 3, two detectives stopped by the apartment of Janecia's eldest sister, Shamika, in Inglewood asking if she knew Janecia.

"Yes, she's my sister," she told them.

"Can we come in?" the detectives asked.

"No," she said. "Is she okay?"

"Can we come inside to talk to you?" they asked again.

"Is she okay?" Shamika repeated.

She had been murdered, the detectives told her. She let them in. Shocked, Shamika, 32, sat silently as police passed along a few details. She immediately called Laverne to tell her the devastating news, but her mother wasn't at home or answering her cell phone. Shamika called her aunt, who lived around the corner from Laverne, and Shamika's aunt told Laverne she needed to call Shamika.

When Laverne hung up the phone, her thoughts immediately turned to Justin. How was she going to tell him his mother was dead?

While Laverne wrestled with the heartache of losing her daughter, the murder of Janecia Peters would take on a heightened sense of urgency for the LAPD. A few months after her body was found, investigators learned that Janecia was the latest in the long list of victims left behind by an unknown serial killer armed with a .25 caliber prowling the streets of South Central.

CHAPTER 15
THE 800

ON APRIL 27, 2007, FOUR MONTHS after Janecia Peters's body was left to rot in a Southside dumpster, the LAPD's Scientific Investigation Division sent Cold-case Detective Cliff Shepard a fax informing him of a case-to-case DNA hit. The cold-case unit, on the fifth floor of Parker Center, was the repository for all DNA notifications from the Scientific Investigation Division. Detective Cliff Shepard was off that day, so a cold-case supervisor brought the information to the third-floor office of Detective Dennis Kilcoyne, the interim supervisor of Homicide Special's Squad One, which handled high-profile murders and serial cases.

Kilcoyne read the fax. Saliva found on the plastic zip tie at the Janecia Peters crime scene had been linked through DNA to the 2002 and 2003 murders of Princess Berthomieux and Valerie McCorvey. Kilcoyne would soon learn that the DNA also connected the same unidentified killer to the shooting deaths of seven women in the 1980s.

"Let's talk to the captain," Kilcoyne said, and the two cops walked to the office of Kyle Jackson, who headed up Robbery-Homicide.

Kilcoyne shut the door and told Jackson the news. The murder of Janecia Peters was alarming. It proved beyond a shadow of a doubt that the killer was still active and didn't plan to stop.

Jackson had a reputation for getting things done. He told Kilcoyne that they needed to create a task force to find the killer and went off to inform the upper brass of the new development.

An hour later, Jackson was back with the news that the task force was a go and that Kilcoyne would be running it.

The task force couldn't have come at a better time for Detective Dennis Kilcoyne. He was due for a change. His twenty-six years as a homicide detective, working gruesome murder scenes in the middle of the night, were wearing him thin. He was burnt out. He needed a break, and the task force would be a welcome challenge.

Kilcoyne started working at the LAPD on February 14, 1977. After academy training, he worked as a patrol officer in the Hollywood Division and the West Valley Division and later returned to the Hollywood Division.

In the summer of 1982, Kilcoyne got his first big break toward his goal of becoming a detective when he was asked to help out Hollywood homicide supervisor Russ Kuster. Kuster, a veteran homicide detective, took the young officer under his wing. Kilcoyne spent three years learning the detective ropes before he was transferred to the Wilshire Division, which included Koreatown, trendy Melrose Avenue, and ritzy Hancock Park, where he worked robberies and homicide. He was there for a year before he was transferred back to Hollywood to work with his mentor, Kuster, until the senior detective's shocking death a few years later.

It happened on October 9, 1990. Kuster was having dinner at the Hilltop Hungarian Restaurant in Hollywood when he overheard an argument between a parolee named Bela Marko and the restaurant owner. Marko began threatening restaurant patrons, and Kuster intervened. When he approached Marko, the parolee fired four close-range shots, striking Kuster in the chest and heart. Kuster was able to draw his service revolver and shoot Marko three times. Kuster died an hour later at St. Joseph's Medical Center in Burbank. Marko died at the scene.

Kilcoyne, a six-foot-four burly Boston native with a thick head of gray hair and a bushy trademark-cop mustache, had joined Robbery-Homicide in January 1994 and worked on some of the unit's most high-profile cases. That hit list included the murder charges against O. J. Simpson and the 1997 killing of comedian Bill Cosby's son, Ennis. The younger Cosby was murdered late one night after he pulled his dark-green Mercedes-Benz sports convertible off Interstate 405 onto Skirball Center Drive to change a flat tire.[20]

The great-grandson of a Boston police sergeant was a tough-minded, meticulous detective with an easygoing demeanor and sharp wit that made him a favorite among his peers. He also had a more than respectable solve rate.

He had recently solved the infamous case of the Black Widow murderers. Two senior citizens, Olga Rutterschmidt and Helen Golay, befriended homeless men, took out life-insurance policies on them, then staged hit-and-run accidents and collected the money from their policies. The septuagenarians were given the moniker the Black Widows and were charged and later convicted of murdering two men and collecting $2.8 million in insurance money. They were nabbed after a suspicious insurance agent called Kilcoyne. Both women are serving life in prison without the possibility of parole.

Kilcoyne decided to keep the new task force under wraps. He feared the news of a police hunt for an active serial killer might put the whole city of Los Angeles into a panic. Why, he thought, scare the shit out of a grandma in North Hollywood? This would prove to be a bad call, at least as far as community relations were concerned. Kilcoyne and the department would be deeply criticized for keeping the news of an active serial killer from the victims' families and the South Central community.

---

20. Mikhail Markhasev, a Ukrainian-born teen, was arrested for Ennis Cosby's murder in March of 1997 and was later convicted and sentenced to life in prison without the possibility of parole.

But Kilcoyne believed his decision was sound. He didn't want this prolific killer to know police were onto to his latest kill. He didn't want to spook him and send him into hiding. The task force needed time to figure out what they were up against.

The detective felt strongly that this new squad would catch the killer who had been making a mockery of the LAPD for more than two decades.

• • •

Kilcoyne came up with a well-rounded and thorough list of detectives he wanted on the task force.

Cliff Shepard had been working the case for three years and knew the most about the .25-caliber killings. But Shepard didn't think he needed any help, let alone a task force. He would soon realize his ego was getting in the way. He was juggling more than one hundred cold cases and clearly could use the help.

Paul Coulter, Shepard's partner, was a given. Coulter's work ethic, smarts, and writing skills had impressed Kilcoyne on previous assignments. Coulter was well-respected, tenacious, and had a long history with Robbery-Homicide, starting in 1998 after ten years as a homicide detective at the Wilshire Division. He worked more than two hundred homicides in his thirty years as a police officer, including the shocking 1998 murder of *My Sister Sam* actress Rebecca Schaeffer. The 21-year-old was killed in the doorway of her West Hollywood apartment building by a psychotic fan. Coulter also investigated the murder of writer Susan Berman, the daughter of Davie Berman, the Las Vegas mobster who in 1947 replaced murdered mobster Bugsy Siegel as the boss of the Flamingo Hotel. Susan Berman was found dead at her rented Benedict Canyon home on Christmas Eve, 2000, shot once in the back of the head. Coulter suspected her close friend, real estate scion Robert Durst, bumped her off.[21]

---

21. Robert Durst was charged in 2015 with one count of first-degree murder for killing Susan Berman. The charge was brought the day before the airing of an HBO documentary about him, *The Jinx: The Life and Deaths of Robert Durst*, in which he seemingly confesses to the murder. He has maintained his innocence, and his trial is pending.

Kilcoyne also recognized the need for task-force members with knowledge of South Central and a good rapport with its residents. "Dollar" Bill Fallon, a Homicide Special detective, had worked patrol shifts at Southeast Division Station with Shepard in the 1980s. Fallon was easy to get along with, and Kilcoyne wanted the talented detective to act as a buffer between the police and the South Central neighborhood. At Fallon's recommendation, Daryl Groce, a black robbery detective who had worked the Southeast and Seventy-seventh divisions, was also brought on.

South Central had a large Hispanic population, and Kilcoyne wanted a Spanish-speaking detective on the team. He singled out Rod "El Guapo" Amador, who had worked with the Hollenbeck Division homicide unit before joining Robbery-Homicide as a robbery detective. Kilcoyne also wanted a female detective and someone experienced in sex crimes. He got them both in Gina Rubalcava, a sex-crime investigator with a background in rape investigations.

The task force was given office space on the eighth floor in the department's former television and sound room—Room 800. The place was an abandoned wreck. There were no phone lines. No computers. The carpet needed to be replaced, and the walls were in desperate need of a coat of paint. It was also empty of furnishings. While Kilcoyne and Coulter picked up tables, chairs, and cabinets from the city's salvage yard, Shepard scoured the hallways looking for abandoned office furniture, computers, and fax machines.

Once the space was set up, the team attempted to come up with a name for their newly formed task force. Several suggestions were tossed about, such as the Alleyway Killer and Western Avenue Slayer, but they couldn't agree.

It was Coulter who came up with the name after one of the LAPD brass asked him what they planned to call the task force.

It'd be the 800 Task Force, he said.

"Eight hundred," gasped the brass. "Do you think there are eight hundred victims?"

"No," said Coulter. "That is the number on the door."

The 800 Task Force was composed of seven veteran cops with close to one hundred years of combined service. But even to them, this case was a mystery. Although Shepard had made some headway, they were pretty much starting from scratch. Kilcoyne didn't have to tell them how difficult this case would be to solve. It had mystified detectives for more than two decades. And at this point there wasn't a lead that could be called anything more than lukewarm. Shepard was in the midst of tracking down Shelly Brown, the police informant who had falsely told police that Dennis Pinkney, Let Loose, and Jimmy Lewis were responsible for the 1986 murder of Henrietta Wright. Both were subsequently ruled out, but Shepard felt, based on her knowledge of unreleased details of the killing, that Brown knew someone involved in the murder.

Detectives Coulter, Kilcoyne, Fallon, and Shepard each had less than five years until retirement, and they were all determined to solve this final challenge before the end of their watch.

CHAPTER 16
HUNTING A SERIAL KILLER

GOOD DETECTIVES ARE GOOD THINKERS and like challenges, and these detectives of the 800 Task Force were determined to connect the dots by revisiting all the evidence. They knew that any leads that previously existed had long gone cold. Suspects and witnesses would now be difficult to track down. Some of the witnesses may have ended up in the morgue or, if they were still around, might not be of any help, as memories fade over time. Another problem was the detectives were dealing with crimes in a neighborhood that didn't trust police. Although the LAPD had made great strides in improving community relations since the days of the Watts Riots in 1965, there was still a lot of bad blood between the police and the residents of South Central.

The 800 Task Force detectives needed to create a profile of the killer. They knew he preyed on weakness and chose vulnerable women he could take advantage of. He was an opportunistic killer, who most likely lured the women into his car with a mixture of drugs and charm. He was elusive; that was obvious. If he weren't, he would have been caught in the '80s. But the new task-force detectives had an advantage the 1980s detectives didn't have: the killer's

DNA. Advancement in DNA testing had provided a much-needed edge. Kilcoyne was adamant the case would be solved by DNA technology. All he needed was a suspect to compare to the DNA profile they already had.

Kilcoyne's plan was to get fresh eyes on the murder books to find a detail, a clue, something the '80s detectives overlooked. The detectives would whittle down the list of suspects, witnesses, and boyfriends, checking for them in the local, state, and federal databases. If they were not there, the task force would track down each suspect and get a DNA swab.

Most serial killers hunted in familiar territory, and they believed this man was no different. He either lived in South Central or once did.

As detectives dug in and the profile of the targeted serial killer took shape, puzzling pieces to this particular killer started to appear.

The detectives understood that murder fueled a rush for serial predators, and that it took more and more killings to satisfy their sick needs. So why was it that this .25-caliber killer took a thirteen-and-a-half-year break? Maybe he didn't. It could be he was a military man who moved around to different bases and was continuing his killing spree elsewhere. That could explain the hiatus. Or, maybe, he was in prison during the gap and had not been swabbed because he hadn't been convicted of a murder or a sexual assault, an offense that would have caused him to be swabbed in the '90s.

Unlike other serial killers, this suspect had kept a low profile. He was not gloating as did the infamous Zodiac Killer, who boasted of his murders in letters to San Francisco Bay Area newspapers, or the BTK Killer, Dennis Rader, who sent letters and morbid cards to the police and media. The definition of a serial killer had evolved over the years beyond the stereotypical smart white male between the ages of twenty and forty that profilers previously identified. The likes of the charismatic Ted Bundy, who defiled beautiful young women who reminded him of a former girlfriend who scorned him, was no longer the boilerplate.

The detectives spent the summer of 2007 huddled at their desks digesting the murder case files. They compiled a broader profile of their suspect and then focused on his traits. Then they asked themselves more questions. Who was this killer? Was he a doting dad, like Rader? Or a sex addict like Green River Killer Gary Ridgway, who claimed to have murdered up to eighty prostitutes in the Seattle-Tacoma area beginning in the '80s?

Maybe their killer was taking revenge on women who reminded him of his mother. Or was it even less personal, more callous? Was he killing drug-addicted black females because he knew he could get away with it? Did he think the women were getting what they deserved? Was he able to keep himself from killing until his urges overwhelmed him? Did he spend long periods of time diligently plotting out his killings and then pounce? Whatever the motivation, when he did strike, he was as deadly as a tiger.

Wherever he vanished to for more than thirteen and a half years, he picked up right where he left off. Kilcoyne was certain he would strike again. Most serial killers don't stop killing until they are caught, and when this guy did kill again, Kilcoyne wanted his team at the crime scene. He alerted every South Central police division to contact him if a female was found dead in an alleyway or dumpster. He also notified the coroner's office to tell him if and when they came across a female body dump in Los Angeles County. If another body surfaced, the 800 Task Force would be ready.

Task-force detectives, meanwhile, went back twenty-three years and pulled the files on 150 murders of black women in South Central—cases that were both solved and unsolved. It would be arrogant to think that everything their killer did came complete with a lab report and DNA, Kilcoyne knew. A lot of their suspects were repeat offenders and were in local, state, and felon databanks, but this guy was different. He wasn't in the usual police databases. Maybe they had missed some of his murders.

The detectives knew of ten homicides they could pin on this

killer, but Kilcoyne suspected that was only half of the murders he committed. The madman discarded his victims in garbage dumpsters and alleyways. It was not a stretch to assume that some of the women ended up in landfills. The question was how many.

• • •

As the 800 Task Force dug into the murder books, a cluster pattern started to emerge. The bodies of Bernita Sparks and Janecia Peters were found in the same alley in South Central. Lachrica Jefferson once lived in the apartment building next door to Othus S. White's house, where lone survivor Enietra Washington was taken before she was shot by her attacker. Mary Lowe's body was found six blocks away from White's house. Princess Berthomieux's body was discovered just four blocks away.

The task-force detectives, like the detectives in the '80s, were intrigued by the phone call from the anonymous tipster in one of the 1987 killings. The caller said he'd witnessed a man dump Barbara Ware's body out of a blue-and-white van that was later traced to the Cosmopolitan Church. But why didn't he identify himself? The detectives were left to wonder if he was affiliated with the church. Kilcoyne wondered if a closer look at church members could lead to identifying the caller.

With that in mind, the detectives tracked down male members of the church, from the pastors down to the congregation members. Maybe they would recognize the voice on the tape?

Meanwhile, Detective Shepard sent the three unidentified fingerprints found in the church van in 1987 to the Integrated Automated Fingerprint Identification System, or IAFIS, the national fingerprint system maintained by the FBI. It took a few weeks, but Shepard was pleasantly surprised when one of the fingerprints lifted off the van's inside rear passenger window came back as a match to congregant Arthur Wilson. Wilson's mother, Yvonne Carter, worked at the church's bookstore and beauty parlor. Wilson, then 22, and his sister Shawnece were at the church the night of Ware's murder and at the time were interviewed by detectives. At that same time, Wilson was subjected to a gun-residue test, and no residue was found.

Wilson was easy to find. He was in the Walton Correctional Institution in DeFuniak Springs, Florida. He had been arrested on June 3, 2007, for cocaine possession. Kilcoyne sent Shepard and Coulter to Florida on December 5, 2007, with the tape of the mystery caller to see if Wilson recognized the voice and to get a DNA swab. During the same trip, the detectives would stop in Orlando to interview his mother and sister.

Wilson was cooperative but told the detectives he didn't remember much.

After a few minutes of general back and forth, Shepard played the tape. "Let us know if you recognize the voice," he said. "Maybe we will be lucky and you will be able to identify this guy."

Wilson said the voice sounded like a light-skinned black man who was older than he was, who would come to church sometimes.

"How much older?" asked Coulter.

"Five or six years older," Wilson said.

"What about his face?" asked Coulter. "Mustache? Smooth skin?"

"He had, like, a not-big Afro, but he had about an inch on his head and it was kind of curly. A pretty-boy type of guy."

"Did he live in the area?" asked Coulter.

"I don't know if he lived in the area or not but I think we dropped him off."

"You don't remember this guy's name?" asked Coulter.

"No," he said.

"Why do you remember this guy?" asked Shepard. "Because of the voice, or did he do something at the church?"

"A lot of time people come to church and I am very quiet and I watch a lot of things," said Wilson. "Some people, you look at them and there is something different about them. It seemed like this guy had some type of problem now. I don't know his name."

"Did he have anything else to do with the church?" asked Shepard.

"I don't know if he was a member, but I know he came a few times," Wilson answered.

"So are you saying this voice sounds like him?" asked Coulter.

"When I heard the voice, that is the face I put to it," said Wilson.

"How often did you talk to this guy at the church?" asked Coulter.

"The only thing I probably said to him is hi or about God or something like that. We didn't have a lot of members, and at the church everyone would get together in the hallway and talk to different people. I am listening and seeing faces and stuff like that."

"Do you remember this guy's car?" asked Shepard. "Or did he show up in a work uniform? Or did he dress fancy?"

"He didn't dress fancy," said Wilson. "I don't think it was a regular type of work uniform, but it was work pants like Dickies you work in. Something like that."

"A big guy?" asked Shepard.

"I would say he was five foot eight," said Wilson.

"Stocky?" asked Shepard.

"Medium," said Wilson.

Wilson couldn't add more, so the detectives moved on with questions about the van.

Wilson told detectives that if the van disappeared during the service that night, no one would have noticed.

"Who had keys to the van you know of?" asked Coulter. "Or were they just kept in the office?"

"I think they were kept in the office," said Wilson.

Coulter and Shepard realized that anyone could have taken that van.

The detectives wrapped up the interview and obtained a DNA swab from him. The next day they flew to Orlando to speak with Wilson's mother Yvonne Carter and his sister Shawnece, who lived together in a gated community.

"I thought the van was stolen," Yvonne Carter told detectives.

"This is what I had heard. We used to use the van for picking up the members."

"Where were the keys to the van?" asked Coulter.

"Inside the office," she said.

"Who had access to the office?" asked Coulter.

"Sister [Ineal] Poole, Fred, everyone who worked there had access," Carter told them. Fred Thomas was the van's usual driver.

"We are going to play you a tape," said Coulter. We want you to listen to the tape. I know it's been twenty years, but we want to see if you can recognize the voice."

They played the tape.

"In a way it sounds like Fred's voice," said Carter.

"Do you want to hear it again?" asked Coulter.

"Yeah, let me hear it again," said Carter.

They played the tape a second time.

"When you first started it, it really sounded like Fred. Now, I could be wrong."

Shawnece Carter was in another room while they interviewed her mother. She was 16 the night police interviewed her in 1987.

"Someone that night called our communications about the blue van," said Coulter. "Listen and see if you recognize the voice."

"Does it sound familiar?" he asked after playing the tape.

"Can you play it again?" Shawnece asked. "Stop it. Play it again. That sounds like Fred . . . It is beginning to sound like his voice."

The detectives were feeling hopeful when they flew back to Los Angeles. On January 22, 2008, the LAPD's surveillance unit followed Fred Thomas to obtain his DNA. It didn't take long. He bought a drink from a vending machine, and when he tossed the cup in a trash can, a detective discreetly collected it for DNA testing. Four days later, on January 26, a Scientific Investigation Division criminalist called Shepard: The DNA profile obtained from Thomas's cup did not match their killer.

• • •

Undeterred, the detectives followed up on their next lead, police informant Shelly Brown. On January 30, Shepard and Coulter went to the women's correctional facility in Lynwood to talk to Brown, the now-41-year-old former informant who was in jail for a probation violation. Brown had falsely claimed, at various times, that three different men—Dennis "Pinky" Pinkney, Let Loose, and Jimmy Lewis—were involved in Henrietta Wright's murder.

After a few minutes of pleasantries, Shepard got to the point. "Do you remember the woman on Third Street and Vernon Avenue in '86?" asked Shepard.

"The lady that got stabbed or cut up?" she asked.

"No," said Shepard.

"It is very hard for me to remember," she said.

"Do you remember your boyfriend at the time?" Shepard asked.

"I was on a lot of drugs at that time," she said.

"What about Dennis? You called him Pinky?"

"Oh, Pinky," she said. "I had amnesia. I hit my head seven years ago. Some black guy hit me in the head with a gun in Inglewood by Hyde Park."

"You had Dennis arrested?" said Shepard.

"Okay."

"You claimed Dennis killed a girl?" said Shepard.

"I don't remember," she said.

"Do you remember Jimmy? You had him arrested too," said Shepard.

"It was so long ago," she said.

"Do you remember this woman?" asked Shepard, showing her a photo of Henrietta.

"Yes, I remember her."

"Could she be the woman in the alley?" asked Shepard.

"Yes, she is the one who was killed. I am trying to remember how they killed her. I can't remember nothing."

The detectives paused a moment to let Brown calm her mind.

"I didn't see her personally get murdered," she said.

"Her first name is Henrietta," said Shepard, "and you said you saw what happened through the window."

"I can't remember. I remember a bed over her."

"You didn't happen to see the police setting up the [crime scene] tape?" asked Shepard. "You were very, very specific about what happened to this girl."

"Whatever I told you had to be the truth because . . . ," she said.

"But you admitted you lied about Pinky," said Shepard.

"That's true," she said.

"Then you said Jimmy did it, and I have doubts about Jimmy doing it," said Shepard. "That is why we are talking to you."

"I don't know," Brown said. "I can't remember."

"I am very certain you saw it," said Shepard. "We need you to think about it. We will give you some time and come back and talk to you."

With that, the detectives left the jail.

• • •

On March 17, 2008, Shepard sat down for an interview with Fred Thomas at his house in Hawthorne, a city near LAX. The former Cosmopolitan church driver, who was ruled out as the killer through DNA, was asked if he recognized the voice on the tape.

"The voice doesn't sound like anybody?" asked Shepard.

"After listening to it, it almost sounds like me," said Thomas. "It really sounds like me."

"Did you call?" asked Shepard.

"I don't remember making any calls," he said.

Feeling he'd hit a dead end, Shepard ended the interview.

One month later, on April 15, inmate Arthur Wilson was ruled out as the possible killer.

With Thomas and Wilson no longer suspects, detectives Shepard and Coulter moved on to former church employee Ineal Poole. On August 5, 2008, Poole told detectives in an interview at her home that she remembered that January 1987 night vividly. She was in the back office, talking to church secretary Marva Lawson when the police knocked on the door.

"They said there was some murder," Poole continued. "I said we just got in." Poole told Shepard and Coulter that police zeroed in on her son Dwayne and accused him of being the killer.

"They handcuffed him," she told them. "They said he is going up and he is going to get some years for the killing of the girl. I said he didn't kill nobody."

Luckily, she said, they released Dwayne and took them back to the church.

Poole went on to describe seeing a man in a car cruise the alley behind the church and a vision she had of her son's arrest.

"I had told my son Dwayne, I said there is an El Camino that goes through the alley by the church," she said. "It is strange. Every night he goes through here around one or two o'clock. Dwayne said he see it, but I don't pay no mind. I said to Dwayne a bunch of detectives . . . I said they are coming, and you be careful because they are going to handcuff you and accuse you of a murder you didn't do. I said this guy in the El Camino that rides through here, he did it. That was two weeks before it happened. That was my vision."

"What did the guy in the El Camino look like?" asked Coulter.

"It was dark. He was tall."

"The girl that was killed used to come into the [church beauty] store and get products sometimes," she said. "She was like a little cheerleader."

"How do you know that?" asked Coulter.

"Because I used to work at the church and my son James would see her. Because he got acquainted with all of his customers and knew who his customers were. He would talk to them, and when they come in and get the product he would tell them what to use and what not to use. He remembered faces. And I seen her when she had the little yellow skirt and little top on. And I said is that the girl who came through here, and he said yeah."

"How do you know it is the same girl who was killed?" asked Coulter.

"I know," she said. "It was shown to me."

"They showed you a picture?" asked Coulter.

"This was a vision," she said. "I had seen the girl before at the store, and my son, since he dealt with them, he said, Mama, this is the girl that got killed."

• • •

By spring 2008, the 800 Task Force detectives had run down numerous fruitless leads and were trying to not lose hope. Then, out of the blue, a little-known forensic tool was approved by the State of California that gave them plenty.

In the meantime, I stayed busy covering other crime stories at the *L.A. Weekly*, but the serial killer never left my mind. I kept wondering if the killer would strike again.

Little did I know that he already had.

CHAPTER 17
THE GRIM SLEEPER

CLIFF SHEPARD'S MIND RACED faster with every word he read. This could be the tool that could turn around years of depressing dead ends. The 800 Task Force detective was at his desk reading a newspaper on the afternoon of May 12, 2008, when he came across an article about familial DNA testing. California Governor Jerry Brown had recently approved the controversial test, which would allow police to broaden a DNA search to include a close relative of a crime-scene suspect. In other words, if a search of felon DNA databases did not produce a match, which would be the case if the suspect had never been swabbed by the authorities, the search could be widened to look for someone who shares part of the suspect's DNA, such as a brother, uncle, or father.

While familial searches had been permitted and used to crack some high-profile cases in England since 2002, ethical concerns in the United States had many states slow to embrace the technology. Civil libertarians worried that familial searches were an invasion of privacy and could lead to innocent family members becoming targets of a police investigation, especially families of blacks and Hispanics in prison. They were concerned minority families would be subject to a greater number of familial searches than other ethnicities.

Shepard learned as he read further that the California Department of Justice was limiting familial searches to cases involving sexual assaults and homicides where there was a serious risk to public safety. A search would only be authorized after all other investigative leads had been exhausted.

Shepard felt that two decades of carnage qualified their case on all scores. So, two days later, Coulter, Shepard, and Kilcoyne flew up to Sacramento to meet Jill Spriggs, the bureau chief with the California Department of Justice.

Over lunch Spriggs agreed with the detectives that their serial murderer was the perfect test case for the new familial DNA search tool. They had an active serial murderer whose DNA was not in the felon databases, and the police department had spent thousands of dollars testing potential suspects' DNA and traveling across the country interviewing hundreds of people, all to no avail. They were running out of options.

Two weeks later, the LAPD put in a formal request to California's Department of Justice's Bureau of Forensic Services to conduct a familial search of convicted offenders in the state felon DNA databank.

Before that could happen, however, a special software program had to be built. The detectives had a new approach to finding the killer, but, for the time being, all they could do was wait.

• • •

Two years had passed since I started investigating the serial murder case. It didn't seem like the police were making any progress with the killings, but that didn't mean I had dropped it. Far from it. The unsolved murders in South Central always interested me.

I was as perplexed as Detective Cliff Shepard about the crimes and who committed them—especially regarding the thirteen-and-a-half-year break between the killings. I, too, wondered whether the murderer was in the military and moving from place to place or whether he was already in prison. And I, too, was looking for the answers to those questions.

I kept in regular contact with Shepard, checking in to ask about any new developments. We would meet up to dissect the case. A few times, we drove around the South Central neighborhoods together. I constantly pressed Shepard for details about the investigation. Had he ruled anyone out? Did he have a suspect? He wasn't having any luck hunting down the killer, he would tell me time and time again. Still, I badgered and badgered. And, finally, one afternoon in the summer of 2008, my tenacity paid off. Tired of being peppered with the same questions over and over for two long years, Shepard opened up.

"There is another one," he told me. "He killed someone else since our last victim."

Shepard offered no details. No name. No date. No location. All he said was that he was now part of a new task force looking into the murders.

Back at my office, I ran what Shepard said over in my mind. I had to find a way to track down the new victim. I decided to contact Ed Winter, who was now deputy chief of investigations with the Los Angeles County Department of Medical Examiner-Coroner. After all, it was Winter and his list of thirty-eight women, some found dead in South Central alleyways and parks, that had started my search for the serial killer two years before.

I didn't tell Winter I already knew there was a new victim when we met up, but I did tell him how I was still in pursuit of this story, despite its endless frustrations. I explained my plan to look at autopsy reports of dead women who had been murdered after June 2005, the month the last woman on his list was found dead.

He agreed to provide me with the autopsy reports, and I said I would let him know if I found anything. He looked at me suspiciously but didn't say anything. I suspected he knew something more was up but decided to wait till I let him know.

It took a few weeks, but a large brown envelope from the coroner's office did finally land on my desk. Inside were twelve autopsy reports of women killed since June of 2005. The mode of death varied: shootings, stranglings, beatings. Most of the victims were African American or Hispanic.

As I looked through the reports, the January 1, 2007, murder of 25-year-old Janecia Lavette Peters stood out. She fit the profile of the serial-killer victims: she was black, and her body was dumped in a South Central alley. She had also been shot—the only difference was that she was shot in the back, not in the chest like the other victims.

I needed to learn more about the case. I called a detective at the Seventy-seventh Division, where the investigation was being handled, to get details about her death. The detective told me the case had been transferred downtown to Robbery-Homicide.

"Robbery-Homicide?" I asked. "Why is it there?"

"You would have to ask them," the detective said.

"You don't know?" I asked.

"It's not our case anymore," he said, unhelpfully.

The LAPD's Robbery-Homicide Division was sent mostly high-profile cases involving celebrities, complex scenarios, and serial killers. It handled fewer cases than division detectives and so was afforded more time to dig in. Because Janecia's case had been transported downtown, I was convinced her case was linked to the serial murders. My next call was to the Inglewood Police Department, the police agency handling the Princess Berthomieux case. A detective there confirmed what I already suspected: that Janecia Peters was in fact connected to the elusive killer and that her murder prompted the LAPD to set up a task force.

I sent in a request to speak to the new police chief, Bill Bratton, and was put in touch with Detective Dennis Kilcoyne, who identified himself as the supervisor of the 800 Task Force handling the investigation.

He agreed to talk face-to-face.

• • •

A few days later, Kilcoyne and I were sitting across from each other at a Starbucks down the block from police headquarters. My first impression of Kilcoyne was that he was a friendly, likeable, charming guy.

I told him about my plan to write a story about the secret task force and the murder of Janecia Peters. Kilcoyne confirmed that Janecia's death was linked to the unsolved series of killings, and that they started the task force in April of 2007 after they discovered Janecia's murder was linked through DNA evidence to the nine murders by the serial gunshot killer who had been haunting South Central for decades. Janecia, he explained, was found in a garbage bag, and the killer's DNA was on the zip tie used to secure it.

At this point, the 800 Task Force had been working on the serial murders for more than a year, and, Kilcoyne conceded, the detectives were no closer to capturing the killer than the detectives were in the 1980s.

It was his decision, he said, to keep the task force a secret despite the reservations of Chief Bratton, who had become L.A.'s top cop in 2002. Kilcoyne didn't want the killer to know they were onto him. A media onslaught could send him underground, never to be found again.

I told him I had heard that the LAPD planned to attempt a familial DNA search to unearth the killer.

"No comment," he said.

Later that day, I called Janecia Peters's mother, Laverne Peters, hoping to interview her about the murder of her daughter at the hands of the unidentified serial killer and to talk about the new task force set up to track him down. She was surprised by my call, mostly because, at the exact moment her phone rang, she was searching the Internet for stories about Janecia. Laverne couldn't find anything online. The quiver in her voice gave away her emotions. She felt no one cared about her daughter's murder and was eager to talk to me about her. We made plans to meet.

A few days later, a striking woman in her early 50s sat down across from me at a family restaurant in Fontana. Laverne was an articulate, elegant, well-spoken woman, but her daughter's murder had clearly shattered her. She was raising Janecia's now-6-year-old son, Justin, and wore the weight of her situation in her subdued demeanor.

"He misses his mother every day," she said. "We all do. I do my best, but I am not his mother."

Laverne told me detectives from Robbery-Homicide visited her about six months after Janecia's murder. They had all kinds of questions for Laverne but offered no information about their investigation. Laverne was upset that police didn't tell her that her daughter was the random victim of a serial killer.

If the girls weren't black or killed in a black community, the police department would have made this serial killer known to the public, she told me. They also wouldn't have kept the new task force a secret from the community or the victims' families. If the victims were white, she said, they would have made the serial killer known for fear of blowback.

Laverne also took issue with how the media reported Janecia's murder and black crime in general. When Janecia's body was found in 2007, her murder didn't make the six o'clock news, unlike the giant splash made by the disappearance of Natalee Holloway, the blonde high-school student who vanished in May of 2005 while on a graduation trip to Aruba in the Caribbean. The media couldn't get enough of the Holloway case. Reporters were sent to the exotic island paradise to investigate. When Laverne's daughter was found in a trash bag in a dumpster, no reporters were sent to investigate. There was no press conference. No offer of a reward.

"No one cares about her," she said flatly.

Janecia Lavette Peters came into the world eleven and a half months after her big sister Jovanna. No mother could have been any happier. And now no mother's heartache could be any greater.

Laverne Peters wasn't the only one upset that the LAPD kept quiet about the serial killer.

• • •

When I showed up unannounced at Porter and Mary Alexander's front door in the summer of 2008, I wasn't sure what to expect. I didn't know much about South Central, and, frankly, I was scared about venturing into the area alone. I brought up my apprehension to my petite and trendy older sister, Amanda, who agreed to tag along—as long as I bought her lunch afterward.

We drove through the streets of South Central in Maude Jr. I was dressed in a work blouse and pants, and my sister wore her trademark platform heels, short shorts, and tank top. On her arm, she toted her prize possession, a Gucci bag.

The plan was for her to wait outside in the car until I finished my interviews. When the Alexanders opened their door, I let them know I was writing an article for the *L.A. Weekly* about the unsolved slayings, which included their daughter Monique's murder. They were surprised to see me because no one had come by in more than twenty years to ask about her death. They also expressed their gratitude that someone had taken an interest in Monique's case. Finally, someone was there to hear what they had to say.

They welcomed me inside, and within a few minutes my sister was calling me, asking when the interview would be complete. She was getting scared waiting in the car. I told the Alexanders that my sister was waiting outside.

"Please invite her in," Mary told me.

Amanda joined me on the couch in the living room. Mary pulled out a photo album and began sharing memories of Monique, a young girl full of life and with a future. I could see that Mary was fighting back tears as she turned the pages. So was Porter, a rough-and-tumble cowboy from Stockton, who wore his heart on his sleeve. "She was my baby," Porter said, staring at a photo of a teenage Monique staring back at him. Even though their daughter's case had not been solved, the Alexanders had not spoken with police since the detectives paid a few cursory visits following her murder in September of 1988.

Monique's death still appeared to haunt Porter. I could see it in his eyes. They welled up with tears when he said her name. He blamed himself for her death and her drug addiction. In his mind, he hadn't done enough to protect her from the dangers of the street. His pain was as fresh as the day she was taken from them.

"We were a working family," said Porter of their lot in life in the 1980s. "Our youngest was doing things that we couldn't combat at the time."

"I'm not making excuses," he added. "It was so sad I had to end up losing one of my kids. Monique was our baby. She was loved by everyone."

"I wonder what she would have been like," Mary said. "I haven't been able to rest too much."

Mary sat mostly silent as I outlined what I knew about the murders. "She was very dear to me," Mary said soberly.

Mary and Monique had shared a special game where they would lie on the couch, put their feet together, and pump them back and forth like they were riding a bicycle. And when Mary was lying down, Monique would come in and lie down beside her. And when Monique would come home after a visit to Beverly Hills, she would always excitedly tell her mother, "Mommy, I been to Billy Hills."

Monique's death sent Mary into a downward spiral for a time. She couldn't stand to see her nieces or nephews, or any of Monique's friends. It hurt too much. She questioned why she should go on. She spent days in her room, crying. Her remaining children, Keevin, Anita, Donnell, and Darin, didn't think she would ever recover. Her health deteriorated. She had a pain in her head that would never leave, and she spent years going back and forth to doctors. Holidays came and went, and the Alexander family just went through the motions.

Porter had a different way of coping. He eventually packed up Monique's belongings and put them in storage. Then he became fixated on her gravesite and had her remains moved if things were not the way he wanted. He once removed her remains and put them into a crypt because he couldn't stand the thought of tractors mowing the cemetery or driving over her burial plot. He later moved her remains again because there were too many gnats in the area. He finally found a crypt where he and Mary and Monique could be entombed next to each other and stuck with that.

Porter, much like Laverne Peters, was upset that the police didn't tell them Monique had been the victim of a serial killer, much less that her death was part of the Southside Slayer Task Force and the more recent 800 Task Force.

At times, when Porter was fixating on Monique's murder, he tried to piece the killing together in his head. He figured his daughter's killer was familiar with the area and knew when to lie low. That is why he got away with all the slayings for so long, Porter believed.

He couldn't have been more right.

• • •

Mary Lowe's mother, Betty, and Mary's younger sister, Kenneitha, were equally shaken when I stopped by their home—my sister still in tow—later that same day. Betty said she was convinced the police didn't care about finding her daughter's killer because she was a black girl who did drugs.

Kenneitha was especially close to her older sister despite a six-year age difference. The sisters shared bunk beds growing up. At one point, they started a singing group with their cousin called the Little Emotions and would perform for their families and at the local park. Mary was the leader of the group and made their costumes.

Mary was a popular teenager. She was a *Soul Train* dancer, and the neighborhood girls looked up to her. When Kenneitha became a dancer on *American Bandstand*, Mary acted as her manager. She gave her direction and encouraged her.

It was Kenneitha and her father who answered the door on that dreaded first of November day in 1987 when the police stopped by with the news. Kenneitha, who was seven months pregnant at the time, was 20 years old. She soon had a son her sister would never meet.

• • •

I had arrived at each interview feeling excited and left each interview saddened. I could see the despair in the faces of the victims' families and hear the injustice they felt. They were all convinced that the murders hadn't been taken seriously or actively pursued.

All the homicide cases that I covered in my five years as a crime reporter had been devastating, but the pain these families were living with was palpable.

Though the LAPD had made progress in the last twenty years, not a lot had changed in the relationship between the black community and the police. The lack of communication had developed into a contemptuous lack of trust.

• • •

On August 28, 2008, a few weeks after I interviewed the families, my exclusive, most in-depth *L.A. Weekly* story yet, "The Grim Sleeper Returns," hit the newsstands. It was the first time the nickname the Grim Sleeper appeared in print. Jill Stewart, a brash, intelligent, no-nonsense editor insisted we name him. Keeping the story in the public consciousness by giving him a name seemed the best way to do that. Everyone remembered BTK, Zodiac, and Son of Sam. We wanted this serial killer to be remembered long after the initial shock and news coverage ran its pace.

There were still a few days before the story would be published, and we sat in Stewart's office brainstorming for a suitable moniker to best describe this killer. We considered and then rejected Western Avenue Killer, because it wasn't catchy enough, and Ripper Van Winkle, because it was terrible, before we landed on the Grim Sleeper. We both liked it because we felt it embodied this killer who took a thirteen-and-a-half-year respite between murder sprees.

The story delved into the 2007 murder of Janecia Peters, and it broke the news that it was at the hands of the same serial killer who had terrorized South Central in the '80s and that the LAPD had been running a secret task force for fifteen months to hunt down the Grim Sleeper.

There was an interview with 800 Task Force Supervisor Dennis Kilcoyne and a reference to the fact that the relatively new scientific tool of familial DNA searching was now part of the 800's arsenal of weapons. I also included my interviews with relatives of some of the victims who expressed anger about not being notified that a serial killer was active in their neighborhood. And some of them also spoke about the racial injustice they perceived.

• • •

The article lit a fire under the Los Angeles City Council and particularly resonated with Councilman Bernard Parks, who was chief of police before William Bratton took over. Parks's district encompassed the area where the bodies were found, and he pushed the city council to offer a reward. A week after the story ran, the city council announced a $500,000 bounty—the largest in the city's history—for information leading to the arrest and conviction of the Grim Sleeper.

Stewart and I were ecstatic the story was being taken seriously and had prompted the reward. As a journalist, I wanted to make a difference, and I was hoping this reward would help bring in valuable clues to catch the killer.

One thing I didn't expect was the number of calls I fielded from people with potential tips. For the most part, the callers were fearful that a neighbor or a friend might be the Grim Sleeper. Some of the callers I heard from refused to call the LAPD because they didn't have any faith in the police department. I was getting a taste of what the detectives were going through, as the 800 Task Force received dozens of phone calls after my story broke, most of which had to be investigated in order to be ruled out.

I did find talking to tipsters pretty interesting. At first, most of the callers seemed credible. Actually, on more than one occasion, I ran to Stewart's office declaring, "I think this person knows the killer," only to be let down when the tipster started talking about their phone being bugged by the CIA.

To my amazement, many of the women who called cast blame on their husbands or boyfriends. It became hard to discern whether the women were just being vindictive or seeking revenge for an infidelity or if they truly believed what they were saying. I passed on the information to the police.

One morning I was at my desk when the phone rang. A woman with a French accent was on the other end of the line. She said her name was Marnie, and she wanted to talk about her best friend, Barry. "I think he might be the killer," she said.

Early on, those words would have sent me into overdrive, but after hearing so many such calls, I was getting weary. "Why do you think he is the killer?" I asked.

"It's just a feeling," she said. "I study psychology, and I think I know the signs of a serial killer."

That's it? I thought. She just has a feeling?

Barry was an attractive black man in his 40s, she told me. A swarthy Casanova type with a love for the ladies. But, he also had a mean streak and had been violent with a previous girlfriend.

Her friend, she said, was very sexual and had the temperament of Motown legend Marvin Gaye and the cunning of serial killer Ted Bundy.

"He also lived in South Los Angeles in the '80s," she said, adding that at the time he was unhappily married and cheated regularly on his wife with drug-addicted prostitutes.

"There are a lot of people who fit that description in Los Angeles," I said. "Is there anything else?"

"Yes, he is obsessed with the case," she replied. "How can I find out it is him?" she asked.

I suggested she call the police and tell them what she told me.

"Out of the question," she said. She didn't trust the police, and, besides, she didn't want her friend getting harassed by the police if he was innocent.

Her next statement stopped me in my tracks: "I'm having dinner with him tonight. If I get his DNA, would your paper be able to analyze it?"

I told her the *L.A. Weekly* wasn't in the business of testing DNA. She asked me if I could bring the sample to the police without them knowing who she was. "I guess I could do that," I said. "I could ask them." I asked her for her number, but she refused to give it to me.

"I'll call you," she said, and she hung up.

I'll never hear from her again, I thought. But I was wrong.

Two weeks later, after I had completely forgotten about her, Marnie called again. "I have the sample," she said. "Can I drop it off later?"

I was again taken aback. I didn't expect that she would go through with it. What have I got myself into? I wondered. Marnie agreed to stop by the *L.A. Weekly* later that afternoon, with the package in hand. After we hung up, I called Detective Cliff Shepard. "I spoke to a woman who is convinced her friend is the killer," I said. "She is bringing over his DNA sample later. Can I bring it to you to test?"

I was met with silence . . . at first.

Shepard was skeptical but agreed to take the sample.

"You never know. He could be the killer," I said.

"Maybe," he said, and then he hung up.

Later that afternoon, *L.A. Weekly*'s office manager Peter Fletcher called me to say Marnie was in the lobby. Fletcher suggested I meet her in a private room near the reception desk. The room was used by the advertising department to collect money from clients and had a video camera. If Marnie turned out to be dangerous, he would have it on tape. Lucky me, I thought.

When I arrived at the front desk, she was already in the private room. I found a pretty white woman in her mid-30s, sitting behind a glass partition. Marnie was annoyed with the arrangements, but I didn't care. All I could see was the white plastic bag in her hand. "Is that it?" I asked, pointing to the bag.

"Yes," she said. "It's a fork." Marnie explained she had dinner with her friend at his house—she made fettuccini Alfredo—and once they finished, she brought the plates into the kitchen and stole the fork.

"I'll pass it on to the police," I told her.

"How long will it take?" she asked.

"I really don't know," I said. "At least a few weeks."

She didn't seem pleased.

"I'm assuming," I said as I tried to reassure her. "Give me your number, and I will call you as soon as I hear anything."

"I'll call you," she said. She then got up and walked out the door.

As soon as she left, I ran up the one flight of stairs to Jill Stewart's office, which faced Sepulveda Boulevard, the main thoroughfare before the 405 Freeway.[22] I watched Marnie cross Sepulveda. She walked about one hundred feet and she stopped. She waited about five minutes before a brown sedan pulled up. I didn't get a good look at the male driver, but I did scribble down the license plate number. If the DNA turned out to be from the Grim Sleeper, I at least had a plate number to pass along to the police so they could find Marnie.

I met Shepard in the lobby of Parker Center.

"Here it is," I said, handing him the bag with the fork inside.

"I'll let you know in a few weeks," he grumbled.

Shepard knew he couldn't take the chance to dismiss it.

"How come it is going to take that long?" I asked.

"We are testing a lot of samples," he said. It was true. In fact, over the course of the police investigation, the lab tested more than one hundred DNA samples, of which I gave two.

Over the next few weeks, Marnie called me every two days. She was nervous it was taking so long. They are testing a lot of samples, I said, trying to calm her.

A week later, I got the call from Shepard.

"It is not a match," he said.

---

22. By the summer of 2008, the *L.A. Weekly* had moved from its office in Hollywood to an office building in Culver City.

When Marnie called me back, I gave her the news. She wasn't happy. She was convinced her friend was the killer and the police screwed up.

"It's not him," I told her. "You should be happy," I said before hanging up on our final conversation.

• • •

A few days later, I got a call from another woman who was certain her husband was the Grim Sleeper. Once again, she didn't want to give me too much information, but she did offer up her name, Pauline.

Pauline said her husband grew up in South Central and had been acting suspiciously ever since the news broke about the serial killer. She couldn't say exactly why she suspected him, only that she had a gut feeling. "I just want to know one way or another," she said. Like Marnie, she wanted him ruled out through DNA evidence, but she didn't want to go to the police. She didn't want her husband's life turned upside down if the police got involved and started investigating him and he wasn't the killer. "Is there a way of doing it anonymously?" she asked.

Again, I agreed to pass the DNA along to the detectives. We hung up, and this time I only half-expected I would never hear from her again. However, like with Marnie, a few weeks later she called and said she was able to get a sample. She suggested we meet at an office building in West Hollywood the following afternoon.

"What do you look like?" she asked.

"I have long blonde hair," I told her.

"I'll find you," she said.

The next day was brutally hot and unusually humid. The temperature had reached ninety-five degrees. I planted myself on a park bench underneath a tree within eyeshot of the front entrance and waited for Pauline. A few minutes later, a slender pretty-well-dressed middle-aged black woman took a seat at the end of the bench.

"There's a cup inside," she said, nodding toward the bag she was holding. "And a napkin with semen on it."

"I thought you were going to bring me saliva from a fork?" I said squeamishly.

"This is the best I could do," she said.

On my way back to Maude Jr., I called Detective Kilcoyne. "I have a semen sample from a woman who believes her husband is the killer," I said. "Can I bring it over?"

Silence.

"I'm out of town," he then said. "Can you bring it by Parker Center tomorrow morning?"

"Okay, but do I need to keep it cool?" I asked. "It is hot as hell out."

"Yeah, put it in your fridge."

"Seriously?" I said.

"Yeah, put it next to your salad dressing and veggies," he said, taking a jab at my vegetarian eating habits before hanging up. I actually put it in my fridge next to my ketchup and mustard.

The following morning, I met a female detective in the lobby of Parker Center who escorted me to an interview room. "You know you are going to have to testify if it comes back a match," she said. I hadn't thought about that and instantly started to sweat in the air-conditioned room.

A few weeks later, Kilcoyne informed me there was no match. He was used to dead ends, but I wasn't. I was hoping this was the killer.

Psychics also called and emailed me. One psychic, who claimed Saint Germaine was helping guide my coverage, said her visions revealed the killer's name was Michael and his victim count was thirty-three. Michael lured his victims to motel rooms, where he killed them and then dumped their bodies in the alleys of South Central. He was a married lawyer whose wife suspected him of infidelity but didn't know he was a killer, the psychic said, adding that he was young and physically was a cross between Tiger Woods and O. J. Simpson. A cute, bad-boy type, she said.

One day I received a letter with no return address. I opened the envelope to find a single sheet of paper with at least eight photocopied color photos. Half of the photos were of the same black man having sex with different black women. The man, who appeared to be in his late 30s or early 40s, and the women were posing for the photos. A few of the shots were close-ups of vaginas. One photo showed the same man, dressed in some sort of traditional African garment, accepting a certificate at an event.

Could this be the killer? I wondered. Why would someone want me to see this?

I photocopied the page and passed it along to Detective Shepard. Maybe he could track down the man.

CHAPTER 18

MORE DEAD ENDS

THE 800 TASK FORCE DETECTIVES were not yet finished investigating members of the Cosmopolitan Church. The day before my "Grim Sleeper Returns" story appeared, detectives Rod Amador and Paul Coulter flew to Macon, Georgia, to interview Bishop F. P. Matthews. The charismatic preacher left the Cosmopolitan Church in the late '80s and continued his work in Georgia. He claimed to have a large following around the world and was known in some circles as God's Miracle Man. In his sermons, he said he was a prophet who had been raised from the dead five times.

Matthews was surprised to see the detectives, who showed up unexpectedly at his large two-story home outside of Macon, but he agreed to answer Amador and Coulter's questions about the Cosmopolitan Church. Matthews informed the detectives that his close friend, Pastor Owen Malone, also a church minister at the Cosmopolitan Church, was interred in a five-foot-high and three-foot-wide concrete crypt in the front yard of the home. The detectives' interest in Malone was piqued when Matthews told them that before he died, in April of 2007 at 74, Malone occasionally returned to Los Angeles. If Malone was the killer, that might account for the long break between the murders.

As unsavory as the idea was, the detectives knew they had to get a DNA sample from Pastor Malone to rule him out. Once back in L.A., Coulter contacted the Georgia Bureau of Investigation and wrote up an affidavit to take a DNA sample from Malone's remains. He and another detective returned to Georgia and were there when the mortuary popped the seal on the crypt and rolled out the casket. The crypt was taken to the local medical examiner, who removed the femur and jaw bone from Malone. Inside Malone's casket was a little tin box. When the medical examiner picked it up, it rattled.

Could it be the .25-caliber pistol? the detectives wondered. Coulter immediately called Kilcoyne. For a moment the detectives' hopes were up, only to be dashed, again. The rattle in the box turned out to be from the collar of Malone's dog. The dog had died within a few days of his master and had been cremated.

The 800 Task Force detectives sent both Bishop F. P. Matthews's DNA and the forensic samples from Malone's body to Spriggs's DNA lab. Less than forty-eight hours later, the two men of God were exonerated by men of science. Neither of their DNA samples matched the human detritus the Grim Sleeper left behind.

• • •

Frustrations were mounting as suspect after suspect was ruled out when a promising lead walked right through the front door of police headquarters. A middle-aged Texas woman who arrived with her adult daughter told the front-desk clerk that she wanted to talk to a detective handling the Grim Sleeper case. In an interview room on the third floor, she told detectives Coulter and Amador she had flown from Texas to speak with the task force.

Her ex-husband was the killer, she told them. The couple lived in

South Central in the 1980s, and she suspected that her ex could have killed women during that period. He beat and raped her repeatedly during their relationship, and he sexually abused his stepdaughter. Her daughter had seen the media coverage of the Grim Sleeper and noticed that the timeline closely matched her stepfather's absences and his actions during the '80s.

Detectives checked to see if her ex, who remained living in L.A., was in prison during the Grim Sleeper murders and discovered he was not. The following day, task-force detectives asked the surveillance unit to follow this new suspect and try to obtain a DNA sample.

The woman called detectives later with more information. She recalled that years earlier, her eldest son found Polaroid photographs of naked women in his father's shop. When she confronted him at the time, he got upset and told her that the photos belonged to a friend. They never discussed the matter again.

Surveillance unit detectives followed the suspect to Tam's 23 Restaurant on Alameda Street in Compton and watched him discard a Styrofoam cup with a straw as well as two forks. Detectives recovered the cup and the straw and booked them into evidence. But there wasn't enough DNA on the sample.

Coulter and Shepard visited their suspect at his home in Compton. They only told him they were investigating a sexual assault. The man agreed to give the detectives his DNA, and in no time the lab determined he was not the Grim Sleeper.

• • •

Kilcoyne was in his office when California Department of Justice Bureau Chief Jill Spriggs called him on December 2, 2008. He was hoping for good news but was bracing himself for bad. He was right.

The new familial DNA search tool, which he and the 800 Task Force were hoping would recharge the manhunt by locating a relative of the Grim Sleeper, had come up empty.

This was a huge blow to the 800 Task Force. Morale plummeted to an all-time low.

"You get tired of getting beaten down, and at that point we weren't close to anything," Kilcoyne confessed not long after he heard the news.

CHAPTER 19
THE SURVIVOR

A FEW MONTHS AFTER THE GRIM Sleeper story came out, I tracked down the woman who, at that time, I believed was his only survivor: Enietra Washington.

Enietra, then a 30-year-old mother of two, had miraculously lived through an attack in November of 1988 after accepting a ride from a man near the liquor store on Normandie Avenue. The man shot her, sexually assaulted her, and then took her picture with a Polaroid camera before dumping her from his car. I wanted to find out what she remembered about her attacker and the details of her assault. After five phone calls and no response, however, it seemed she wanted to leave what happened to her buried with time.

So I was surprised when she eventually left a message on my answering machine at work—although it wasn't the message I was hoping for.

"I'm not interested in talking to you," she said in a flat, indignant tone that I would come to know as Enietra's no-nonsense personality. Rather than give up, I took her call as an opening to try again. I dialed, expecting the phone to go straight to voicemail, but I was caught off guard when she picked up. I introduced myself. Her response was as terse as the message she had left.

"Yeah, I know who you are. You've left me too many messages."

Did I also mention she was blunt?

"Why should I talk to you?" she asked.

I told Enietra what I knew about the case—which wasn't much, yet—and told her I wanted to write about what happened to her. After a few minutes of back and forth about the police investigation, she asked me if the police had any suspects.

"I don't think so."

After a slight pause, she said: "I believe he is a policeman."

"Why do you think that?" I asked. It was a theory that I had heard before through my three years investigating this story.

"He is too organized," she said. "And, he could get away with it."

I wondered if she just didn't want to believe that someone in her community could be responsible for such heinous acts.

Before we hung up, Enietra agreed to meet me at a soul food restaurant on West Century Boulevard—as long as I drove her to a manicure appointment after our lunch.

I could tell by her demeanor on the phone that she was a tough broad. Still, I wasn't sure what to expect when we met in person. In many ways I was her exact opposite. I was a blue-eyed blonde of Bulgarian descent who grew up in Ottawa—a sleepy government town where the annual average for murders was probably less than one. She grew up in L.A., where the annual murder rate in the '80s was closer to one thousand.

What we did have in common was our brash and sometimes in-your-face attitudes.

As we entered Bertha's Soul Food Restaurant, men raised their heads, and I watched their approving eyes follow my striking fifty-year-old lunch date as she passed their tables.

"How you doing?" one called out. Enietra ignored him and sat down at a nearby table for four. She gazed at the menu, called over the

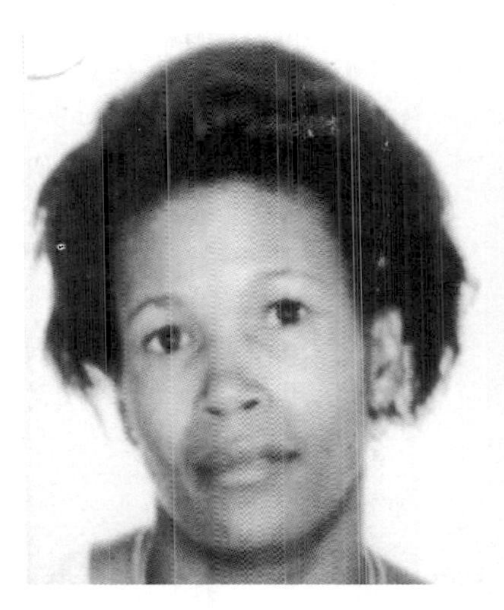

The body of cocktail waitress Debra Jackson, 29, was found under a discarded red carpet in a South Central alley on August 10, 1985. *(L.A. Superior Court Exhibit)*

Henrietta Wright, a 34-year-old mother of five, was found fatally shot on August 12, 1986. *(L.A. Superior Court Exhibit)*

Police were tipped to the January 1987 killing of 23-year-old Barbara Ware by a mystery caller who said he'd seen someone dump a woman's body from a blue and white van. Police discovered the van belonged to the Cosmopolitan Church. *(L.A. Superior Court Exhibit)*

Bernita Sparks, 26, accepted a job as a school monitor preparing lunches for students at the Ninety-second Street Elementary School days before her death. *(L.A. Superior Court Exhibit)*

Mary Lowe, 26, was a *Soul Train* dancer. Neighborhood girls looked up to her. *(L.A. Superior Court Exhibit)*

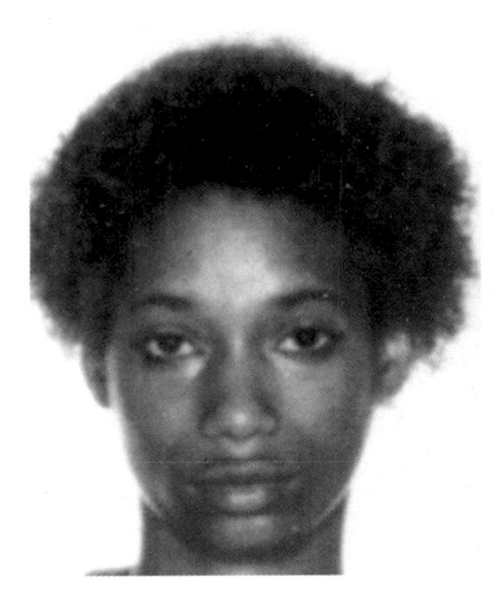

Lachrica Jefferson, 22, was known as L.A. Crisha. A napkin with the word "AIDS" handwritten in pen covered her nose and mouth when police found her body. *(L.A. Superior Court Exhibit)*

Alicia Monique Alexander, 18, was affectionately known as Moo or Moo Cow by her closeknit family. She was last seen getting into a Pinto or Chevrolet Vega. *(L.A. Superior Court Exhibit)*

Enietra Washington was a 30-year-old mother of two when she miraculously survived an attack in November 1988 after accepting a ride from a man near a liquor store on Normandie Avenue. The man shot her, sexually assaulted her, and then took her picture with a Polaroid camera before dumping her from his car. *(Courtesy of Enietra Washington)*

800 Task Force detectives swabbed around fifty suspects and traveled across the country looking for the Grim Sleeper. 800 Task Force detectives (left to right): Paul Coulter, LAPD employee, "Dollar" Bill Fallon, Cliff Shepard. *(Courtesy of the author)*

Valerie McCorvey, 35, was "a sweet person, and she wanted more, but she couldn't because the drugs had her," said her ex-boyfriend's daughter Lucinda Nobles. (*L.A. Superior Court Exhibit*)

The body of Princess Berthomieux, a 15-year-old runaway, was found in an Inglewood alley on March 9, 2002. She was strangled to death. (*L.A. Superior Court Exhibit*)

A homeless man looking for recyclables discovered the body of Janecia Peters, 25, in a plastic garbage bag on January 1, 2007. Her death prompted the LAPD to start a task force looking into the Grim Sleeper murders. (*L.A. Superior Court Exhibit*)

Georgia Mae Thomas, 43, was one of four additional murders linked to Lonnie Franklin after his 2010 arrest. Her body was discovered along a dirt sidewalk in a warehouse district on East 57th Street on December 28, 2000. *(L.A. Superior Court Exhibit)*

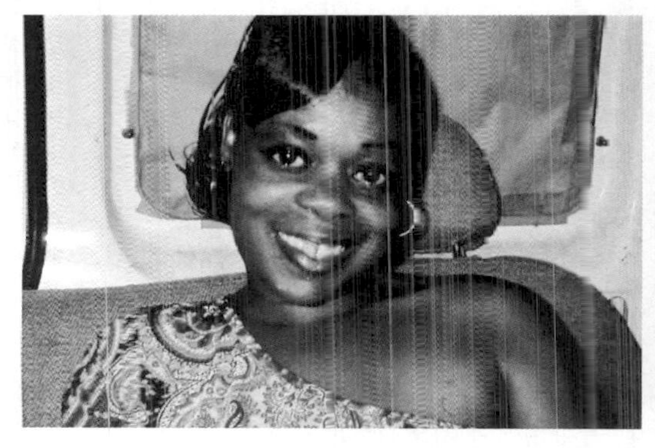

Rolenia Morris, a 31-year-old mother of two young children, vanished under mysterious circumstances on September 5, 2005. During a search of Lonnie Franklin's home, detectives found photos of Rolenia in an envelope in the mini-fridge in his garage. Her body has never been found. *(L.A. Superior Court Exhibit)*

Sharon Dismuke, 21, was discovered on the floor of a men's bathroom in an abandoned gas station. The same Titan .25-caliber semiautomatic used to kill Janecia Peters in 2007 had been used in the murder of Sharon twenty-three years earlier. *(L.A. Superior Court Exhibit)*

Aerial photo of Lonnie Franklin's bungalow (center, with three-car garage) on West 81st Street and the surrounding South Central neighborhood. (*L.A. Superior Court Exhibit*)

More than 800 pieces of evidence, including 20 cameras and 15 phones capable of taking pictures and hundreds of sexually explicit photos of naked women, were collected from the house and garage during the three-day search by the LAPD. (*L.A. Superior Court Exhibit*)

Lonnie Franklin Jr., a father of two and former LAPD garage attendant and sanitation worker for the city of Los Angeles, was caught in July of 2010 through familial DNA testing. (*L.A. Superior Court Exhibit*)

Lonnie Franklin defense attorney Seymour Amster. *(Courtesy of San Fernando Valley Bar Association)*

Los Angeles Councilman Bernard Parks, whose district encompasses the area where the bodies were found, and LAPD Detective Dennis Kilcoyne (in police uniform) at a Grim Sleeper press conference. *(Courtesy of the author)*

Prosecutors and family members at a press conference after Lonnie Franklin's guilty verdict. LEFT TO RIGHT: Diana Ware, Marguerite Rizzo, and Beth Silverman.

The Hat Squad (left to right): LAPD detectives Rich Haro, John St. John, and Brad Magrath. *(Courtesy of Rich Haro)*

Monique Alexander's father Porter (left) and 800 Task Force Detective Daryn Dupree after the guilty verdict. *(Courtesy of the author)*

Mary Alexander (left) and reporter Christine Pelisek after Lonnie Franklin was found guilty of killing Mary's daughter Monique and nine other women. *(Courtesy of the author)*

waitress, and ordered collard greens and chicken and rice smothered in gravy before I had even picked up my menu.

"I'm starving," she said. "What do you want?"

"What's good?" I asked.

"Everything," she said. "As long as you aren't a vegetarian."

"I eat fish," I said meekly.

She looked at me like I was from outer space.

Enietra had told very few people about her attack, and I could quickly tell that, in many ways, twenty years later, it still defined her.

During our lunch she kept pushing back her black blouse and touching the top of her chest, where there was a loss of pigment due to scarring.

"Is that where you were shot?" I asked.

"Yeah," she said, quickly dropping her hand to her lap.

At lunch, she offered no details about the attack, and she told me that she wanted me to attend her church, where we could conduct the interview.

I agreed.

A few days later, I arrived thirty minutes early at Freewill Missionary Baptist Church on South Figueroa Street. I spotted Enietra, who was wearing a long flowing yellow dress with a matching headdress, and she ushered me into the kitchen and invited me to join some churchgoers who were gathered in a circle, holding hands, praying. Every Sunday before the service, a handful of parishioners met in the kitchen to pray for friends and church members who were going through hard times. Enietra prayed for a young girl caught up in gang life. An older man in a striking pressed blue suit and matching clip-on tie asked God to look out for a neighbor who had just been diagnosed with cancer. An elderly woman prayed for her daughter who was going through a divorce. A man asked for prayers for his wife who was suffering from emphysema.

"Amen," said the group after each prayer.

Soon the church was buzzing with activity, and we joined the other members in the chapel.

"Take a seat with my son Jahman," said Enietra, pointing toward a handsome clean-cut teenager dressed in a suit and tie. He was born in 1993, five years after his mother's attack. "Jahman, sit with Christine," she told him.

"Yes, ma'am," he said politely.

"Jahman is going to be a professional baseball player," she said proudly. The ninth grader was a catcher with the South Bay Rockies, a youth team that chose its players as much for their character as they did for their baseball ability.

As she walked to the front of the church to join the choir, she left us by saying, "God is good and wise."

After that, Enietra and I met on numerous occasions at various soul food restaurants to talk about the case.

During one of our meetings, Enietra told me matter-of-factly about her recurring fear that her attacker was following her. She lived in constant angst that he would come back to finish her off.

"Sometimes I get this sense he is keeping track of me," she said. "He knows I survived, and he wants me dead. There have been times at home when I have received calls in the middle of the night, and I pick up the phone and it seems like someone is listening but not hanging up."

One day, she confided, she noticed a man staring at her on the bus. It was one or two years after the attack.

She had lost her purse and identification during her 1988 attack and suspected he still had it. A week after the bus incident, the same man walked down her street and asked her, "Do you know me?"

She remembered responding, "Am I supposed to?"

He turned and walked away. She didn't think it was him at first but then thought, Oh, my God! That's him. But she shook it off.

She didn't like calling the police, she said, because one time when she talked to the police about the attack, a detective accused her of being a streetwalker.

She admitted to doing coke the night she was assaulted, but not because she was a fiend or anything. She had more personal reasons.

"I was trying to be skinny."

She was smarting from a break-up, and she wanted to lose some weight and flaunt it in her ex's face, she told me.

Mostly, during our talks, she spoke about how difficult it was readjusting to life after the shooting. A proud, dignified woman, she was embarrassed she had become a victim. She kept the attack secret from most of her friends and even some family members. She was afraid to tell her boyfriends because she was afraid of their reaction.

Instead, she found solace in the church.

"I've always been close to God," she told me. "But I got even closer to him after this."

My arrival in Enietra's life was an outlet she never knew she needed. She was a walking powder keg about to explode.

Then one day she defiantly announced: "If I have to be the bait, I will be the bait." On two or three occasions, before we had lunch, we drove the streets of South Central looking for the house where her attacker had briefly stopped to speak to a relative. Her plan, if we found the house, was to march right up to the door to see who answered, and if it was who we were looking for, then whatever might come would come. We never did find the house. If we had, out of concern for her safety, I told her I would never let her get out of the car.

During these drives, she would fault me for driving too slowly and needle me for not paying attention to her directions.

"I have to drive slowly so we can look at the houses," I said.

"Not that slow," she retorted.

It was the first time in my life I'd been accused of driving too slowly. And then she got on the size of my tiny Toyota. "You need a bigger car," she quipped.

One day when retracing her steps, we started in front of the store where she had first seen her assailant. As we drove up and down the streets, she picked out close to a dozen houses that fit the description she remembered: a white house with a hedge in the front yard. I would snap photos of the homes along the way.

"Were there bars on the window?" I asked.

"I don't remember," she said. "I know he went around to the side of the house, so we are looking for a home with a side door you can see from the street."

While she remembered the house clearly after the attack and had been able to lead police to it then, it had been more than twenty years, and the neighborhood had changed.

We drove around the streets for two more hours that day until she suggested lunch. I agreed but begged her not to choose another soul food restaurant. She laughed when I told her I couldn't eat another bite of collard greens or macaroni and cheese.

"Would it kill you to have a salad every once in a while?" I teased.

"Not only do you drive like an old lady, but you eat like one too," she all but hollered.

We griped back and forth like we had known each other for years.

• • •

After spending time together, talking on the phone, driving around, and meeting up with people who gave us clues about who the killer might be, Enietra eventually opened up and told me about her life.

Her mother, Carolyn Matthews, grew up in the Episcopalian religion in Galesburg, Illinois. She participated in beauty contests, and her good looks landed her modeling jobs in magazines and newspapers. Carolyn moved to Los Angeles when she was eighteen to study psychology at the University of Southern California. She was married briefly before she met Enietra's father, Nathaniel Joseph Washington, a Cajun Catholic from New Orleans. He served in the U.S. Army and was stationed in Okinawa, Japan, before he met Carolyn when he was a UCLA student on a football scholarship.

They married on New Year's Eve in 1958. Enietra, the first of two children, was paralyzed on the left side of her body during a difficult delivery on October 17, 1958. Thanks to her father's persistence and determination, she learned to walk at age five without the help of braces. Her sister Chemette was born in 1961. Carolyn later returned to the workforce as a spokesmodel for a bank and then became an escrow officer helping families get mortgages. Enietra's father was a successful carpenter, but his real passion was doting on his daughters.

The family lived in a duplex in South Central until Enietra was five. Then they moved into a comfortable middle-class life in Inglewood.

"The neighbors used to think my daddy was my mom's chauffeur," she said, because he drove around a beautiful woman in an expensive car in a white neighborhood.

Theirs was a charmed life. The family would ride horseback in Griffith Park when Enietra and her sister were young. Saturday was Enietra and her sister's day with their mom. They would go out for breakfast and then shop. Nathaniel was the hairdresser in the family and would line up the kids at the sink to wash their hair. He showed them how to polish their shoes.

Enietra and her sister attended an affluent private school where just 10 percent of the students were black. "If you got into a fight with someone, you had to sit and hold hands all day. I only did it twice."

She spent her summers in New Orleans visiting her paternal grandparents and planned to go to high school there until her father got sick. He was diagnosed with leukemia in 1972.

Instead, she became her father's chauffeur, taking him to his doctor's appointments at the Veterans Affairs clinic when he became too weak to drive. He would lie in the backseat while she drove. He used to tell her he needed to buy her a chauffeur's cap.

Nathaniel Washington was 43 years old when he died at his home in January of 1974. He was waiting for a bone-marrow transplant. Enietra, 15, took his death very hard.

"I was angry, hurt, resentful, and I didn't want to be bothered by anybody," she said. "I was angry at the world."

The loss affected her schooling. She started ditching classes and sometimes drove her Monte Carlo to Beverly Hills High, where she would walk the hallways and occasionally sit through a random class. She always made sure she was back at Inglewood High by 2 P.M. for volleyball practice.

She skipped school a few too many times, and after school administrators called her mother, Enietra lost her driving privileges for six months.

Enietra was a natural-born entertainer. She loved ballet and tap dancing and had childhood dreams of taking over for Lola Falana at her shows in Las Vegas. In her senior year of high school, she was offered a job in a dance troupe, but her mother wouldn't sign the permission slip, she told me. She wanted her daughter to be a doctor.

Enietra eventually gave up on dancing and started taking classes to become a physician's assistant. She was taking the classes when she found out she was six months pregnant.

She went into labor on the same day as one of her final exams. In 1977, Enietra, 19, had a boy, Nathan James.

She then had a daughter, Cherez, born in 1983.

Five years later, her life would be shattered in a way the strong-willed vivacious woman could never have imagined.

CHAPTER 20

THE HOT SEAT

IN STARK CONTRAST TO THE HUSH-hush birth of the 800 Task Force in the spring of 2007, by the end of February 2009, Kilcoyne and his team were desperate to get the media to focus on the Grim Sleeper.

Billboards offering the $500,000 reward had been plastered around South Central, but they generated few leads. The unveiling of the first billboard, which went up on the corner of Western Avenue and 98th Street, was covered by a large media contingent. However, the later billboards drew far less attention.

In December of 2008, the detectives released three sketches of the Grim Sleeper drawn by an artist who worked with The National Center for Missing and Exploited Children. The sketches were based on a sketch artist's drawing done in 1988, after Enietra Washington described her assailant.

Kilcoyne told me he wanted the public to have the three versions because twenty years after Enietra's assault, the police had no idea what the Grim Sleeper looked like. One of the sketches showed minimal aging, another depicted aging with a healthy lifestyle, and the other one showed aging taking its toll, perhaps as a result of drug or alcohol abuse.

"Every few months we have to tickle the media to get it on the front page," Kilcoyne told me, irked at the fact that he now had to kowtow to the press, including me. This was, after all, the same guy who decided two years before not to inform the public about the serial killer and the task force. He had, begrudgingly, done an about-face.

He knew the public could help solve this mystery and needed the media to repeatedly remind them of it. It was, he was well aware, the promise of a reward by a gossip magazine that led to the capture of the killer of Bill Cosby's son, a case Kilcoyne worked in 1997.

Kilcoyne was now hoping the media and the public could reverse the task force's failure in identifying the anonymous caller who implicated the Cosmopolitan Church members in the Barbara Ware murder. He decided to dust off the tape and play it to the media—front-page fodder for sure. "I know what the media is looking for, and the media will be in a frenzy over it and we will get mileage," he told 800 Task Force detectives. "If the public wants to solve this thing, let's let the public solve this thing. Let's pacify the press. Let's get our phone to ring."

Los Angeles Police Chief Bill Bratton called a press conference on February 25, 2009, in a city building next to Parker Center. It was a huge success, in terms of media coverage. Bratton, a media magnet during his years as New York City's police commissioner, was enough on his own to bring out the big guns: CNN, ABC, NBC, as well as local and international press.

It was the first time since my Grim Sleeper story broke in August of 2008 that Bratton spoke publicly about the case. Bratton told the crowd of reporters that the Grim "Sleepa," as he pronounced it with his thick Boston accent, was "the only still-outstanding serial murderer working in the city currently."

Bratton's use of the nickname surprised both the detectives and me. The detectives hated the name and shot me dirty looks when Bratton used it.

After the press conference, the 800 Task Force was inundated with more than a hundred calls into the tip and text line. (They would receive 250 calls in total during the course of the investigation.) There were a few promising leads. But in the end, once again, nothing panned out.

• • •

There was one important call, however, that came right after the press conference. It was from Barbara Ware's stepmother, Diana. And she was angry.

"Why did I have to hear about Barbara on NBC?" she laid into Kilcoyne. "This is the second time this has happened to me." Diana, who had been living in West Covina, an eastern San Gabriel Valley city nineteen miles east of downtown L.A., had seen the press conference on television, as did many of Barbara's other relatives, and they were devastated they had not been notified it was going to take place.

Kilcoyne was gobsmacked. He had been told that Barbara Ware had no living relatives. He knew immediately he had made a huge mistake by not contacting them before going to the media. Diana had every right to be upset.

"We haven't heard from the police in twenty years and when we do it is at a press conference?" Diana Ware fumed.

Diana was aware of my story, and of the Grim Sleeper, but she still had not heard directly from the police about any impact all this might be having on the search for her stepdaughter's murderer.

Kilcoyne was embarrassed. "We should have called you," he told her. "I apologize. I'd be more than happy to meet up with you and your family."

"We want to know everything you have so I don't have to see it on TV," she said. Diana told Kilcoyne she would be in touch.

On the misty morning of March 2, 2009, Kilcoyne and Detective Silvina Ynguez drove through the historically black Crenshaw

District to meet with Barbara Ware's family. Kilcoyne had no idea what to expect. He brought Yniguez, a soft-spoken woman, to act as a buffer if things got heated. "I was hoping they wouldn't yell at me as much because there was a young woman with me," he related later.

He and Yniguez walked down the quiet tree-lined street appointed with tidy 1960s-era homes. They reached the given address at the same time as five black men in business suits. Diana Ware, always impeccably dressed, greeted them at the door. Her demeanor was stiff, but she answered Kilcoyne's hello with a polite smile and invited him inside, where at least twenty of Barbara's relatives were drinking coffee and eating pastries by the kitchen counter. Kilcoyne was ushered straight through to a large living room where the furniture had been arranged into the shape of a horseshoe. At the open end of the horseshoe was a single white plastic chair. He observed correctly that the hot seat was reserved for him.

As soon as he sat down, he felt he'd been punched in the face by the years of frustration the family endured over the handling of Barbara's murder investigation. Diana spoke first. "We were blindsided," she told him, her relatives nodding in agreement. "Why weren't we informed of the press conference? I was at home and I turned on the television and this is what I saw."

Kilcoyne, in his calm, relaxed demeanor, listened and apologized. It was something he would do for the next hour.

Family members took turns peppering Kilcoyne with questions and comments about the investigation. Most were disappointed with the department's lack of transparency and what they believed to be a shoddy police investigation back in the '80s. They couldn't fathom why the anonymous call wasn't played back then. Family members were also upset that the police had labeled some of the girls as prostitutes. Barbara was not a prostitute, they insisted. Another point of contention was the fact that police didn't inform them Barbara's murderer was a serial killer.

Kilcoyne didn't understand why that mattered, though he certainly kept that to himself. It wasn't going to bring Barbara back, he thought. But he did feel terrible. After twenty years of silence, this family turned on the television to hear a tape recording in which an anonymous caller callously referred to their much-loved relative as a "dead body or something in the alley." It was unacceptable.

But Kilcoyne was thinking like a cop, not a sympathetic bystander or a victim. The family members, he felt, were blaming the police for the crime, but the police were not responsible. Their job was to solve it.

After an intense hour on the hot seat, Kilcoyne raised his hand. "It is my turn to talk. I agree we should have done better and told you about the press conference," he said. "And I am very sorry. It will not happen again. I screwed up. It was my fault, and I am sorry. I should have got a hold of you.

"I know you are angry and frustrated. I listened for an hour, and I need to say a few things. I cannot change what has happened. I can't change what happened in the '80s and what your perceptions are of the police department. A lot of resources went into the cases in the '80s. I can't defend what happened. I can't change what happened back then.

"What we need to do is move things forward, and I need your help to do that. We need to work together. You need to work with me. Let's try and come up with ideas to move forward and solve the case. Together maybe we can find an answer to this."

When Kilcoyne finished, he noticed a few of the family members nodding their heads in agreement and felt slightly more at ease. He had made his point, and it seemed to resonate. He was hopeful that they could work together. As the meeting drew to a close, he passed around a paper and asked family members to provide their phone numbers and email addresses. He would make sure they were notified anytime the LAPD held a press conference about the Grim Sleeper case.

"They were accepting, but I still wasn't a best friend," Kilcoyne told me later. "It was still very businesslike. I accepted that. We crossed a big bridge there, and I thought progress was made. Their frustration isn't unique. When a family member is murdered, it doesn't matter what color you are or your background; you are frustrated and angry and want an answer and [the investigators] are the closest thing to beat up on. You are the guy they can vent to, and if it doesn't get solved, you are looked upon as the guy who didn't solve the case. 'It is the LAPD who didn't treat us right.' People want to blame someone for what happened. They aren't going to analyze their child's upbringing or guide him away from being a gangster; they want to blame someone. It is just human nature."

During an investigation, Kilcoyne said, you become very close to families. "You are the person they vent to or share personal things with, and when it is over, it is over. And they cut you off because you were part of that nightmare."

During the meeting, Diana Ware suggested a gathering of all the families. "Maybe some of these girls knew each other," she told him. "Maybe there is a connection with the victims that has been overlooked." Kilcoyne thought it was a good idea.

A few weeks later, they settled on a date. However, finding a place to hold the meeting proved to be a problem. Kilcoyne's suggestion of the community room at Seventy-seventh Division Station near where some of the families lived didn't go over well with Diana and some of the other families. They wanted neutral territory. It was Enietra Washington who came up with an acceptable solution.

Laverne Peters, the mother of Janecia, called to tell me about it. The LAPD, she said, was meeting with family members the following morning, April 5, at the Freewill Missionary Baptist Church.

"What's the meeting about?" I asked.

Detectives wanted the families to meet to find out if any of the victims knew each other or hung out with the same crowd, she said. "Would you come?" she asked.

"Yes, I'll be there," I told her.

After I hung up, I wondered how task-force detectives would react when I showed up. At this point in time, Kilcoyne and his detectives weren't exactly my best buddies. They resented having to go public about the case and blamed me for it. They had taken a public berating after my story broke, and they didn't take kindly to it. The LAPD was used to disseminating the information they wanted to get out and didn't appreciate being on the defensive. They were under a lot of pressure to solve the case.

I decided to let Kilcoyne know I would be at the meeting. I didn't want to blindside him.

"I can't tell you not to go," he said wearily when I reached him on his cell phone. "But it is just for the families."

"Laverne invited me," I emphasized.

"Other families are going to be there," he said. "They might not want you there."

"Why don't we leave it up to them?" I said.

"If one person says they don't want you there, you have to leave," he said.

"That's fine," I agreed.

I arrived at the church the next day at 11 A.M. The pastor escorted me back to the kitchen, where about thirty members of the families of the murdered women were milling about, talking to each other. Detectives Kilcoyne, Shepard, Coulter, and Fallon were there, too, all dressed in suits and ties. They stood together near the Costco submarine sandwiches, soft drinks, and bags of potato and corn chips they had brought for the meeting.

I immediately spotted Monique Alexander's parents, Mary and Porter, seated at one of two large cafeteria-style tables covered with pink-and-white-checkered tablecloths. They smiled and waved at me as I walked in.

Laverne Peters, who was with her daughters Shamika and Jovanna, beckoned me over to her table. We hugged, and I sat down with them. I was, after all, her invited guest. Everyone, even the usually stoic Diana Ware, appeared to be slightly nervous. I was, too, but for a different reason. I was expecting the detectives to toss me out of the church at any moment. The tension in the room was palpable. So was the veil of pain that hung in the air. Every family member in that room had lost a daughter, a sister, or a mother to the Grim Sleeper.

Many of the family members had never met before but were now forever linked by one sick killer.

The sentiment in the room was clear. The families were dissatisfied with the way the police handled the investigation, in the past and in the present. They felt slighted and were angry they'd been kept in the dark about a serial killer on the loose. Some of their daughters and granddaughters walked alone on the streets to go to work or school, unaware that a serial killer lurked. The majority of the relatives had not spoken to a detective since the 1980s when the bodies of their loved ones were found abandoned in dumpsters and alleyways. Bitterness had a long time to fester. The wounds were deep and had not healed. Nonetheless, for the first time in more than two decades, most of the ever-grieving relatives in the room started to feel some real hope that the killer would be found.

As I looked around and took in all the faces, many of whom I did not know, I saw Enietra Washington standing alone near the doorway and went over to her.

"I don't feel good about being here," she told me.

Surprised by her comment, I asked her why.

"I don't belong here," she said. "I survived."

Enietra was one tough cookie, but she couldn't mask her survivor's guilt.

At 11:15 A.M., the pastor welcomed everyone to his church and asked family members to join hands in prayer with the task-force detectives. We all walked toward each other and formed a circle. I couldn't help but smile when I saw the steely detectives, cloistered in a group, awkwardly reach out to hold each other's hands. After the short prayer, the pastor asked the family members to take seats around two large tables.

I watched as the families of the murdered women sat down together for the first time.

The Alexanders sat near Henrietta Wright's daughter Rochell Johnson, who was only a toddler when her mother died in 1986.

Across from them sat Diana Ware and her daughter, Larina. A few feet from them were Laverne and Janecia's two sisters.

After the opening prayer circle, Kilcoyne went to the front of the room, and he cut to the chase. "We have a reporter here from the *L.A. Weekly*," he said. "We had mentioned this was a private meeting with family members and not with the press. If anyone wants her to leave, please raise your hand, and she will be gone."

"We don't want her to leave," said Laverne.

"We would like her to stay," said Mary.

"That's right," Porter added. "She can stay."

I wasn't sure what to expect, but I was happy for the support and relieved none of the family members raised a hand. Kilcoyne sighed before he said, "Okay. She can stay."

Then, Kilcoyne got straight to the point. He told the room of thirty family members that he needed their help.

"We are looking for any family connections. Did the girls know each other? If so, how?"

But it was soon clear the families wanted to talk about the investigation first. They had plenty of questions and were looking for answers. Why was the killer so hard to catch? Are the killings ritualistic? Is he still out there? Could he be killing elsewhere? These were questions the detectives asked themselves daily.

Then they tried to connect some dots, talking back and forth about any and all possibilities of crisscrossing lives—neighborhoods, families, jobs, church groups, community activities, schools, friends. But the paths of the murdered women didn't appear to have crossed.

Lachrica Jefferson's aunt, Yvonne Bell, said she recognized some of the girls but couldn't place where she knew them from. That was about it.

All the family members had heard the news that the familial DNA test conducted by the California Department of Justice in 2008 didn't unearth a relative of the killer. Laverne wanted to know if there was a time limit on the task force.

"No," said Kilcoyne, although he secretly wondered himself.

CHAPTER 21
THE COALITION RESURRECTED

IN BETWEEN LETDOWNS AND BAD leads were more letdowns. In one instance, the 800 Task Force detectives' interests were piqued when Seventy-seventh Division officers stopped a businessman from Diamond Bar cruising for prostitutes on Western Avenue. The man, who had a family, spent his nights prowling the streets in his Mercedes-Benz. Kilcoyne asked the surveillance unit to follow him. Like clockwork, he left his home at 3 A.M. and trolled the streets of Western, occasionally bringing the girls to a home in South Central where, detectives learned, his mother used to live. He then drove home, changed clothes, and went to work. His routine also included drives along prostitution strolls during his lunch breaks, detectives noted. The surveillance team surreptitiously collected a sample of his DNA, but he was soon ruled out.

"He was just a horny dude," said Kilcoyne.

• • •

The morale of the 800 Task Force detectives dipped more and more as each day passed with no breakthroughs. To keep their minds active, Kilcoyne told detectives that besides focusing on the calls that came in, they were going to refocus on the neighborhood where Barbara Ware was found. They would find out who lived in the neighborhood in the '80s, track them down, and see if they recognized the voice of the mystery caller. "We will try to recreate what went on in that neighborhood in 1987, and if that means going through archive records or real estate records, that is exactly what we will do," he said.

Kilcoyne knew it would be a difficult undertaking. The South Central neighborhood had changed over the past twenty years. Once made up predominantly of middle-class blacks, it was now the home of Hispanics, mostly from Mexico. The 800 Task Force detectives had recently canvassed the area for people who lived there in the '80s but found no one.

Kilcoyne believed the anonymous tipster lived in the neighborhood where Barbara Ware's body was found and had called from a payphone at a corner store less than one block away. During the call he said he would not come forward because too many people knew him. Kilcoyne theorized that he most likely watched the killer dump the body in the alley and watched as he drove off.

Since police could trace landline calls, the tipster, like most South Central residents, leery of police contact, probably chose to use the pay phone so he wouldn't have to identify himself. Kilcoyne didn't think the caller was the killer because the actual killer wouldn't have spent as much time on the phone with the dispatcher. However, as time went on and the killer remained at large, Kilcoyne vacillated in his thinking about the tipster-killer connection.

• • •

After a few weeks task-force detectives tracked down the now-retired postman who delivered mail in the neighborhood. He told them it was his habit to hang out at the neighborhood liquor store with the locals and have a few beers after he finished his route. But the two weeks spent tracking him down turned out to be a bust. The postman only remembered a couple of names. More importantly, he couldn't recognize the voice of the mystery caller.

Task-force detectives also planned to canvas the neighborhood where Othus S. White, the older man whose house Enietra identified as the home where her attacker stopped, lived. It was on the list of things to do. At that point, everything was a long shot.

Meanwhile, Detective Bill Fallon received a letter from a Veteran Affairs investigator on February 17, 2009, regarding a written confession given to a nurse at a VA medical clinic.

In the letter, the patient claimed he had killed several prostitutes and planned to arm himself and go to local schools. Fallon tracked down the patient's father and learned that his son was mentally ill and had been missing for a week. Before Fallon could get worried, the investigator called to say the patient was currently in custody at the VA hospital's mental ward on Wilshire Boulevard.

The following day, Amador and Fallon interviewed the patient. With the patient's consent, they obtained a saliva sample. He told the detectives he was riding an emotional rollercoaster. He was frustrated with the doctors and the medical care he received over the last decade. When detectives asked him about the threatening letter, he admitted he wrote it, but said he was just venting. He was soon ruled out.

Shepard now switched his attention to Ronnie Lewis, Monique Alexander's boyfriend at the time of her death. Lewis's background, Shepard learned, was not without legal entanglements.

Lewis had been arrested on April 19, 2001, for two separate murders. But, before the case went to trial, the Los Angeles County District Attorney's office dropped the charges against him after DNA linked two other men to the slayings. Lewis had spent four months in jail.

Now married and living in Highland, a city near the San Bernardino Mountains, Lewis was not in any felon database. Shepard discovered a sample of Lewis's DNA had been taken after his arrest for the two murders, and the LAPD lab still had it. The detective ordered the police lab to compare the sample with the Grim Sleeper. Lewis was soon excluded as a suspect.

• • •

Not surprisingly, some community residents, activists, and family members continued to express displeasure with the slow progress the task force was making. I reached out to Margaret Prescod, the community activist and founder of the Black Coalition Fighting Back Serial Murders who'd staged protests in the '80s decrying the police work in the Southside Slayer cases. She was completely surprised to learn that there was still an active serial killer dating back to those years.

Prescod had become a radio host with KPFK. Her public-affairs show, called *Sojourner Truth*, focused on how local, national, and international policies affected women and minority communities.

Prescod, whose once-short Afro was now a mane of brown-blonde dreadlocks, told me she had thought the arrest of L.A. County Sheriff's Department Deputy Rickey Ross twenty years before had put an end to the serial killings. Chagrined at the turn of events, Prescod organized a flurry of protests and press conferences over a period of a few months, starting on May 29, 2009, including a sidewalk vigil outside of Parker Center.

The Southside Slayer Task Force in the '80s was much different than the 2009 version. While the police brass in the '80s considered Prescod's rhetoric to fall somewhere between unproductive and asinine, Kilcoyne and the task force were willing to help Prescod get the word out. Prescod wanted an open relationship with the police. Kilcoyne wanted the same with Prescod. At least to a point. He had no plans to share police information with her, but he was more than happy to organize press conferences and print fliers for the coalition.

Prescod, who was used to having an adversarial relationship with the police, wasn't sure what to make of Kilcoyne's gesture. "We will see how it goes," she told me, for an article I wrote for the *L.A. Weekly.*

Prescod resurrected the Black Coalition Fighting Back Serial Murders and contacted family members of the victims. Diana Ware and Porter and Mary Alexander were at the May 29 press conference she held outside of Parker Center, where the 800 Task Force was criticized for a lack of information and progress in the case. While Prescod scolded the police, Diana Ware and the Alexanders held up signs that read: "Every Life is of Value," and "Black Women's lives count," sentiments that would later be echoed in the Black Lives Matter movement.

"South Los Angeles residents have no idea that there is a serial killer out there," she said to the small gathering of media in attendance.

Prescod was particularly perturbed that it took more than two decades for the police to release the tape of the anonymous caller in the Barbara Ware case. During the press conference, she issued a series of demands to the police, asking for the release of a bimonthly report on the status of the task-force investigation, compensation for the victims and their families, and the publication of the actual number of unsolved murders of black women in South Central.

Prescod ended with the call for an investigation by the United States Department of Justice into the handling of the Grim Sleeper murders.

In the afternoon of June 25, I was heading to another one of Prescod's press conferences in South Central, this one being held across the street from Jesse Owens Park, near the alley where Janecia Peters and Bernita Sparks were found dead. I had my car radio on when the news broke that Michael Jackson had died. I arrived at the press conference to find Prescod, Diana Ware, and a small group of activists. A member of the Spanish press and I were the only media. All of the other members of the press were at the Ronald Reagan UCLA Medical Center reporting on the tragic saga that was Jackson's life.

Despite the lack of media, Prescod announced the start of a community crusade called Stop the Serial Murders Community Information Campaign, with an aim of raising awareness of the Grim Sleeper case by plastering the area with the composite sketches.

The murders were not a high priority for the police, the mayor, or the media, she told me.

Prescod was miffed that Los Angeles County Sheriff Lee Baca had not spoken publicly about the murder of Lachrica Jefferson, who was killed in the sheriff's territory in 1988. Prescod was incensed that Baca had not tried to get a reward offered for her slaying as the LAPD had done for their victims.

"Should her death be dismissed because Baca can't be bothered?" she asked at the press conference.

When the press conference was over, Prescod, Diana Ware, and a few church members dispersed across the neighborhood and passed out fliers to businesses and passersby. I was surprised at how few South Angelenos knew about the Grim Sleeper case. One female church worker I spoke to told me that the serial murders were disconcerting but the community was more concerned about drugs, gangs recruiting school children, and drive-by shootings, where innocent lives were lost. The women's deaths were a tragedy, but getting into a car with a stranger was just plain foolish.

• • •

While the 800 Task Force was spinning its wheels tracking the Grim Sleeper, its work on the case did help the LAPD to clear up other previously unsolved cases, including the capture of the so-called Westside Rapist, who had terrorized elderly white women in the '70s.

LAPD Sex Crimes Detective Diane Webb was one of the detectives who helped solve that case along with the cold-case unit. Webb's job involved monitoring L.A.'s registered sex offenders, and when she read my Grim Sleeper Returns story, it sparked an idea.

She could design a database for the city's 5,212 registered sex offenders that could search for men who fit the Grim Sleeper's profile.

From that list, she would then be able to figure out if any of them had somehow evaded the mandatory DNA test required of all of them.

Webb brought her plan to Detective Dennis Kilcoyne, who gave her a thumbs-up. Webb's database search for black sex offenders between the ages of 40 and 100 found ninety-two sex offenders who fit the criteria of the Grim Sleeper and who had not been swabbed. Once she got their names, Webb asked officers to track down each man and get a swab of their DNA.

John Floyd Thomas, a then-72-year-old state workers' compensation fund insurance adjuster, walked into LAPD's Southwest Division Station on October 22, 2008. He told the duty officer at the desk he had received a call and was told he had to provide the police department with a sample as part of Webb's sweep. Thomas, who had served time for sexual assault, did just that.

A backlog at the lab delayed the test for five months, but his cheek-swab DNA was eventually matched to murders from the 1970s and '80s linked to the so-called Westside Rapist. His modus operandi was the same for each victim—he sought elderly white women, raped them, and then strangled them using his hands and powerful forearms. His victims lived in the Mid-Wilshire area of Los Angeles; Westchester, a Westside neighborhood of Los Angeles County; and Inglewood.

Ethel Sokoloff, 68, was Thomas's first known victim in 1972. Cora Perry, 79, followed on September 20, 1975. Then, the partially naked body of Elizabeth McKeown, 67, a retired school administrator, was discovered in her '65 Chevelle, near her apartment in February of 1976. Maybelle Hudson, an 80-year-old retired schoolteacher, was found in her home in April of 1976. Miriam McKinley, 65, was murdered in her garage two months later. And in October, 56-year-old Evalyn Bunner was raped and murdered by the brutal Thomas.[23]

The database hadn't yet identified the Grim Sleeper, but catching the Westside Rapist was a worthy consolation prize for the LAPD.

---

23. In April of 2011, John Floyd Thomas pleaded guilty to seven murders. He is serving life without the possibility of parole.

CHAPTER 22
AN ARREST

THE 800 TASK FORCE, WHICH HAD begun three years earlier with so much fervor and promise, had by 2010 dwindled down to four depressed detectives following dead end after dead end. Overtime hours had been cut, the keys to the squad cars turned in. Of the four detectives—Dennis Kilcoyne, Cliff Shepard, Bill Fallon, and Paul Coulter—only Kilcoyne kept his take-home police vehicle.

The three other detectives, Rod Amador, Daryl Groce, and Gina Rubalcava, had been reassigned to new cases in different departments.

With morale at an all-time low, Kilcoyne asked his boss if his team could take a break from the Grim Sleeper case and catch some fresh homicides. It wasn't going to happen. The Grim Sleeper case was a huge priority for the LAPD.

Kilcoyne was surprised the task force was still operational. Most task forces he had participated in disbanded within three to six months if there was no progress.

Politics. That is what kept this task force going, he concluded. The department had dedicated a lot of money and manpower to the

Grim Sleeper case and still had not found a viable suspect. Former Chief Bratton and his replacement Chief Charlie Beck would not dare anger the black community or the black city council members by closing down the task force altogether, Kilcoyne believed. This pleased Kilcoyne, though he welcomed the distraction of other investigations to keep the detectives' minds working.

Then, in early March, during a break at the California Homicide Investigators Association conference in Las Vegas, Kilcoyne was talking with California Department of Justice bureau chief Jill Spriggs, who suggested it was time to try another familial search.

Since the first search in 2008 failed to get a hit, the California DNA database of felons had grown from one million to 1.4 million. Kilcoyne got his hopes up again that the new tool would find a relative of the Grim Sleeper among the four hundred thousand felons added to the database.

The LAPD formally requested that California's Department of Justice lab perform a second familial search on March 31.

One month went by, then another. By late June, Kilcoyne figured it was another dead end.

But on Wednesday afternoon, June 30, he got the call that, finally, would change everything.

• • •

Kilcoyne was initially caught off guard. When the phone rang and it was Spriggs, he assumed she was calling to remind him about their monthly breakfast plans the following morning. Spriggs had been flying into Bob Hope Airport in Burbank from Sacramento once a month to attend a meeting with local law enforcement. She would usually rent a car and drive to the Cathedral of Our Lady of the Angels in downtown L.A. and park across the street from the office of the Los Angeles County Board of Supervisors, where the meetings were held. Kilcoyne would pick her up for breakfast. Police Chief Charlie Beck was scheduled to join them this time, but

Spriggs told Kilcoyne she had to cancel and asked him to relay the message to Beck.

"I'll let him know," Kilcoyne said.

Then Spriggs asked, "Aren't you going to ask me why I have to cancel?"

"You are a busy gal, and you are in charge of thirteen labs," Kilcoyne said. "I figure you have a good reason. You don't need to tell me why."

"Aren't you even a little bit curious?" she pressed.

"Okay," Kilcoyne said, taking the bait. "What's this about?"

Spriggs told him to go somewhere quiet where they could talk.

Kilcoyne stepped away from his desk and walked past Coulter, Shepard, and Fallon to the secretary's office down the hallway. He thought Spriggs had some gossip she wanted to share. "What's up?" he said.

"Are you sitting down?" she enquired.

"No, I'm not sitting down."

"Then sit down," she said.

Kilcoyne sat down.

"It's about the Grim Sleeper case," she said matter-of-factly.

Kilcoyne jumped up from his seat.

"Did we get a hit?" he shot back.

"I can't tell you that," she told him.

She did tell Kilcoyne she would be in L.A. on Friday, two days hence, and asked him to set up a meeting at the city and county's DNA lab at Cal State University, Los Angeles. She told him to make sure Los Angeles County District Attorney Steve Cooley and Beck were there. "But you can't tell anyone," she added.

"Well, I can't walk up to Beck and tell him 'you need to go to the lab' and not tell him anything," Kilcoyne said. "Old Dennis isn't that high up on the food chain."

She brushed him off. "You will be happy, and you will need to make this meeting happen," she told Kilcoyne.

"Did we get a hit?" Kilcoyne asked again.

"I can't tell you," she said.

"Is he alive?"

Spriggs wouldn't budge.

When Kilcoyne hung up, he felt like he was going into shock. He actually wasn't sure if he heard Spriggs right, and he called her right back.

"Am I dreaming?" he asked. "Did you really call me and tell me you are bringing me some information?"

"Yes, I just called you," she told him. "Just make sure there is someone to pick me up from the airport."

"I'll be there," he told her.

While nothing specific was said, the seasoned detective heard plenty. Spriggs wouldn't have called a meeting unless there was a familial hit.

"My mind was going one hundred miles an hour," he later told me. "I want to bust and start yelling out, 'We got it,' but I can't. I am thinking to myself, You don't want to be the guy who ruins it for everyone by not keeping your mouth shut."

However, he was able to release a bit of that pressure. He had to inform his captain, who was driving home on the 60 Freeway when Kilcoyne reached him on his cell phone. "You need to get off the freeway and call me back," Kilcoyne told him.

A few minutes later, Kilcoyne was informing his boss of his conversation with Spriggs.

The rest of the day was a haze for Kilcoyne, as was the fifty-mile drive to his home in north L.A. County near Santa Clarita. His wife and their two sons were in Florida visiting her parents, and, for the first time, Kilcoyne was grateful they weren't home—he was afraid he wouldn't be able to contain himself. The detective pulled up a chair and sat on his side patio, lit a cigar, and cracked open a cold beer. It had been a long and frustrating ride. Kilcoyne wondered if the 800 Task Force's journey was finally coming to an end.

That night, he barely slept. He crawled out of bed at 4:30 A.M., got dressed, and drove the one and a half hours back to police headquarters. At 7 A.M., Kilcoyne and his boss went to Beck's tenth-floor office and filled in the chief of police on the latest news. Kilcoyne told Beck he was certain they had a familial hit. Why else would Spriggs ask for a meeting?

When Friday, July 2, finally arrived, Kilcoyne picked up Spriggs and the chief of Department of Justice investigations at Bob Hope Airport and drove them to the city and county lab at California State University, Los Angeles for the meeting with Beck, Pat Dixon from the district attorney's office, and the head of LAPD's forensic lab.

Spriggs got straight to the point. The lab did get a familial match, she said. The search had produced a list of two hundred genetic profiles of people in the database who might be related to the Grim Sleeper. Among the top five hits, only one shared a common genetic marker with the DNA found at the crime scenes.

The profile belonged to 28-year-old Christopher John Franklin. He had been in the state DNA database of felons since the summer of 2009 after he pleaded guilty to a felony firearms charge. As a convicted felon, he was required to provide the state a sample of his DNA. Christopher's DNA was in the system for just ten months before lab workers did the second search.

The Department of Justice had narrowed the search for Christopher's relatives down to two men before meeting with the police. The first, a possible uncle in Riverside, California, was later discovered to be no relation. The other was Lonnie David Franklin Jr., a longtime South Central resident and, according to birth records, Christopher's father.

Spriggs showed the group of lawmen a Google map of where the murders occurred and compared them to where Christopher's father lived.

Spriggs reiterated that it was just a lead.

Kilcoyne's first call when he left the meeting was to Task-force Detective Paul Coulter, who already suspected something big was happening. Kilcoyne asked him to do a background search on Lonnie David Franklin Jr.

"Find everything you can about him," he told Coulter. "But I don't want anyone putting Christopher Franklin's name in the computer. He is not under investigation. I don't want any record to later pop up at trial."

Kilcoyne knew that organizations such as the American Civil Liberties Union thought familial searches were tantamount to a witch hunt because police were investigating relatives who may not have committed a crime. Kilcoyne wanted to make sure no one went near Christopher Franklin or even typed his name in a computer. He wanted to avoid a legal challenge in court.

Coulter had a report prepared on their suspect by the time Kilcoyne got back to the office: Lonnie Franklin Jr., 57, and his wife, Sylvia, lived at 1728 West 81st Street since 1986, the epicenter of where the Grim Sleeper murders took place. Their mint-green bungalow was three doors down from where Enietra Washington's attacker stopped briefly before driving on and shooting her. Franklin, a grandfather, also fit the description of her attacker. Princess Berthomieux was discovered within four blocks straight down 81st Street. Lachrica Jefferson was last seen at Jody Gatewood's apartment on the corner of 81st Street and Western Avenue, half a block from Franklin's house. Franklin had not been in jail or prison during any of the Grim Sleeper murders.

The detectives exchanged looks. They were certain they had their man.

It was now up to the LAPD's surveillance team to confirm what Kilcoyne and Coulter knew deep in their gut: Lonnie David Franklin Jr. was the Grim Sleeper.

• • •

The team of undercover detectives got their assignment around 10 P.M. on July 2, 2010.

The covert operation was simple: in shifts, follow Lonnie Franklin Jr. twenty-four hours a day and pick up anything he discarded that could yield DNA and use it to prove their case.

One hour later, a surveillance team made up of members of the High Intensity Drug Trafficking Area (HIDTA) Task Force was surreptitiously camped outside Franklin's bungalow. They were there for less than twenty-five minutes when Franklin left his house, got into a dark green 2005 Honda Accord, and drove to an apartment building on Buckingham and Palmyra roads, about five miles away. He was oblivious to the undercover detectives following him. The surveillance team watched as a black woman, who they later discovered was Franklin's girlfriend, Sonia, walked out of the apartment building and slid into the passenger seat beside Franklin.

The surveillance team followed Franklin and Sonia to a gas station in Hollywood and then to Original Tommy's Hamburgers drive-thru on Roscoe Boulevard in North Hills, in the north central San Fernando Valley. The team tailed the car onto the 405 South Freeway and followed for twelve miles until it got off at the Santa Monica Boulevard exit. Franklin eventually turned into Dolores Restaurant and Bakery. Detectives shadowed Franklin and his girlfriend inside the bakery and observed as they ordered take-out at the counter and then got back into the Honda Accord. Franklin and Sonia drove back to her apartment, arriving at 2:38 A.M. Franklin, a married man, stayed the night.

The same team of detectives was back on Franklin detail the following night. They watched as Franklin drove around his block to talk to an unidentified black man and then run errands. Franklin came home and stayed inside until after 2 A.M. on July 4, when the surveillance team watched him get into a black 1992 Nissan, drive to a local gas station, and then troll the area of Western Avenue and 43rd Street, where two prostitutes were standing on the corner. Franklin drove past the women three times before he pulled up along the curb near them.

What happened next was beyond the mandate of the surveillance team. They needed direction on how to proceed.

Kilcoyne was at home in bed when his cell phone rang, waking him up.

"Franklin is slowing down to talk to the girls," one of the undercover detectives told him. "What do we do if a girl gets in the car?"

"We aren't going to let him kill anyone," responded Kilcoyne. Kilcoyne told the officers to keep watching Franklin and that if he picked up anyone to get a patrol car to pull him over and "get the girl out of the car and send him on his way."

"Should we get a DNA sample from him?" the undercover detective asked.

"No," Kilcoyne said.

He didn't want to blow this. Kilcoyne knew that by law the officers couldn't randomly ask for a sample. In order for it to stand up in court, Franklin had to discard something with his DNA in a public place. "If they had asked him to stick a swab in his mouth, it would have been an illegal search," said Kilcoyne. "We can't go to his porch, his house, his car, or his trash. If he spits on the sidewalk, it is open game. It is considered abandoned."

Fortunately, the undercover detectives didn't have to intervene. A few minutes later, a patrol car cruising the area, unaware of the surveillance team, pulled up behind Franklin and flashed its lights. Franklin quickly drove off.

The surveillance team followed Franklin to Sonia's apartment, where he parked outside the building and made a cell-phone call. Twelve minutes later, he drove home.

Later that July 4 day, as revelers across the city celebrated the holiday, the same surveillance team followed Franklin and Sonia to a Ralph's supermarket and then later to the Los Angeles Coliseum near the University of Southern California, where Franklin and Sonia watched the fireworks. Once again, the undercover detectives were unable to get a sample of DNA from Franklin, who didn't so much as toss a cigarette butt.

• • •

While the surveillance team was following Franklin, Detective Cliff Shepard was off the clock. He was driving a rented U-Haul on the 5 Freeway that Sunday morning of July 4, on his way to Laguna Woods in Orange County to empty furniture from his deceased mother's condo, when he got the call from Coulter about the big break in the case.

"They are following a suspect," Coulter told him.

Shepard was stunned. This significant development appeared to come out of nowhere.

Adrenaline was coursing through his body. He turned the U-Haul around and returned home, took a shower, put on a suit, and drove to police headquarters. When he arrived, Coulter was at his desk dressed casually in a shirt and jeans.

"What do you have?" Shepard asked Coulter.

Coulter told him they had been given two names. The man in Riverside was one, but he was not related. The remaining suspect, Lonnie Franklin, lived on 81st Street and Western Avenue.

When Shepard learned that this possibly momentous development occurred two days before, he was outraged that Kilcoyne had kept him in the dark.

You people knew this Friday, and you didn't have the courtesy to tell me, he thought. After all the time he had invested, not to be informed felt like a slap in the face. However, Shepard decided not to confront Kilcoyne. He was, after all, his boss, and Shepard didn't want to risk being removed from the task force for complaining. He wanted to see the investigation through to the end.

And, the fact was, Shepard wasn't totally surprised with Kilcoyne's actions. Kilcoyne had hinted now and then that he thought Shepard had leaked information to me, and Shepard figured that was why he was kept out of the loop on this latest development.

He put aside his ill feelings and focused on the task at hand. The last six years of the most important case in his career as a detective was about to pay off. When Coulter told him the address of the prime suspect, everything clicked. It made perfect sense. The man was literally hunting in his own backyard.

The next day, Monday, July 5, the undercover detectives following Franklin finally caught a break. Shortly after noon, Franklin drove his wife's silver Honda van to pick up Sonia and her two daughters, who were waiting down the street from his home. They drove the twenty-five miles to Orange County to John's Incredible Pizza Company in the Buena Park Mall. Undercover Detective Art Stone watched as Franklin and company made their way to Party Room 4, where a kid's birthday celebration was in progress. Franklin, who was dressed in a beige short-sleeve shirt and beige pants, took a seat at the edge of a long table covered with a purple tablecloth. The kids watched a restaurant employee blow up balloons, and the adults took trips to the buffet for slices of pizza.

This was the opportunity Stone was waiting for. While Franklin chowed down on pizza, Stone went to the restaurant manager with a request. Within a few minutes, Stone was dressed in a company blue shirt and blue baseball hat, clearing Franklin's table. If anyone became suspicious that a middle-aged white guy was bussing tables at a kid's birthday party, he would say he was the owner's brother-in-law learning the ropes.

Stone placed the dirty dishes in a large black plastic tub. Inside the tub was an eight-by-twelve-inch stainless steel metal tray, where he separated Franklin's dirty dishes and utensils from the others.

In a few hours, Stone had what he needed. He collected a fork, two napkins, two plastic blue cups, a discarded pizza slice, and a white ceramic plate with a piece of partially eaten chocolate cake on it—all from Franklin. With enough evidence to test for DNA, he turned in his uniform and headed to a nearby Kohl's department store parking lot, where the rest of the undercover team members were waiting. They packaged and photographed the evidence before they turned it over to Coulter and Kilcoyne. Kilcoyne booked the evidence with the property division, and then he checked it back out and that day hand-delivered it to the crime lab for comparison with the Grim Sleeper's profile.

The lab technician told him the profile would be complete the next morning. Kilcoyne was ecstatic.

But the following day, the technician called to inform him of a mix-up. The test results wouldn't be back until the next morning, Wednesday, July 7, because of the holiday weekend. Kilcoyne would get his answer by 5 A.M., she said.

Exhausted and frazzled, Kilcoyne went home. There was so much riding on this case, and he was feeling the pressure. Capturing the serial killer would be huge for the police department. And this was the biggest case of his long and distinguished career. Nothing had come close to this.

• • •

I was in Ottawa visiting my parents when I got a call from my *L.A. Weekly* editor, Jill Stewart. She had been tipped off that something big was happening at the LAPD and they were about to make a big arrest in a cold case. Stewart had an inkling that it involved the Grim Sleeper.

"I'll check with the detectives," I told her.

I hung up and called Shepard. He didn't pick up. My next call was to Kilcoyne. "Hey, I heard you guys are about to make an arrest in a cold case. Does it have anything to do with the Grim Sleeper case?" I asked.

"Nope," Kilcoyne said.

"Are you sure?" I said. "If it isn't the Grim Sleeper case, what case is it?"

"No clue," he said.

"You aren't lying to me, are you?"

"No," he said adamantly.

I called Stewart back and told her what Kilcoyne had said.

• • •

At 5 A.M. on Wednesday morning, July 7, 2010, Kilcoyne was at his desk waiting for the phone to ring. It didn't. An hour later, he called the lab. No answer. He was so anxious he was ready to pull out his thick gray hair.

He waited and called the lab again. Again, no answer.

Kilcoyne's phone finally rang at 6:30 A.M., but it was Coulter. He had been parked outside the house of Los Angeles Superior Court Judge William Pounders for the last hour armed with a warrant for the judge to sign that would allow police to legally search Franklin's home once his DNA linked him to the murders. The search warrant asked the judge for permission to search Franklin's home for weapons, including a .25-caliber pistol; any cameras or Polaroid pictures; and "any news or magazine articles regarding any of the alleged crimes described herein, including those related to the 'Grim Sleeper,' i.e. *L.A. Weekly*, *America's Most Wanted* video clips, CNN website/blogs, or photographs of related billboards, or articles related to additional unsolved similar crimes." Coulter, who wrote the search warrant, knew serial killers were infamous for keeping stories about their murders.

"I think the lab is screwing with us," Kilcoyne told him. "We still haven't heard from them."

Fifteen minutes after Kilcoyne hung up with Coulter, he received a text from the lab. The text simply read: "Positive results."

Kilcoyne learned that saliva found on the pizza and two napkins matched the Grim Sleeper's genetic profile. The cheese on the pizza slice had hardened enough that there was a nice solid surface from which to pull a sample. The lab couldn't get a DNA sample from the utensils. They were too oily from the salad dressing.

The second he read his text about the positive results, he called Coulter back.

"It's our guy," Kilcoyne told him. Coulter got out of his car and walked up to Judge Pounders, who was standing outside his house on his porch. He invited Coulter inside, read the search warrant, signed it, and wished Coulter good luck as he left.

Game on.

Undercover detectives from the Special Investigation Section, who were regularly tasked with tracking down the city's most violent offenders, were assigned to take Franklin into custody.

Franklin was on the street outside his house about to move a car when the detectives swooped in to pick him up at 9:30 A.M.

Franklin didn't resist. There were no dramatics. In fact, Franklin exhibited a placid resignation that would be the manner in which he presented himself throughout his case.

The detectives escorted Franklin to Seventy-seventh Division Station. Franklin was standing outside the police car when Coulter and Kilcoyne pulled into the station parking structure.

"We stopped by to introduce ourselves, Mr. Franklin," Kilcoyne said as he finally set his gaze upon the man the LAPD had been hunting for more than two decades.

Franklin, a robust man who looked as though he lifted weights, was wearing a khaki long-sleeved work shirt over a white T-shirt and a pair of Dickies. Kilcoyne noticed that the writing above Franklin's shirt pocket was similar to what a mechanic or gas attendant would wear. He couldn't help but remember Enietra's interview, during which she said her attacker wore a type of uniform worn by mechanics.

On finally seeing Franklin, Coulter's first thought was, This is the little shit we have been looking for all this time. He was reminded of another serial killer he investigated and interviewed, Michael Hughes. Like Hughes, who terrorized South Central in the '80s and early '90s, Franklin seemed soft-spoken and compliant.

Kilcoyne and the 800 Task Force detectives would soon discover that Franklin was a car mechanic who, in the 1980s, worked as a garage attendant with the LAPD and then as a garbage collector with the Department of Sanitation.

"We have an investigation going on, and we have a warrant to search your residence and for your arrest," Kilcoyne told Franklin, who was handcuffed and leaning on the police car. "We are going to take you downtown, and we will explain more to you."

Franklin didn't ask any questions. He was polite and respectful. "Okay. Thank you," he responded in an even tone.

Franklin was escorted to police headquarters in downtown L.A. and taken to interview room 582 to wait for Coulter and Kilcoyne, who had stopped by Franklin's house to see what the search warrant had turned up. Detectives had found a .25-caliber pistol in the pocket of a jacket hanging inside a hallway closet. As they then drove to police headquarters, Kilcoyne called the office secretary to tell her to contact the victim's family members. "Tell them to come to police headquarters as fast as they can," he instructed. "Don't tell them why. Just tell them they have to come now. If they don't have transportation, get detectives to go get them."

"It was a big priority to call the families," he told me later. "We were trying to avoid hurting people's feelings, and after the incident with Diana Ware, it really brought it home for me."

When Kilcoyne arrived at police headquarters, he called the Alexanders. Mary Alexander answered the phone.

"Are you sitting down?" Kilcoyne asked her.

"No," said Mary. "Should I?"

"Yes," he told her. "We got him. You need to come down here right away." Before he hung up, he could hear Mary screaming her husband's name.

Kilcoyne had already decided that he and Coulter would conduct the interview with Franklin. He had seen Coulter in action and recognized his talent for drawing information out of people. There was a lot hanging on this interview. Their first challenge would be to get Franklin to talk. It would be the interview of their careers, and they knew that every move they made would be dissected by the top brass, as well as the district attorney's office. A lot of high-level eyeballs would be watching from the video room.

When Coulter and Kilcoyne entered the interview room at 12:50 P.M., the room was dark, and Franklin had fallen asleep. They woke him and noted he did not appear concerned that he had been arrested.

• • •

After general questions about where he lived, his profession, and the names of his wife and children, Coulter got down to business.

"Do you know why you are here?" Coulter asked, taking a seat across the table from Franklin.

"No, I don't," said Franklin in a calm, relaxed tone.

"We are working on an investigation," said Coulter, "and there is a warrant for your arrest, and we are charging you with a count of murder."

"Murder?" asked Franklin.

"Yes, sir," said Coulter. "I can see by your expression you have a lot of questions to ask us, but we have a couple of questions to ask you too."

Coulter read Franklin his Miranda rights, basically informing him he had the right to clam up, as well as the right to an attorney. The seasoned detectives, of course, hoped Franklin would waive that right and open up to them there and then. If Franklin asked for an attorney, they couldn't even ask one question. The interview would be over before it started.

"Do you want to sit here and talk to us about it?" asked Coulter.

"I don't know what it is about," Franklin said casually, with no hint of surprise or outrage over his arrest.

"Do you want to sit here and talk about the warrant and what the charges are against you?" asked Coulter.

"Yes," Franklin responded.

Coulter told Franklin that the LAPD had been investigating a 2007 homicide.

"I am going to show you a photo of this young lady and see if you recognize her," Coulter said, and he placed a photo of Janecia Peters in front of Franklin.

"No, I don't," Franklin said, looking at the photo of a smiling Janecia.

"We didn't just pick your name out of a hat," said Coulter. "You have been identified with this young lady. Do you understand that?"

"Yes, I do," answered Franklin.

"Do you have any questions about that?" asked Coulter. "Why would you be identified?"

"I don't know," shrugged Franklin. "I know a lot of people, but I don't know her."

"I am sure you probably heard about DNA," Coulter said.

"Uh-huh," responded Franklin.

"Well, your DNA was identified in relation to this lady's death," said Coulter. "How could that happen?"

"I don't know," answered Franklin.

"You have never seen this lady before in your life?"

"No, I haven't."

Coulter began showing Franklin photos of three more dead women: Valerie McCorvey, Princess Berthomieux, and Monique Alexander.

"And again, it is all linked to you," said Coulter. "You tell me once maybe you met the gal and you had a little relationship with her and she turns up dead and maybe it is a coincidence. But I just showed you four people. I mean, your coincidences are getting pretty slim. Wouldn't you say?"

"Yes, sir," responded Franklin.

The detectives could see how callous the man in front of them was. He displayed a completely cavalier attitude. It was pure arrogance, Kilcoyne thought. Kilcoyne had the urge to reach across the table and smack Franklin, but he remained polite and levelheaded, addressing his suspect as Mr. Franklin. Kilcoyne was known to jump up and get into a suspect's face. Sometimes it worked, and other times it didn't. Today was not the day to do that. His gut told him that an in-your-face approach would not work on Franklin. This guy was too passive. By being too aggressive, Kilcoyne feared Franklin would shut down entirely. The longer he kept him talking, the better off they were.

Franklin didn't appear to be nervous at all, Coulter thought. He seemed calm. And he wasn't saying much. What the detectives needed was for Franklin to slip.

"Do you go to church?" Kilcoyne asked.

"Yes I do," said Franklin. "As a matter of fact, I am supposed to be at church tonight."

"Do you remember a church that used to be on Normandie, the Cosmopolitan Church? Do you remember that?" asked Kilcoyne. "Were you a member there?"

"No, I wasn't," said Franklin.

"Did you used to drive their van?" Kilcoyne continued.

"No, I didn't," responded Franklin.

"Did you know people that went there?" Kilcoyne asked.

"No, I don't," said Franklin.

Coulter showed Franklin a photo of Mary Lowe.

"I don't know her," said Franklin, looking at the photo. "She looks like a girl who lived in Rialto. One of my wife's friends, but her name is . . . I couldn't tell you."

"That is another one," said Coulter as he placed a photo of Bernita Sparks in front of Franklin. Franklin denied knowing her. Nonetheless, he made a crass comment.

"Wow, she looks heavyset," said Franklin. "I just say she look fat. I don't know her."

Again, the detectives changed course.

"Did you ever own any weapons?" asked Coulter.

Franklin told detectives he owned a .22 long rifle, a .38 revolver, a 9mm, and a .22 pistol. "The 9mm—I sold it but I got it out of Texas," Franklin told the detectives. The .38 revolver had been his father's, he said. "It was stolen years ago. The house was broken into some years ago. They stole the car in 1988, but they broke in the house in '91. I lost two guns."

The other gun he lost was a .22 pistol, he said.

"So is that all the handguns you owned?" Coulter asked. "You don't own any more handguns?"

"No more," said Franklin.

"What about the .25 caliber there in your closet?" asked Coulter.

".25 caliber?" asked Franklin. "Is that a rifle?"

"No," responded Coulter.

"A .25 caliber," Franklin responded. "A pistol? No, that is not mine."

"It is not?" asked Coulter.

"That is my brother-in-law's. I have two things of his. He got evicted. We just picked up his stuff last week."

"What is the other thing you got?" asked Coulter.

"A shotgun," said Franklin. "In the same closet."

Coulter then placed a photo of Barbara Ware in front of Franklin.

"Never saw her before," Franklin said, shaking his head. "Know nothing about her."

"Again, I am really feeling insulted here. We are grown men here. I am not playing games with you. I am laying my cards right here on the table just like this," said Coulter as he spread the pictures out in front of Franklin. "Laying my cards right here. Maybe one I would say okay. Two I wouldn't be going to Vegas if I were you because your luck isn't that good."

Franklin chuckled.

"Look at all of these," snapped Coulter. "Your luck is running out fast, so unless you can come up with some kind of explanation. I am not hiding anything from you. I am telling you straight up."

"I understand that," Franklin responded.

With that, Coulter showed Franklin a photo of Henrietta Wright. "No recollection at all?"

"No recollection," said Franklin. "I don't know her. Butt ugly. I don't know her."

"What?" asked Coulter.

"Butt ugly," Franklin giggled. "I don't know her. Sorry. I don't know her."

The detectives didn't have a lot of information to challenge Franklin with at this time. They could only confront him with what they knew, or the interrogation could backfire. Franklin was playing coy. He wasn't volunteering any information. It appeared that he was waiting to hear what the detectives knew.

Coulter showed him the last photo—Debra Jackson.

"All these people that you say you don't know," Coulter said, referring to the pictures of the dead women, "through scientific evidence are all pointing the finger at Lonnie David Franklin Jr. Sit there and look at their faces all staring at you and pointing that finger at you. Don't insult my intelligence."

"I am not trying to," shrugged Franklin. "I'm not trying to insult anybody."

"I am gray-haired," said Coulter. "I am going bald. I am getting close to the end here. I have done this a lot. Just like you. You have been around. I respect your experience. You are probably the best mechanic there is out there. You are good at what you do. And we have been doing this for a long time, too. You wouldn't be here if we weren't absolutely convinced that you did this to these young ladies. Give me an explanation?"

"I don't have no explanation to give you for something I didn't do," Franklin replied.

"So you are just saying you just got a run of bad luck?" asked Coulter.

"I'm not saying I had a run of bad nothing," insisted Franklin. "I don't know these people."

"There are my cards," said Coulter as he looked down at the photos. "There is my deck right there. I think my hand is a lot better than yours right now, Lonnie. Your bluff ain't cutting it. You a poker player?"

"No," said Franklin. "I don't play cards."

Kilcoyne decided to change strategies, again. Maybe Franklin would open up at least a bit if he appealed to him as a father.

"Mr. Franklin, you have a major problem today," he said. "You would creep out. You pick up these young ladies that are working Western or Figueroa in the middle of the night. You have sex with them. You kill them and then you dump their bodies in alleys throughout the city of Los Angeles, most of them not too far from your house."

Pointing to the photos of the women, Kilcoyne went on. "You

see the number of faces here? That's how many families that are affected by this. Families that have been suffering with this for twenty-five years . . . What do you think it would feel like to have your little girl murdered, dumped in the alley, and not know how that came to be for twenty-five years; but somebody left their DNA signature like their thumbprint on my little girl?"

"And that is your little girl out there and some guy that has got a problem and he keeps picking them up, having his way with them, killing them, dumping them in alleys like they are trash, but he is leaving his mark, like a dog pissing on a fire hydrant. That is you. You are leaving your mark every single time you do this. Well, now the science has caught up with you. Mr. Franklin; your signature is on every one of these young ladies. There is no denying that. There is no getting out of it. You need to man up and start talking to us and tell us about what in God's name caused this to happen. Caused Mr. Lonnie Franklin, when he is not working on a car, when he is not with his wife and children, when he is not driving the trash truck or fixing a police car in a garage somewhere, why he is out creeping at night. He can't control himself. How did this happen? These families just like you would want to know."

"I don't creep at night," said Franklin, who for the first time during the interview seemed agitated. "I have a place to go. I have a girlfriend."

"We also know that you cruise Western Avenue looking for whores every night," said Kilcoyne. "You were out there last night. The cops shined their light at you, and you skedaddled on home. You were out there a couple of nights ago. Saturday night."

"I saw the cops when he shined the light on me on Forty-eighth and Western cause I pulled over," Franklin said quickly, referring to the night that police made him move along. "If he didn't notice, I was using my cell phone."

"What was the Saturday out there on Forty-first and Western?" asked Coulter, referring to the same evening.

"I was with a friend that night," responded Franklin. "His girlfriend . . . that was . . ."

"Let me stop you right here," said Kilcoyne testily, "because I don't want to hear your bullshit. I'm not going to waste my time in here listening to bullshit about talking on the phone. How are you going to explain away your one-and-only-on-earth DNA attached to all of these young ladies over a twenty-five-year period?"

"I can't explain it," said Franklin

"You haven't seen the news over the last several years?" said Kilcoyne. "Do you know what the news calls you? You tell me what the news calls you. I know damn well you know."

"I know they talk about some guy on the news," said Franklin.

"What do they call him?" asked Kilcoyne.

"What is it? The Reaper?" asked Franklin.

"The what?" said Kilcoyne.

"The Grim Reaper?" asked Franklin.

"The Grim Sleeper," said Kilcoyne.

"I know it was something like that," said Franklin. "I saw it on TV. I am into TV."

"So here we are sitting here, Paul and Dennis, are sitting here having a chat with the Grim Sleeper, and that is Mr. Lonnie David Franklin Jr.," said Kilcoyne.

"It is not me," said Franklin. "I'm sorry. It is not."

"Okay. Then you tell me how all of your DNA got on every one of these gals," said Kilcoyne.

"I don't have a clue," said Franklin, laughing. "I haven't been with these girls. I don't know how my DNA got there."

"You are laughing," said Coulter. "This is not funny."

"When you tell me something like that," said Franklin. "You know I wasn't with them."

"Okay. Then how did your DNA juice get on these bodies?" asked Kilcoyne.

"I don't know," said Franklin.

"Your little DNA," said Coulter. "All your little markers go back to all of these women, and they are staring at you right now."

"They deserve an answer," said Kilcoyne, about the victims'

families. "Why did this happen to their little girls? I have got to agree with them. I have met with the families many times over several years, and some of these people have lived with an unknown for twenty-five years, and I think they deserve an answer from you. You are not going to wiggle out of this. There is no way in hell you are going to wiggle out of this. Your DNA signature is on every one of these daughters here, and you are going to sit here and say, 'I don't know, last night I pulled over to talk on the cell phone.'"

"I know what I did because me and my girl," said Franklin, trying to steer the conversation back to the night he was caught trolling on Western, "I had just left my girl's house, and we were talking and that is when she called. I already got one ticket for talking on the cell phone, so I pulled over and I was talking to her."

"Lonnie, that is a minor thing," said Coulter. "You have much bigger problems than whether or not you were going to get a ticket for talking on a cell phone in the car. This is your problem, and I guarantee, Lonnie, we are going to do everything in our power that you never see the light of day outside of a prison again. You understand that?"

"I understand that," said Franklin. "But I had nothing to do with it."

Franklin, Kilcoyne mused, was talking about getting pulled over for his cell phone? What made this man tick?

"You have worked on your last car," said Kilcoyne. "You have instantly become a billboard celebrity off Western Avenue, unless you start talking and tell us what happens to Mr. Lonnie Franklin to cause this to happen. What goes on? Are you two different people or something? Is there another little side of Lonnie Franklin that we are unaware of that snaps in the middle of the night and every couple of years he goes out and kills somebody?"

"I haven't killed nobody so I don't know," said Franklin.

"One of these gals survived, and she is going to have a grand time sitting in a courtroom looking down at the man who did some terrible, terrible things years ago," said Kilcoyne. "These girls can't talk, but we got one that can."

"Lonnie, you will be 58 next month," added Coulter. "You are not going to be getting out. Now is the time . . . at least us in the twilight of our careers can go back to the family members with an explanation. Don't you think they are owed that? Wouldn't you be owed that if someone was showing a picture of [your daughter] Crystal?"

"Yes," responded Franklin.

"That is what they deserve," Coulter told him. "You are done. Life as Lonnie Franklin knew it is over."

"You have trolled Western Avenue for the last time," said Kilcoyne.

"You think once you are locked up they are really going to care where Lonnie is?" asked Coulter. "They are going to move on with their lives, as well they should. Your own family's lives are going to be changed tremendously after today."

Kilcoyne decided to give an out and see if Franklin would go for it.

"I know you are a gentleman," said Kilcoyne. "I know you have a conscience and you have a soul. And you, inside, have a problem, and that problem has caused all of these tragedies to happen, but along the way you left your mark," said Kilcoyne. "All of these years that have gone by finally, and probably a blessing to you, science has finally stopped what Lonnie Franklin inside can't control. And that is what brought us to today. I know you are an intelligent man, that you have a conscience. That you have a soul inside and I think you want to tell us. I think you want to tell these family members of these young ladies that can't talk anymore that you are sorry and you don't know how this happened. You have to open up and tell us. We don't have all of the answers yet, but we are working on it. So what is the deal, Lonnie?"

"There is no deal," said Franklin. "I don't know any of these people. I am sorry."

"Maybe you don't remember their faces?" said Kilcoyne. "You picked up trash for a living in alleys, but you are dumping them like they are trash. You are disposing of these young ladies in the alley or in the trash bin, and you are piling stuff on top of them. They are trash to you. How do you get there in your brain? . . . This isn't something that your neighbor did or your son did, or your uncle or brother-in-law. This is something you did. Talk to us, Lonnie."

"I have nothing to say," said Franklin. "I don't know none of these people."

"You think that is just going to make it go away?" asked Kilcoyne.

"I didn't say it would make it go away," said Lonnie. "I just have to get an attorney because I didn't know none of these people. It is as simple as that."

"I don't know what else to say," said Kilcoyne. "I guess he wants an attorney now, so . . ."

Kilcoyne informed Franklin that they would need a blood sample as well as a saliva swab from his mouth.

"Any questions?" asked Kilcoyne.

"No questions," Lonnie told him.

The two detectives got up, left the interview room, and rode the elevator to the tenth floor. Family members, including Diana Ware and Porter and Mary Alexander and their sons Donnell and Darin, were gathered in a conference room. They were told the news. Mary Alexander started to cry, and the others followed.

Kilcoyne was struck by the tears pouring down the faces of Darin and Donnell, two tough men who were familiar with the hardened ways of South Central. It got to him. It got to Coulter too when he gazed into the glistening eyes of the stoic Diana Ware. He took her into his arms and hugged her.

PART THREE

TRIALS AND TRIBULATIONS

2010–2016

CHAPTER 23
LONNIE

THERE WERE NO NODS OF encouragement or waves of support from Lonnie David Franklin Jr.'s family members as he was escorted to his seat at the defendant's table in the windowless courtroom on the ninth floor of the Clara Shortridge Foltz Criminal Justice Center. None of them were there. Sylvia, his wife of more than thirty years, was a no-show. His two children, Crystal, 37, and Christopher, 34, whose DNA profile led to his father's arrest, didn't make an appearance either.

Instead, on this day, February 16, 2016, the four rows of long wooden benches in the spectator's gallery were thick with a mix of media, police, deputy district attorneys, and family members of the women Franklin was accused of murdering.

After so many years of not knowing what happened to their loved ones, and an additional five-plus years after Franklin's arrest for the case to wind through a morass of judicial vagaries, the long-delayed trial was about to get underway.

Monique Alexander's parents, Mary and Porter, sat with their two sons Darin and Donnell in the second row of spectator seats in courtroom 109. Next to them sat Barbara Ware's stepmother Diana Ware, who showed up despite having the flu. Lachrica Jefferson's sister Romy and aunt Yvonne Bell sat together. Princess Berthomieux's sister Samara Herard was also there, as were Henrietta Wright's daughter Rochell Johnson and Henrietta's sister Alice.

On the shorter benches on the opposite side of the gallery aisle were 800 Task Force detectives Dennis Kilcoyne and Paul Coulter. This vantage point put them just a few yards behind the man they'd worked so many years to bring to justice. Both detectives, by this time, were retired, but they held a burning interest in the outcome of the case, having spent the final three years of their careers hunting the Grim Sleeper.

Deputy District Attorney Beth Silverman was about to deliver her opening statement, 2,050 days after Franklin's arrest.

Franklin sat at a table next to his defense attorneys across the aisle from Silverman and her co-counsel, Marguerite Rizzo. They all faced Los Angeles Superior Court Judge Kathleen Kennedy.

Franklin looked different from the day in 2010 when the world first saw his mug shot. Five and a half years behind bars had changed him. Once a burly man who appeared strong enough to toss a body into a dumpster, this now-bespectacled 63-year-old sat slouched next to his defense team. He appeared to have shriveled since his arrest. His long-sleeved light blue shirt and dark blue slacks hung loosely on his now-thin frame.

Beyond his diminished look, Franklin was clean-shaven, his salt-and-pepper hair clipped short. He resembled a college professor or a bookish grandfather, not a stereotypical serial killer.

The man now known as the Grim Sleeper appeared unfazed and emotionless, never once turning his dark eyes toward the spectator gallery behind him. He just stared straight ahead at the courtroom wall, seemingly oblivious to the family members' hostile glares burrowing into the back of his head and the unblinking stares of the mass media recording his every movement.

Almost everyone in the courtroom was convinced of his guilt, but none could fathom why. Was he simply a man who hated women and killed them when they made him angry? Or were his motives more complicated?

One burning question was whether or not he actually took a thirteen-and-a-half-year break between killing sprees. Police suspected he never did and that some unidentified and unlucky victims ended up in landfills.

• • •

Lonnie Franklin, in many ways, was a chameleon.

He was born in Los Angeles on August 30, 1952. His mother, Ruby, was a strong-willed former beauty-school student from Texas, and his father, Lonnie Sr., was a laid-back longshoreman. The timeline is somewhat vague, but not too long before Lonnie Jr. was born, possibly while Ruby was still pregnant with him, his parents got into a head-on collision, and his mother was thrown from the car. Doctors had to reattach her left ankle.

She survived, and Lonnie Jr. grew up in South Central on East 78th Street, then Grand Avenue, and then 85th Street, with her and his father and his sister, Patricia, who was five years younger than him. Otis, Ruby's older son from another relationship, grew up in Texas with relatives but visited the Franklin home during the summer.

Franklin was somewhat of a sickly child. He had perpetual colds and suffered debilitating migraines that left him throwing up and forcing him to lie still in darkened rooms. These subsided in his early 40s. As an adult, he was afflicted with bleeding ulcers.

Franklin was a poor student who had problems with reading and writing. When he was in the fifth grade, Ruby hired a college student to tutor him, but the extra studying didn't help his grades. He struggled throughout high school and changed schools before he transferred to Dominguez High School in Compton, where he enrolled in the work-study program—he went to school in the morning and then to a job in the afternoon.

Franklin wasn't book smart, but he excelled at fixing cars. Being an accomplished gearhead became a lifeline for the social teen to impress girls and show the local gangsters he was somebody they could go to. His dad taught him to drive when he was 7. When he was 14, his dad gave him his first car and allowed Franklin to drive it around the neighborhood.

As a youngster, Franklin was a fast-talker and a flirt, always ready with a compliment.

His first childhood crush was on a neighborhood girl when he was 7 or 8. In the eighth grade, he fell for a girl named Kate and lost his virginity to her when he was 14. They were a couple for about a year. In ninth grade, he dated a classmate named Shannon, until she moved to another state at the end of the school year. Franklin told some people he got Shannon pregnant and she had a son by him. It's unclear if Franklin had anything to do with the child or if the story is even true.

Franklin's next major romance was with Rachael. They dated through grades eleven and twelve.

At this youthful point in his life, he appeared to others to be a mild-mannered, respectful young man with a gift of gab.

But then he started to change.

In 1969, just 16, Franklin was arrested twice for grand theft auto. The following year, he was arrested for burglary.

Then he was expelled from Dominguez High School for getting into a fight with a classmate, just two weeks before graduating. He worked as a box boy until his father suggested he join the military.

On July 26, 1971, one month shy of turning 19, Franklin joined the U.S. Army. He did his basic training at Fort Ord, in Monterey Bay, California. In January of 1972, he was deployed overseas and stationed with the Seventy-first Air Defense Artillery at the Kelley Barracks in Stuttgart, Germany.

That was where Franklin's true sexual deviance began to emerge.

CHAPTER 24
A RAPE IN GERMANY

ON APRIL 17, 1974, AT 12:30 A.M., 17-year-old Ingrid W. was on her way home from her boyfriend's place when life as she knew it took a horrific, everlasting turn. She was waiting to catch a train home at the Zuffenhausen train station to Asperg, a town nine miles north of Stuttgart, when three young African American men in a Fiat pulled up alongside her. Two of them stepped out of the car to ask for directions. Ingrid was more than happy to help, if she could, but, before she could answer, one of the men grabbed her by the shoulders, pushed her into the backseat of the car, and piled in behind her. One of them had a foot-long white-handled butcher knife to her throat.

"I'll kill you," he threatened.

The apprentice who did data entry for a mail-order catalogue barely spoke English, but those words she understood. Terrified, she leaned back against the car seat, the knife still pressing against her skin. She turned toward the window as they drove away from Zuffenhausen train station toward the city of Ludwigsburg, thinking, I'm going to die.

After what felt like half an hour, the driver pulled off the road and drove into a dark empty field. He turned off the engine, and that's when Ingrid's hell truly began.

The driver forced her to take off her clothes, and the three men took turns raping her at knifepoint. They intermittently cut her on the stomach and threatened to kill her. They took pictures of their attack, holding up a flashlight for light.

Ingrid's instinct told her not to fight. She hoped being compliant would spare her life. She even struck up a conversation with the driver between assaults, hoping to win his sympathy.

The rapes continued until just before dawn. When it appeared it was over, Ingrid played along in order to get the men to take her home. On the way there, she gave her phone number to the driver, hoping it would help the police later.

Once home, she slipped inside the apartment she shared with her mother, drew a bath, and scrubbed off as much of the ugliness as she could. She eventually fell into a fitful sleep.

Later that day, Ingrid took a train to the police station in Ludwigsburg to report the attack. She detailed the horrifying hours to the police and told them the driver had called and asked her out on a date.

The detectives were skeptical of her account. For one, why would one of the rapists ask her out? It didn't make sense. They wanted to know if she was a working girl.

Infuriated, Ingrid told them no and wondered whether she'd made a mistake reporting the assault, as now she was sure the police thought she was lying. However, the detectives soon changed their thinking after learning of another similar assault. Three men fitting the same description had attempted to grab an 18-year-old girl one hour before Ingrid said she had been abducted. That girl told police that she had walked her boyfriend to the bus and on her way home she noticed a Fiat passing slowly by. She didn't think anything of it and stopped at a vending machine to buy cigarettes. The next thing she knew, a man grabbed her from behind, put his hand over her mouth, and dragged her to the car. Another man sitting in the backseat attempted to grab her legs and pull her inside. She felt a blow to the back of her neck, then heard someone yelling for the police.

A local resident who witnessed the attempted kidnapping told police she heard the loud skid of a car outside her bedroom window and then a woman's voice shouting, "Help" and "Please don't." She ran to the window and saw a woman being dragged into a car and a tall black man hit the woman twice. The witness's husband called out the window for the police. The couple saw the man drop the girl and jump into the car and watched it drive off without the headlights on.

The police, realizing they had an opportunity to catch three rapists, asked Ingrid for her cooperation. Based on her descriptions, the police notified the U.S. Army of the incident, and, the following evening, Ingrid was standing outside Ludwigsburg station waiting for her purported date. Officers from Ludwigsburg and the U.S. Army were watching nearby. Ingrid was to drop a handkerchief from her pocket once she spotted her assailant. The police would take over from there.

When the man approached, the handkerchief fell to the pavement, and the police swiftly moved in. The fresh-faced young black man looked surprised but didn't resist, even when officers found a large knife tucked inside his boot.

When Ingrid saw the knife, she turned pale. She suspected it was for her.

Police took the man's identification and learned his name was U.S. Army Private Lonnie David Franklin Jr., a 21-year-old stationed at Kelley Barracks in the outer Stuttgart district of Möhringen

Franklin was a kitchen supervisor and resident cook and had obtained the rank of specialist fourth class. In March of 1973, he received the Thirty-second Army Air Defense Command Award for "Best Mess" for the third and fourth quarters of 1972.

He had a few minor disciplinary actions, including one for going AWOL in July of 1972 when he was late returning from leave, for which he was demoted in rank.

Franklin claimed he missed his flight back to Germany because he was looking after his mother, who was suffering from complications from a car accident that happened years earlier, and he was the only person available to care for her.

Franklin was taken into custody on May 5, 1974, and charged with the rape and kidnapping of Ingrid and the attempted kidnapping of the 18-year-old woman who escaped. Franklin's two accomplices, also in the U.S. Army, were charged with the same crimes.

Franklin denied any wrongdoing. He told the German police that on the night of the attack, he had borrowed his friend's car because the clutch went out in his Volkswagen. He met up with the two Army privates in a local pub. Franklin said they were on their way to see a friend when one of his Army buddies recognized a young woman on the street. Franklin pulled over, and the two men got out of the car but quickly realized they didn't know her. The woman became frightened and screamed and they quickly drove off.

About one hour later, his story went on, they were driving by the train station when they came across a young female hitchhiker. They pulled over, and she got in the car.

Franklin said that on their way toward Ludwigsburg, the gas pedal came loose, and he pulled off the road to fix it. His two buddies got out of the car, and he sat in the backseat with the young woman.

Franklin claimed she told him she was high and didn't have a boyfriend and would have sex with him if he drove her home. Franklin said he tried to have sex with her but couldn't get an erection. Instead, his two buddies did.

After they were finished, the hitchhiker jumped into the front seat with him and gave him her phone number.

Franklin said he never attacked the girl. However, he did see one of his buddies with a knife, but he didn't know what he did with it.

One of the other men told police he was high on heroin that night and denied attempting to pull the 18-year-old girl, the one who successfully ran from them, into the car. He said he just asked her where to get gas. He said his buddy grabbed her arm and tried to get her to take a ride with them, but not to rape her.

He said he then fell asleep in the car and woke up when Franklin had pulled over to the side of the road. A young woman, referring to Ingrid, got in beside him. He said he tried to talk to her but he couldn't understand German. Franklin stopped the car, and he and Franklin changed places and Franklin had sex with her. They swapped spots again, and he asked her if he could have sex with her. He said she didn't say anything and didn't resist, so he did. Once he was finished, he said he took pictures of his buddy having sex with her. He denied owning or carrying a knife and insisted the sex was consensual.

The other alleged rapist told authorities another story. He claimed it was his buddy who grabbed the 18-year-old girl's arm and not him. He tried to get her to stop screaming, and when he couldn't, they drove off. He denied that anyone hit her or attempted to force her inside the car.

He said they later came across the hitchhiking Ingrid and that Franklin pulled the car over to talk to her. After Franklin spoke a few words to the teen in German, he said, she pointed at a sign for Ludwigsburg and got into the car. They pulled off the road, and Franklin climbed into the backseat and had sex with her. He said once Franklin was finished, the hitchhiker pointed toward the other soldier, and when he was finished having sex with her, he went next. After they were done, he said, she jumped into the passenger seat, started kissing Franklin, and gave him her address. They drove her home.

He denied having a knife but said his friend did.

The case was going to be handled by the German courts. As a rule, German courts had allowed the U.S. military to discipline its soldiers when they ran into trouble with the law in that country. But in this case, the German prosecutors were concerned that

Franklin and the other two Americans would get off with only a slap on the wrist. Ingrid was a German citizen and so it was decided the men would be prosecuted under German law.

Franklin's mother, Ruby, flew to Germany to support her son. She stayed in Germany for three and a half months and sat with a representative of the U.S. Army in the spectator's gallery during the trial, which was held over eight days in November and December 1974.

The prosecutor told the panel of judges presiding over the case that it was the most brutal assault he had seen over the past ten years. He pointed out that the other two appeared to be more dangerous than Franklin.

During the trial, Ingrid and the 18-year-old assault victim testified about the attack.

Also testifying was a juvenile psychiatrist who had examined Ingrid in order to gauge if she lied about the rape. The psychiatrist testified that for a person to make up such an elaborate tale they had to have a motive and a high IQ. He didn't believe Ingrid had either, so he concluded she was telling the truth.

Franklin's defense attorney argued that Franklin would never have committed an attack on his own and that he was under the influence of the two men that night. Attacking women was just not part of his character, his counsel argued. Franklin thought Ingrid liked him, he said.

He asked that Franklin be given a chance to become a good citizen, to make up for the offense, and to return to his family.

The three defense attorneys for the three men on trial all attacked Ingrid's credibility. One of the lawyers cited Ingrid's earlier arrests for theft and a previous false statement she made in court about a car accident. Ingrid explained that in the latter incident she lied because she had come home late and feared her mother's wrath.

In the end, the panel of judges agreed with Ingrid and the other young victim. They believed that Ingrid had no motive to lie and convicted Franklin on December 20, 1974, for her kidnapping and rape, as well as the attempted kidnapping of the other victim.

He was sentenced to three years and four months in a German prison. His two accomplices were given about one year longer. He was serving his sentence in Stammheim Prison in Stuttgart in early July 1975 when a military board hearing was held to determine whether Franklin should be discharged from the Army.

Franklin's commander told the military panel that Franklin ran the mess hall and was always neat and cheerful and the best cook in the unit. However, the commander said that because of the serious charges against him, he didn't want him back.

A first lieutenant pointed out that Franklin was not career-oriented, had few close friends, and appeared to be a loner. He said Franklin spent most of his free time working with or recording music with his stereo equipment. The officer recommended that Franklin be discharged.

Franklin addressed the board about the attack on Ingrid. He tried to put the blame on his friends. He said that when he pulled over to fix the gas pedal, he heard one of his buddies talking to Ingrid loudly in the backseat, then saw him get mad and pull out a knife.

Franklin played the innocent, claiming that after she had sex with his two buddies, they drove back to the train station to drop her off, but she told Franklin she didn't live around there and asked to be driven home. When they dropped her off, Franklin claimed that Ingrid kissed him, gave him her phone number, and waved as she walked off. He said he called her the next day, and that's when police arrested him.

Franklin blamed part of his conviction on his attorney for his outbursts in court that angered the judge and prosecutor. He told the board he was bitter for being accused of something he didn't do.

He contended that his two buddies lied about him having sex with Ingrid because they were just jealous that Ingrid wanted him. He picked her up because he had been stranded before and knew what it was like, he said.

Franklin also claimed that one of the men pulled out a knife and put it in his face.

However, the board didn't buy Franklin's pleas of innocence and recommended a discharge.

The Army first transferred Franklin to Fort Jackson in South Carolina, where, on May 5, 1976, he received a general discharge, making him ineligible for reenlistment. A dishonorable discharge would have made it difficult for Franklin to find city, state, or county work.

Franklin's accomplices were given dishonorable discharges.

Before the Army sent Franklin stateside, he was subjected to a mental-status evaluation. Franklin claimed in the evaluation that during times in his life, he had trouble sleeping; he suffered from mild anxiety and depression, frequent colds, shoulder pain, and chest pains that lasted a few seconds; and he had a bout of gonorrhea in 1972. He was found to have no significant mental illness, a good memory, and a normal thought process, and he was able to distinguish between right and wrong.

Franklin did seem to learn a valuable lesson though from his experience in Germany. When you commit a horrific crime, don't leave the victim alive to turn you in.

CHAPTER 25
A LIFE OF CRIME

AFTER HIS DISCHARGE FROM THE Army, Franklin returned home and soon met his future wife, Sylvia Lino, at Los Angeles Trade Technical College. She was 21. They married a year later and had two children, a daughter Crystal in December 1978, and son Christopher in August 1981.

The family lived on 111th Place in South Central. In 1986, a year or so after Lonnie Sr. died, they bought a bungalow on West 81st Street.

Franklin took on various jobs upon his return to civilian life. He ran a gas station, worked as a patient scheduler with Veteran's Affairs, was a security guard and later a truck driver before a friend hired him to set up parties and do maintenance work for his entertainment company. He wanted health benefits, so he applied for a job with the city and in 1981 was hired as a garage attendant at LAPD's Central Division. He was promoted to a mechanic helper but gave it up a year later when he accepted a job with the city's Department of Sanitation as a garbage man. It paid better and offered the young father more overtime hours.

His time with the Department of Sanitation was plagued with injury claims that suggested limited use of his right arm. Whether Franklin was ever actually injured would be questioned later. Franklin filed his first disability claim for a rotator-cuff injury on January 6, 1983, six months after he was hired. By October 21, 1985, he had filed four injury claims.

Another claim was filed March 21, 1986, five months before Henrietta Wright's murder, and another on November 10, 1987, nine days after Mary Lowe's body was found in the alleyway near the Love Trap Bar. Franklin was still on city leave in 1988 when Lachrica Jefferson and Monique Alexander were found murdered and Enietra Washington was shot and sexually assaulted.

Franklin's reported injuries and their degrees of severity were first called into question on November 5, 1991, after he submitted an application for disability benefits.

Dr. Homer L. Williams and Dr. Melvin R. Stolz, both city-paid orthopedists, disagreed on Franklin's diagnoses. Dr. Williams found Franklin to be capable of working, but Dr. Stolz did not. A third orthopedist, Dr. Stanford M. Noel, was brought in to examine Franklin. He found that "Mr. Franklin must unfortunately be considered disabled."

Franklin now had the time and money—no work, and disability benefits—to pursue both of his passions: running an illegal car-repair-and-sales business from his own backyard, and trolling for prostitutes on the streets of South Central.

• • •

Franklin maintained a public persona as a doting father, and, later, grandfather, and as a kind and thoughtful neighbor who helped needy and elderly people with their car problems.

"He would fix neighbors' cars for free," Franklin's friend and neighbor Paul Williams Jr. told me. "A lot of the people didn't have money. Sometimes he would buy the parts for them. He would do that for a lot of people. He could get parts for cheap, and people trusted him."

Franklin was said to always have a smile on his face. He also loved to talk about sports and his favorite crime shows.

To Williams, Franklin was a chatterbox who loved to gossip, so much so that he nicknamed him Loni Anderson, after the actress who starred in the '70s and '80s sitcom *WKRP in Cincinnati* and who later married and divorced Burt Reynolds.

"He talked a lot," said Williams. "He talked all the time. A lot of the neighbors stay to themselves, but Lonnie was the complete opposite. It was a standing joke. You could be going eighty miles an hour down the street, and he would flag you down. He would walk out on the street and stop you. He would be talking about your business and other people's business. You would have to find a reason to get away from him. We would laugh and say, 'old Lonnie caught me.' You had to stand there and listen to him do all that talking. You had to find a way to get away from him."

Also, Franklin didn't use drugs or smoke marijuana. He was a self-professed teetotaler, though, in reality, he was an occasional social drinker. He had his first drink, a can of stout malt liquor, when he was about 8 years old. He got drunk, and he never touched malt liquor again, but he admitted to having the occasional beer while in the Army.

On the surface, Franklin and his wife appeared to have a good marriage. But, in reality, Franklin had a bevy of girlfriends and prostitutes Sylvia either didn't know about or chose to ignore.

Franklin had at least four girlfriends during his marriage. The first was a woman named Alexis, who he started dating in 1982. They saw each other about every three or four weeks, and the relationship continued for a couple of years. After Alexis, there was a registered nurse he met at a supermarket. Next was a woman named Beverly, whom he began seeing in the mid-1980s.

Sonia was his last known girlfriend. She was with Franklin at

John's Incredible Pizza Company when undercover detectives surreptitiously collected his DNA.

To supplement his girlfriends, Franklin spent time with prostitutes, and those dalliances gradually became part of the regular dialogue among certain friends in his circle.

Franklin bragged regularly about his encounters with working girls to Ray Davis, a fellow car aficionado Franklin met drag racing in the late 1970s. Franklin would emerge from his garage holding different stacks of photos he'd taken of various women, most of them nude. Davis, who would later testify against him at the trial, noted that in some of the photos, Franklin cut the heads out of the frame.

"They are my girls," Franklin would boast to Davis.

Sex seemed ever-present in Franklin's thoughts. When he wasn't boasting about his pictures or a recent sexual conquest, he was showing his confidants a bag full of bras and panties he bought for his "girls." He hid them from Sylvia in his garage and in a camper on his property.

Franklin named his "girls" according to the size or shape of their breasts and other body parts. He referred to one girl as "Droopy Titties." Another was "Big Leg." Another, "Big Butt." Another, "Skinny Leg." If they didn't merit a nickname, he referred to them as "my friend" or "my girl."

Franklin confided to Davis that he would sneak out at night when Sylvia was asleep and search for prostitutes. On the nights that she was awake, police said, he allegedly told her he was going out for donuts.

Franklin, on occasion, would pull up in his car at Davis's gate with one of his trophies in the car with him. "Where did you get this girl from?" Davis asked during one late-night visit. The girl was sitting in the passenger seat quietly. "Oh, I got her last night," Franklin told him.

• • •

Those who knew this side of Franklin not only knew him as an unfaithful husband and a player, but they also knew him as a man who could convince women to have sex with him and pose for his homemade porn collection. He was also known for showing off a .25-caliber pistol he carried in his front pocket.

While they were aware he could get a good price on a TV or air conditioner, none of them were privy to the real evil that lurked within—that drove him to kill unsuspecting women and toss them away like trash.

Franklin also kept another secret from those who thought they knew him well—his regular encounters with the police. He'd been arrested numerous times, for burglary, grand theft, carrying a loaded firearm, possession of burglary tools, and assault with a deadly weapon (a firearm). Despite all that heat, for decades the police were oblivious to his more egregious illegal activities—raping and murdering women.

The police did keep a close eye on his stolen-auto-parts business, though. By 1993, Franklin was considered a major receiver of stolen property in South Central.

The first opportunity to shut him down came on February 25, 1993, with the police-radio call of "car strippers there now"—jargon for stripping a car of its parts. LAPD Patrol Officer Eris Owen was called to investigate. He drove to Franklin's home and surreptitiously watched as Franklin and his then-11-year-old son, Christopher, worked on a red Toyota MR2 in the backyard garage.

Father and son were unaware they were under surveillance until police helicopters whirled overhead. Franklin came out of the garage and tried to hide under a van while Christopher closed himself behind the garage door.

Owen moved in swiftly and asked Franklin who owned the Toyota. Franklin told him, "I just bought it."

Owen ran the Toyota's license plate. It came back stolen. He searched Franklin's property and found several more cars, car parts, and engines stacked on top of each other. He also came across a partially stripped Jeep Wrangler and several engines for different sports cars: a 1988 Chevy Camaro, a 1968 Ford Mustang, a Datsun 280Z, and a 1989 Pontiac Firebird. It would turn out that the VIN number on each engine matched cars that had been reported stolen.

Franklin, now 40 years old, was charged with six counts of grand theft auto. At a preliminary hearing on May 24, 1993, Los Angeles Superior Court Judge Kathleen Kennedy (who, twenty-two years later, would be the judge in his murder trial) ordered Franklin to stand trial for his crimes.

Franklin decided that a trial wasn't in his best interests, so he pleaded guilty to all six counts of grand theft.

A probation hearing was held two months later in front of a different judge, Los Angeles Superior Court Judge Robert Perry. Through his attorney, Winston Parkman, Franklin claimed he had no idea the engines were stolen and that he had purchased them through *Recycler* magazine. He said he later began to suspect they were stolen, so he decided to stop dealing with the clients who used the magazine.

Parkman asked the judge for no jail time and to instead consider formal probation and community service.

"I feel certain that he, after this experience, he will have no further brushes with the law," Parkman said.

Judge Perry, however, had his reservations about Franklin's innocence. Perry was concerned about Franklin's probation report, in which an investigating officer labeled Franklin a "major participant involved in stolen property," who was responsible for the theft of approximately thirty cars over a three-month period.

"Well, yes, he bought the stuff out of ads in the *Recycler*, your honor," said Parkman at the hearing. "He never dealt with anyone who stole the car, that he knew could say for certain stole the car.

"These parts were all advertised in the *Recycler*," Parkman continued. "And I guess he is not sophisticated enough or wasn't at that time—he is now, I am sure—to realize people do steal things and advertise them for sale and get away with it."

Judge Perry asked L.A. County Deputy District Attorney Kent Cahill what his thoughts were about probation instead of jail time.

"A view about 180 degrees different," said Cahill, who then

laid out a laundry list of Franklin's criminal history, starting in 1969 with two auto-theft arrests as a juvenile. "Then we have a burglary as a juvenile. Then we have possession of a gun. Then we have receiving stolen property in 1984. Possession of burglary tools in '89. [A] 245 [assault with a deadly weapon] in '91. No one is a victim of circumstances that many times. And for counsel to come in here and represent that what we have is basically a naïve innocent who got caught up in circumstances just strains credulity to the breaking point, given this man's history. That is just ludicrous."

Cahill wasn't finished. "We have someone with six felony counts to which he now stands convicted," he went on. "We have someone with a criminal history going back to 1969 for theft offenses, burglary, burglary tools, receiving stolen property. There is nothing naïve about this man. On the contrary, I think he is trading in on the hope that the court is naïve."

Cahill then urged time behind bars, saying that anything less than a year in the county jail "would be grossly inconsistent with the history and facts in this case."

After hearing both sides, Perry sentenced Franklin to 365 days in county jail. Overcrowded jail conditions meant Franklin would likely serve just over four months. He was also put on felony probation for three years and was ordered to begin serving his jail time. As part of his probation, Franklin was ordered not to "own, use, or possess any dangerous or deadly weapons."

"Do you understand and accept the terms and conditions of probation?" Perry asked.

"Yes, I do," responded Franklin.

• • •

Franklin's jail experience did nothing to diminish his nefarious behavior.

Over the next nine years, Franklin avoided major jail time despite being arrested for grand theft auto, robbery, and assault with a deadly weapon other than a firearm with GBI (Great Bodily Injury).

In the latter case, Franklin got angry with a woman he was dating. When he drove off with her still in the car, she turned off the ignition and tried to jump out. Franklin allegedly pulled her back inside, hit her, and drove a short distance with her legs dragging. He then stopped the car and attempted to pull her back inside again, but she broke free and ran. A witness intervened and jumped on the car and punched Franklin.

He also never stopped operating his lucrative auto-theft business. And, all the while, his killing spree went on, too. Despite police monitoring his business dealings, no connection was made to the murders of so many South Central women.

In early 2003, Franklin's long stretch of dodging jail came to an end. There was one too many car thefts for a judge to overlook.

This time it was a 1998 Infiniti QX4 reported stolen from the parking lot of the Glendale Galleria on December 22, 2002. The car was equipped with a LoJack anti-theft device, and California Highway Patrol Officer Donna Martinez and her partner tracked the signal the following morning, to Franklin's place. They watched Franklin climb into the car and drive it from one side of the street to the other, where he parked it and then stopped to talk to a friend.

The officers arrested the now-50-year-old Franklin on the spot. His friend, a parolee, was detained along with Franklin after a Ruger .357 revolver fell out of the leg of his sweatpants when he was talking to police.

By this time, Franklin was used to dealing with the police and playing dumb. He agreed to waive his rights and talk to the officers. He spun a now well-rehearsed tale: He had no idea the car was stolen. He had been asked to install a TV and DVD player, and that was it. The Infiniti, he said, had been dropped off four weeks before by a business acquaintance named Mike, who ran a body shop from his home around Normandie Avenue and 50th Street. Mike had parked the car in front of Franklin's house and left the key in his mailbox but didn't leave any money for the work. Franklin claimed he tried to get a hold of him but was never able to. Because of this, the car had sat outside his house untouched. When the police stopped him, he said he was merely moving the car from one side of the road to the other to avoid a ticket on street-cleaning day.

Franklin's parolee friend first told the police Franklin had owned the Infiniti for about one year and that he had seen it parked in front of Franklin's house in the past. Later, under further questioning, he said he had never seen the car until that morning.

Franklin pleaded not guilty on January 14, 2003, to receiving stolen property and car theft. Once again, it was up to the court to decide what to do with him. This time, the probation department recommended that Franklin spend time in state prison.

"In regards to the present offense, it appears that the defendant was motivated by his need and desire for quick cash without the benefit of labor," a chief probation officer wrote in a report to the judge.

"If at this age the defendant is still engaging in criminal activities, and the defendant has had opportunities for probation in the past, the community can best be served by imposing the maximum time possible in state prison," the probation officer wrote. "It is recommended that probation be denied and the defendant be sentenced to state prison with pre-imprisonment credit."

On April 2, Franklin was ordered to spend 270 days in jail and avoided the more-serious prison time. Once he entered jail, Franklin again benefited from Los Angeles's overburdened justice system. Sheriff's officials were releasing inmates early to ease overcrowding in the county's jails. Franklin was one of them.

Franklin wouldn't see another jail cell for seven more years. And when he did, there was much more than grand theft auto on the docket.

CHAPTER 26
LOCAL CELEBRITY

THE CAPTURE OF THE GRIM SLEEPER made Franklin the talk of Los Angeles. There were endless news reports about him and his decades-long killing spree. All of which shook the South Central community to its core.

The neighborhood was angry that one of their own was killing its women, and Franklin's home became a target of that wrath.

Sylvia had since moved out, but Franklin's neighbor and friend Paul Williams Jr. witnessed the fury firsthand. Sitting outside his home one evening, a black Nissan pulled up in Franklin's driveway. He heard someone say, "Is this the house right here?" referring to Franklin's mint-green home. Fearing the worst, Williams went inside. A minute later, he heard gunfire and then a car peeling away. Williams told the police, but they didn't find any bullet holes. "They must have fired up in the air," he said.

Another morning he woke up to find "Raper" and "Killer" written in black spray paint on the front of Franklin's house.

Williams took it upon himself to look after the property following Franklin's arrest. He and a few neighbors painted over the graffiti and repainted the house gray. Mint green was too much of a magnet.

A slew of reporters descended on 81st Street hoping to get a glimpse into the mind of one of California's most notorious serial killers. There were plenty of tales about Franklin. "His personality was kind of flirtatious," neighbor Rosie Hunter told the *Los Angeles Times*. "For 57, he looked really good."

Another woman, Yvette Williams, no relation to Paul Williams Jr., told the *Los Angeles Times* that Franklin was fixing her car one day when he showed her a brown box full of women's underwear.

"That was just Lonnie," she said.

Franklin was trying to sell them, Paul Williams Jr. said about the underwear. "Maybe it was a way to pick up women, but he was definitely trying to sell them," he said. "He was always trying to sell something. People always came to him to buy something."

One neighbor told the *Los Angeles Times* that Franklin spoke regularly about prostitutes and his dislike for them, referring to them as "crack heads."

"He was a nice guy, but he was a freaky old man," said long-time-neighbor Francis Williams, also no relation to Paul Williams Jr. "He just talked nasty. He said he'd get women to do strange things in strange places with him."

One neighbor also talked about Franklin's side business selling electronics, such as televisions and computers. "I got two flat-screen TVs and put one in my son's room and the other in my daughter's room," neighbor Tomia Bowden told the *Los Angeles Times*. "Stolen? Oh, hell yeah. But that don't make him no killer."

Not everyone in the neighborhood was up to sharing stories with reporters or pleased with the accusations leveled against Franklin. Paul Williams Jr. was convinced that police had set up his friend. "I had a problem with the whole case," he told me. "I basically thought Lonnie didn't do it and that it was a major setup. At first when he got arrested, I didn't believe they had his DNA." Williams mostly didn't believe it because he didn't trust the police.

"I have seen them with my own eyes putting drugs on school-age kids. I don't have any reason to trust the police. I thought, There is something wrong with this case."

• • •

Meanwhile, after decades on the hunt for helpless women, Franklin was learning what it is like to be prey, behind bars.

His new residence was the K-10, the so-called high-powered inmate unit at Men's Central Jail in downtown L.A., where notorious or especially violent inmates are kept. His rule as king of his own sick realm meant less than zero behind bars.

Five days after his arrest, Franklin was sucker punched twice in the head by another inmate who decided to give him a beatdown, probably to try to score points with cellmates. The two were in the meeting room used by inmates to talk with their attorneys. Antonio Rodriguez, who had been convicted of sexually assaulting and killing a 5-year-old girl, took his chance when he had just finished a sit-down with his lawyer and was being uncuffed from his seat. Franklin was floored before he knew what hit him. A deputy was able to restrain 29-year-old Rodriguez before he did any serious damage.

CHAPTER 27
JUSTICE DELAYED

BY 2015, FIVE YEARS AFTER FRANKLIN'S arrest had brought such jubilation to the LAPD and Southside L.A., the case of the People vs. Lonnie Franklin Jr. had stalled badly. Franklin had been charged with the murders of ten women and the attempted murder of another, but the victims' families were no closer to finding justice than they had been the day before his arrest. Delays over evidence testing and the constant bickering between the defense team and prosecutors cast a shadow of frustration over courtroom 109.

By this time, the 800 Task Force detectives Dennis Kilcoyne, Paul Coulter, and Cliff Shepard had all given up trying to outlast the bureaucratic delays and retired from the force. Kilcoyne was the last to go, leaving in April 2013.

When Kilcoyne left, responsibility for the case was handed over to Detective Daryn Dupree, a seasoned cop with roots in gang homicide. Handpicked by Kilcoyne, Dupree had joined the 800 Task Force in 2010 just three days before Franklin's arrest. Previously he worked a special DEA task force, dubbed Redrum (*murder* spelled backward), which investigated the possibility that LAPD officers were involved in the slayings of rappers Biggie Smalls and Tupac Shakur.

Dupree was the perfect choice to head the 800. The gregarious black detective grew up in South Central and lived through the crack and PCP epidemic in a house five blocks away from Franklin's parents' home on 85th Street. Dupree was 6 when he started to carry a stick to defend himself against stray dogs and street thugs. Living in the ghetto was like living in a low-key war zone, he later told me. He was 10 years old when he saw his first dead body while walking through an alley on the way to elementary school on 95th Street. As a teen, he listened to his mother talk about the Southside Slayer killings and played football in Jesse Owens Park, across the street from the alley where the bodies of Bernita Sparks and Janecia Peters were discovered in dumpsters twenty years apart.

Dupree became a high-school football star and then went on to San Diego State University, graduating with a degree in economics. In 1991, at the age of 24, he joined the LAPD. He kept his new career path from many of his relatives and friends. Being black and becoming a cop wasn't something to brag about, he told me. It was like being a traitor or going to the other side.

After a patrol stint at the Southwest Division Station, Dupree landed at the Van Nuys Division, where he partnered with Jaime Fitzsimons. Their partnership would later be the subject of the 2012 cop movie *End of Watch*, starring Jake Gyllenhaal and Michael Peña. He joined the Robbery-Homicide Division in 2006. Over his career, he had been to more than five hundred homicide scenes.

While Dupree and Franklin may have lived in the same neighborhood, the detective's childhood was the antithesis of Franklin's in every way. Dupree grew up without a father and had a soft spot for victims of violence after someone he was close to was sexually assaulted.

Out of all the 800 Task Force detectives who preceded him, Dupree was most familiar with Franklin's personality. He regularly listened in on Franklin's calls on the jail phone in the hopes he would slip up and admit to the murders. Franklin never did. But the calls gave Dupree an insight into the mind of the Grim Sleeper.

What Dupree saw was a braggart, a know-it-all, and, as Dupree described it, a "topper."

"If you told Franklin you had sex with four girls, he would tell you he had sex with seven girls," Dupree told me. "He was always trying to one-up you."

Dupree had received tips almost every day since Franklin's arrest and had chased down hundreds of leads in search of more of Franklin's victims. He was in court every two weeks for the pretrial hearings, being the last remaining detective on the 800 Task Force.

Dupree's drive to see Franklin convicted was fueled in large part by his respect for former 800 Task Force detectives Coulter, Kilcoyne, and Shepard. More than that, though, he wanted to bring justice to the victims and satisfaction and closure to their families. Life had not been kind to the relatives of these young murdered women. The sheer magnitude of their suffering hung heavy around them. Many of them were bent and frail and walked with a cane.

One of the biggest obstacles Dupree encountered was trying to convince the family members that the police were not their enemy and that this case was a high-priority for the department. Although they never spoke directly to him about their mistrust, Dupree knew that it was inherent. Police don't care about black people was a popular sentiment. Dupree wanted to prove that wrong.

"I wanted them to see that I wasn't just a suit and tie. I was someone who cared," he told me later. "Everyone in this case really cared about the people. They didn't see race."

• • •

The pretrial hearings took place every two weeks, and Barbara Ware's stepmother, Diana, made her thirty-eight-mile round-trip bus ride to every one. The former office worker would then take an elevator up to the ninth floor of the criminal courts building—

where all high-profile cases are heard—and take a seat on the spectators' bench in Judge Kathleen Kennedy's courtroom.

Diana's husband, Billy Ware, died of cancer at age 67 in November of 2002 and didn't live to see his daughter's killer arrested or brought to trial. So Diana attended every court hearing not just for her stepdaughter but for Billy, too. Her husband had never recovered from his daughter's murder. Barbara's funeral was the first time his other children had seen their father cry, an indelibly enduring memory for all of them.

Diana promised herself that she would see the case through to the end, despite her own failing health. At 74, she had a bad hip and used a cane. Walking the block from the bus stop to the criminal courts building winded her.

She wanted to see Franklin brought to justice. "I just hope I live long enough," she told me early on during the pretrial hearings.

It was a sentiment she would repeat regularly. At each hearing, Diana sat in the second-row bench next to Mary and Porter Alexander. They, too, were frustrated by the long and bumpy road to justice.

• • •

Porter Alexander had lived in South Central for most of his life. He was an honorable man who treated people with respect and expected the same in return. He traveled all over the city for his work as a rent collector and enjoyed the diverse culture. A father and a grandfather, he remained steadfastly devoted to his family.

"I don't understand why this is taking so long," Porter told me after one of the pretrial hearings. "We come down here every two weeks for nothing. The hearings last only five minutes, and we leave frustrated. Where is the justice in that?"

I didn't have a good answer. Death-penalty cases in Los Angeles County almost always take longer to prosecute than other cases, typically four to eight years. Judges are particularly concerned about costly capital cases being overturned by an appeals court and so are generally far more lenient in terms of preparation time for defense attorneys so that mistakes don't happen. At the same time, defense attorneys are motivated to drag out the proceedings in the hope that the state will at some point do away with the death penalty. Whether it be the death penalty, a life sentence, or a lesser sentence brokered by a deal, victims' families for the most part just want things to move as fast as possible so they can get some closure and move forward with their lives.

Porter, Mary, and Diana just wanted to live long enough to see Franklin on death row. The mother of Bernita Sparks was already dead, as was Mary Lowe's mother, Betty, and Lachrica Jefferson's mother, Wanda. This attrition, combined with the relentless passage of time and the families' never-ending ache for justice, prompted numerous letters to Judge Kennedy, beseeching her to set a court date. Still, the delays continued.

Franklin's defense team of lawyers who opposed the death penalty—Louisa Pensanti, a former producer of TV's *The Richard Simmons Show* who took the case pro bono, and Seymour Amster, a seasoned criminal defense attorney with twelve death-penalty cases on his resume—were primarily responsible for the delays, the families believed.

Amster maintained that his only motive was to prepare the best defense he could, but none of the family members were buying it.

"A blind man could see what [Amster] is doing, stalling for time," Porter wrote in a letter to the judge in 2013 asking her to speed up the pace. "The attorney has given one excuse after another, and the court has allowed this to happen for three years . . . He still has not had the ballistic tests done. When will the court finally tell Attorney Amster to conduct these tests and ensure he moves this case forward without further delay? All my family and all of the other families want is justice."

• • •

It wasn't only the defense's strategy that was questioned. Some wondered why Pensanti was even representing Franklin. Although she had handled major felony cases, she had never worked as the lead attorney in a death-penalty case.

Pensanti grew up in Los Angeles and initially chose a career in education. She taught elementary school but soon realized it wasn't for her. Before settling on law, specifically becoming a criminal lawyer, she was a building contractor and a real estate agent, and she later dabbled as an actor, an assistant to a movie producer, and a publicist with clients that included Sammy Davis Jr. and Robin Williams.

It was her persistent manner and her belief in the innocence of all her clients that helped build her legal props. She also had a website that highlighted her numerous impressive court victories, including getting a client released to his home on probation after he was charged with molesting multiple victims as well as negotiating a client's eight-year sentence for operating an illegal-alien smuggling ring down to a twelve-month term at a minimum-security federal penitentiary dubbed Club Fed.

One thing not touted on her website: Pensanti had been disciplined by the California State Bar. She was put on a year's probation in May of 2013 for "failure to perform legal services with competence," according to the state bar website. She hadn't promptly given back unearned fees and had filed a motion on behalf of a client she was no longer representing.

Amster, the other defense attorney, joined Franklin's legal team in November of 2011, following Franklin's indictment by an L.A. grand jury. Pensanti knew that she needed to bring in a second attorney with experience in capital cases, so she reached out to Amster, a member of the Indigent Criminal Defense Program.

The two had met a few years before when Pensanti was a paralegal at a law office where Amster worked as an attorney. They later shared a law office in Van Nuys.

"She truly believed in the innocence of her clients and was able to convey that to the jury," Amster told me. "She could never lose."

Amster, a Los Angeles native, became a lawyer in 1982. He knew in the fifth grade after participating in a mock United Nations trial that he would become a lawyer and represent the underdog. "The nice Jewish boy," he told me, had been picked to represent Egypt, Israel's sworn enemy. "It was obvious I could argue a position even though I didn't believe it and do it dramatically."

Amster is short, wiry, and neurotic, and his courtroom behavior was laced with theatrics, which he says came from his mother's side, on which there was a long line of actresses. His mother, Francine, he told me, had to turn down the ingénue role of Veda Pierce in the 1945 Joan Crawford movie *Mildred Pierce* because her mother was concerned about the lack of morality in Hollywood and feared that her daughter would be taken advantage of. The role went to Ann Blyth, who was nominated for an Academy Award for best supporting actress. Also, his mother's great aunt, Anna Chandler, was a vaudeville star and best friends with actress Fanny Brice, whose life was the basis for the Barbra Streisand movie *Funny Girl*.

As for his courtroom credits, Amster successfully persuaded prosecutors to take the death penalty off the table in the case of David A. Garcia, who pled guilty to first-degree murder in the 2003 slaying of 26-year-old rookie cop Matthew Pavelka.

He also handled the appeal and motion for a new trial, which was denied, in 2006 of convicted killer Sante Kimes after her son, Kenneth, testified against her in the 1998 murder of businessman David Kazdin. Mother and son, who were the subject of two made-for-TV movies, including *Like Mother Like Son: The Strange Story of Sante and Kenny Kimes*, which starred Mary Tyler Moore as Sante, had already been convicted in 2000 of killing Irene Silverman, an 82-year-old New York socialite.

Amster took over the Kimes case on appeal and argued to the Second District Court of Appeal that Judge Kathleen Kennedy, who he would later tangle with during the Grim Sleeper case, made an error by not informing the jury that several witnesses were accomplices and co-conspirators and consequently potentially responsible for the killing of Kazdin. His argument did not persuade the judge.

In his spare time, Amster advocated for the developmentally disabled, at-risk youth, and children from lower socioeconomic families through a non-profit he founded. He believed it was imperative to help these kids early on so they wouldn't become criminals later in life.

Amster was a staunch believer in the government spending more on hiring additional police officers and keeping kids away from crime. Money going toward social programs was much better spent than the millions used to fund the death penalty, he believed. Capital punishment, as he saw it, was an exercise in futility, one that didn't make society better or safer.

Criminals, he posited, never thought about the consequences before they committed an offense; they only thought about getting away with it.

Now a major player in this high-profile case, Amster had reservations about taking it on. He had the experience to know you just didn't walk into a case like the Grim Sleeper without ruminating on its many facets and potential consequences. It was his 16-year-old daughter, Haley, who convinced him he was the only man for the job. "I'm her dad; no one could do better," he said, giggling about her understandable bias.

• • •

Lonnie Franklin's anti-death-penalty defense team was squaring off against a pro-death-penalty team of Los Angeles County deputy district attorneys Beth Silverman and Marguerite Rizzo.

Silverman has been a member of the office's trial unit since 2006. The elite unit had handled the high-profile trial and conviction of Dr. Conrad Murray in connection with the death of Michael Jackson, as well as the murder trials of music producer Phil Spector and former *Baretta* actor Robert Blake, although Silverman didn't work those cases.

Silverman was born in Chicago, but her family relocated to California when she was two. Law wasn't Silverman's first choice of profession. She worked for her high-school newspaper and planned to pursue a career as a photojournalist. After obtaining her undergraduate degree in journalism at the University of Wisconsin in 1989, however, she decided to pursue a career in law, specifically as a prosecutor. She got her law degree at the University of San Diego School of Law and joined the district attorney's office in 1994.

Silverman cut her teeth prosecuting hard-core gang cases in the San Fernando Valley before she joined the Major Crimes Division in the criminal courts building in 2006. Silverman developed a reputation as a brilliant courtroom litigator. She had a keen intellect and a strong work ethic, and she never lost a case. She was the go-to person for death-penalty cases, prosecuting five capital trials and securing convictions in all of them.

Besides batting 1.000 in her death-penalty cases, Silverman was more than qualified to tackle the Grim Sleeper case for other reasons. She was familiar with the alleyways of South Central, having walked through them for years as she prepared to prosecute various murder cases. In 2011, she had successfully prosecuted South Central serial killer Michael Hughes for the '80s and early '90s strangulation murders of three women and a 15-year-old high-school student. He was sentenced to death. Hughes was already serving a life sentence in prison after he was convicted in 1998 for the murders of four women in the early '90s.

Three years later, in 2014, another serial-murder case brought Silverman to the same alleyways. This one was the trial of Samuel Little, who in the late 1980s viciously beat and strangled his three female victims before he dumped their bodies in back alleys and dumpsters in South Central. Like Hughes, Little's DNA linked him to the killings. That same year, Silverman also secured a conviction against Chester Turner, whose DNA was found on four women discovered dead around South Central in the '80s and '90s. It was the second time a jury voted for death against Turner, who was already on death row for the murders of ten other women.

These three killers whom Silverman put away hunted the same dark secluded streets Franklin had trolled. They, too, preyed on black women, many of whom had drug addictions. Silverman later told me she had come up with a formula when it came to prosecuting serial-killer cases. In many ways, she said, they were all the same sick predator with the same sick agenda.

Silverman's co-prosecutor on the Grim Sleeper case was also in many ways her opposite. Marguerite Rizzo, of Italian and Irish descent, was from Paramus, New Jersey, a town whose claim to fame is being one of the largest shopping destinations in the U.S. The fourth child of seven siblings, Rizzo received her Bachelor of Science degree at Northeastern University before she attended Boston University and completed graduate studies in microbiology. Rizzo was a clinical microbiologist at a hospital in Boston before she moved to Palo Alto, California, to work at Stanford University with her husband and then later to Los Angeles.

It was in 1994 when Rizzo, a researcher at UCLA, decided she wanted a career change. She enrolled as a night-school student at Southwestern Law School. Five years later, by then divorced, she joined the district attorney's office.

Early in her career, Rizzo began prosecuting domestic-violence and sexual-assault cases at the airport court. In 2006 she was transferred to the Family Violence Division, where she handled domestic-violence murders, serious child abuse, and child-homicide cases. In one case, a father shot his 2-year-old boy in the head. In another horrific case, a man, frustrated with his adopted infant son's crying, punched the boy with such force his head slammed against the wall. The child suffered major head trauma and died.

Rizzo also prosecuted cases that drew upon her medical and science background. She assisted with the prosecution against UCLA and a chemistry professor for the laboratory fire death of a research assistant. She also co-prosecuted the case of a restaurateur who surreptitiously administered the abortion drug misoprostol to his pregnant ex-girlfriend.

Rizzo was also a member of the office's forensic-science working group and head of the DNA training team when, because of her DNA expertise, she was tapped to work on the Grim Sleeper case with Silverman.

Rizzo had only spoken to Silverman a few times before she was handed one of the largest cases in Los Angeles history. She was at her desk in the criminal courts building late in the afternoon of July 3, 2010, when her boss came into the office and told her that the head of the Major Crimes Division, Pat Dixon, wanted to see her. She took the stairs down to the seventeenth floor, and when she walked into his office, she came face-to-face with Dixon, Silverman, and 800 Task Force detectives Dennis Kilcoyne and Paul Coulter.

Dixon had one question.

"What do you know about familial DNA searching?"

After giving a rudimentary explanation of the science, she was told she would become part of the prosecution team with Silverman.

She had no way of knowing then, however, that the case would be fraught with delays caused by evidence testing, pretrial courtroom outbursts, and accusations of incompetence. And that now, five years in, the thud of the opening gavel was still not close at hand.

• • •

After each hearing, Silverman, Rizzo, and 800 Task Force Detective Dupree would speak to the victims' families outside the courtroom in an effort to keep their spirits up and remind them they were all in it together. The Alexander family and Diana Ware just shook their heads.

The regular pep talks notwithstanding, the families remained disappointed and often disgusted by the delays. But not derailed. Despite the endless hurdles, their eagerness for the trial of Lonnie Franklin Jr. to get underway, and for them to be there for it, never waned. They knew that one day, they would be in the seats up front.

• • •

The biggest pothole in the bumpy five-year ride to trial surfaced early in 2014, and it threatened to bring the proceedings, such as they were, to a standstill. The problem was a grisly decapitation involving a former employee of one of Franklin's defense attorneys, Louisa Pensanti.

It began when John Lewin, a deputy district attorney with the Major Crimes Division, got a call on February 10, 2014.

Valerie Cole, the L.A. County deputy district attorney in charge of the Inglewood Branch, was on the line and wanted to know if he was available to speak to L.A. County Sheriff's Department Homicide Detective Louie Aguilera about potentially interviewing a murder suspect named Oscar Bridges.[24]

Bridges, a 54-year-old twice-convicted child molester, had just been arrested and was in custody for the January 23 murder of 21-year-old Texan Robert Brewer, who had been found partially decapitated in a motel on South Vermont Avenue. At the time of his capture, in San Francisco, Bridges was going by the alias Seth Silverman, a spin on the name of Grim Sleeper prosecutor Beth Silverman.

Bridges wanted to speak to a prosecutor about a lawyer he had worked for whom he said was doing "illegal, unethical things."

That lawyer in question was Louisa Pensanti.

Lewin and Aguilera interviewed Bridges for seven hours the following day, during which he confessed to the decapitation killing but blamed his former boss.

Bridges first met Pensanti when she represented him in 2003 after he failed to register as a sex offender. She later hired him to work for her. During the interview, Bridges alleged that Pensanti unethically poached clients away from other attorneys and, he added, put so much pressure on him that it led him to abuse drugs and alcohol, and to eventually kill Brewer. Then he alleged that Pensanti had "unethically and likely illegally solicited" the Grim Sleeper case.

---

24. Oscar Bridges was sentenced in June 2016 to twenty-five years to life in state prison after pleading no contest to fatally stabbing 21-year-old Robert Brewer.

After listening all day to Bridges's accusations, Lewin, who worked in the same unit as Silverman, wished he had not picked up the phone. The accusations were messy enough had they been aimed at anyone, but since they were tossed directly at Pensanti, the potential for a judicial implosion was disastrous.

Acting on advice from his boss as well as an office expert on ethics, Lewin put the charges in writing and then left it to Grim Sleeper judge Kathleen Kennedy to decide what should be done.

Lewin spoke with Kennedy in her chambers on February 20, nine days after his interview with Bridges.

After listening to Lewin, Kennedy told him there "were always suspicions as to how Miss Pensanti ended up with the representation of Lonnie Franklin, but nobody had ever given any evidence of wrongdoing. It was always, 'Well, how in the heck did she get this case?'"

Kennedy told Lewin she had heard other lawyers complaining that Pensanti had taken clients away from them. Kennedy also added that Pensanti did very little in the Franklin case. "I mean, she rarely opens her mouth except to state her name," she said.

"And this guy has got a right to, you know, a competent attorney," Lewin said, referring to Franklin. "Now, obviously the person making the allegations, you know, is a twice-convicted child molester and has just decapitated a guy."

"Right," said Kennedy. "And he may have his own ax to grind for whatever reasons."

With that, Kennedy thanked Lewin and said she would need to consult with other judges on the matter.

After doing so, Kennedy held a hearing on March 14 with Franklin and his attorneys, Pensanti and Amster, and the prosecution team of Beth Silverman and Marguerite Rizzo.

"Mr. Bridges is supposedly an employee of Miss Pensanti [and he] has been arrested for murder and has provided some information, made some allegations about Miss Pensanti and her competence to practice law," Kennedy told the lawyers.

"Now I don't know anything about whether the information that he provided is true, not true; I don't have any information about that. And the only reason why this is a concern at all is, this court has to be assured that Mr. Franklin is being represented by competent counsel."

Kennedy told the group that she was going to give each of them a transcript of the private hearing she had with Lewin as well as the seven-hour interview Lewin conducted with Bridges. And then, addressing Franklin directly, she made her thoughts very clear about these charges against Pensanti.

"Mr. Franklin, you need to consider whether Miss Pensanti is a lawyer that you want to continue to represent you," she said. "I have no opinion on that matter at all. However, there have been some serious allegations made against her. Whether those are true or false or whether there is going to be investigations concerning her, I don't know."

But, she stressed, Franklin had to decide himself, "whether this is someone that you want to continue to represent you."

Pensanti, she added, "would not qualify to be a court-appointed lawyer on your case. She does not have the experience and the qualifications that would allow the court to appoint her."

"Now, you made a private deal with her, and that's fine," she continued. "You are entitled to have anybody represent you. However, you are also entitled to have competent counsel representing you. You are on notice that there are issues. And you are not going to be able to claim at some point later on that you didn't know or, if you had known, that you would not have continued to have Miss Pensanti on your case if at some point you are convicted and there is an appeal down the road. I just want you to be aware of these things, and I want you to think about them seriously."

Franklin returned to his jail cell with a decision to make. At a follow-up hearing ten days later, Amster told Judge Kennedy that he had consulted with Franklin about "everything that the court brought to our attention." And Franklin, he told the judge, "wants Miss Pensanti to remain as his attorney."

"He understands," Amster said. "I made sure he understands everything."

• • •

I interviewed Pensanti at that time for a story I was writing for the *L.A. Weekly* about Bridges and the Grim Sleeper case. Bridges's allegations, she told me, and I quoted in the article, were a "desperate attempt" to make a deal with prosecutors in his own pending murder case. "He is saying he ran the law office and acted as an attorney," she said. "If anyone wants to believe that, then go ahead. It doesn't make sense. The statements he has made are insane . . . The man is a sociopathic liar."

Pensanti later told me that she had hired Bridges in the hopes that he would turn his life around. "I was giving him a chance to work and do something he was good at and something he had knowledge about," she said. "I was trying to help somebody."

Pensanti said that after Bridges began to abuse drugs and alcohol, she told him he could not work for her anymore. Bridges took it hard. "I never expected him to come after me because I wouldn't hire him back," she said. "This man obviously hated me."

CHAPTER 28
MAKING A DATE

MARSY'S LAW, THE CALIFORNIA VICTIMS' Bill of Rights Act of 2008, was named after Marsalee Nicholas, a 23-year-old University of California, Santa Barbara student who was stalked and murdered by an ex-boyfriend in 1983.

The law called for increased rights for victims and their families in the judicial process. Among them: the safety of victims and their families would be a consideration when setting bail for the accused; mandatory notification of all court proceedings; the right to address the court at every stage of trial proceedings; the right to seek restitution; and the right to a speedy trial.

It was on the speedy-trial mandate of Marsy's Law that the victims' families in the Grim Sleeper case focused a large part of their attention. Silverman and Rizzo agreed with their concern. With the calendar now reading 2015, their endurance was pushing all limits. It had been four and half years since Franklin's arrest. No matter the intricacies of this case, they all felt, that was a ludicrous amount of time to wait for justice.

The next hearing came February 6. Pumped by their ever-growing frustration and armed with the Marsy's Law mandate, there was real hope this would be the day a court date would be set.

There were others in the courtroom for this hearing besides the agitated family members. At most of the pretrial hearings, I was the only journalist in the courtroom, but local radio and print reporters were there. Word of the family's frustration had finally breached Kennedy's courtroom. Silverman, who generally didn't want the family members to talk to the press, had relaxed her anti-media stance.

Only once before during a Franklin pretrial hearing had so many journalists attended the proceedings. That was the day almost a year before when Franklin testified for the first and last time for his own defense, January 7, 2014. The main attraction that day was the issue of Franklin's DNA, more specifically the discarded piece of pizza on which the DNA was found. The legal question was whether or not the undercover LAPD detective who confiscated it at John's Incredible Pizza Company violated Franklin's rights. If the judge ruled that the seizure was unlawfully obtained, it could possibly lead to serious problems for the prosecution. But the prosecutors were holding firm to what is known as the law of abandoned property, which gives police the right to obtain evidence a suspect has disposed of in a public place.

Franklin's counselors, Amster and Pensanti, pushed back, citing a previous court challenge, one involving a cancer patient. In that case, the patient sued researchers who used the composition of his rare blood cells, which had helped him fight his illness, to produce a commercial anti-infection product. The cancer patient lost that challenge, but team Franklin felt the logic was again worth trying to use with their case.

Amster argued that Franklin's DNA was his property and that he never gave permission to the police to take his human detritus. Franklin had a reasonable expectation that his leftover food, chewed or unchewed, would be tossed, uninspected, into a garbage pail and then into a dumpster, along with everyone else's.

Amster told the judge, "So it is our issue that Mr. Franklin allowed his bodily fluid to be taken under control of who he thought was a restaurant employee, and he never agreed for it to be seized, individualized, or turned over to a third party. He believed it was going to be mixed so the individualization of it would be no longer identified and the general public would not have access to it until it was put into a container where you could not identify it individually for himself."

Under oath, Franklin told the judge that he thought his food remnants would end up in the trash.

"Did you have any feeling that the restaurant employees were going to turn over your food, your unused food, to a third party?" Amster asked Franklin.

"No, I didn't," responded Franklin.

"Did you feel or not feel that they were going to keep it individualized?" asked Amster.

"No, I didn't," Franklin said.

"What did you feel?" asked Amster.

"I feel it was going to be mixed with the rest of the trash," answered Franklin.

"And then what did you feel would happen to it once it was mixed with the rest of the trash?" Amster asked.

"It would be disposed of," said Franklin.

"And did you ever consent to your bodily fluids being tested by law enforcement or a third party?" asked Amster.

"No, I didn't," said Franklin.

"Was it ever your intent to abandon your property for the purpose of it being tested by a third party?" asked Amster.

"No, I didn't," Franklin answered.

Amster knew that it was a risk to put Franklin on the stand because he would be vulnerable to cross-examination, but he also was aware he couldn't make his argument without him.

"Every individual has the right to dictate what will happen to portions of his body, including bodily fluid," Amster summed up.

It was then Silverman's turn to cross-examine Franklin. She immediately questioned his credibility to testify as a witness, given his long list of crimes. After Franklin testified about some of his numerous felonies, including battery, grand theft auto, and receiving stolen property, Silverman, who knew this was most likely the only opportunity she would have to interrogate Franklin, went for the jugular.

"Do you know a person by the name of Debra Jackson?" she asked.

Amster quickly raised an objection. "Not relevant to these proceedings," he told Kennedy.

Kennedy agreed. Silverman changed course, questioning Franklin's earlier testimony to Amster that he had attended a birthday party at John's Incredible Pizza Company with a church group on the day the undercover unit followed him. "Isn't it actually true that you went with your girlfriend, Sonia,[25] and her daughter to a birthday party?"

"I was invited by the pastor of the church," answered Franklin.

"And isn't it true that you went to this birthday party with your girlfriend, Sonia?" she asked again.

"She wasn't my girlfriend," insisted Franklin.

"She is not your girlfriend?" asked Silverman. "What is your relationship—or what was your relationship in July of 2010 to Sonia?"

"She is an employee," responded Franklin.

"She is an employee?" asked Silverman. "An employee of who?"

"Employee of mine," Franklin answered, possibly referring to the small cleaning business he started in 2009, which police believed was nothing more than an excuse to pull the wool over his wife's eyes.

It seemed to me that Franklin didn't like that bit of dirty laundry being unfurled in the courtroom. He hardly seemed bothered about the murder charges leveled against him, but when it came to calling him out as a philandering spouse, that was another story.

At the end of the hearing, Judge Kennedy called Amster's argument about Franklin's DNA "specious and ridiculous," stating

25. Sonia's last name has been omitted from the court testimony to protect her privacy.

that no reasonable person would wonder about how his or her trash would end up unless the police had him or her under surveillance.

"And if he were really concerned about such things, as I said, either he wouldn't eat or he would take his trash with him," Kennedy said. "The fact of the matter is that the defendant ate his food like anybody would eat their food. And when his items were taken away, that was the end of his association with those items, and the property thereafter is abandoned property.

"Whether it has evidentiary value or doesn't have any evidentiary value is kind of irrelevant to the issue of whether he had a reasonable expectation of privacy in those items. And once those items were discarded, he no longer had a reasonable expectation of privacy."

• • •

So now, February 6, 2015, just over a year after Franklin's appearance on the stand energized courtroom 109, the courtroom again was pulsing with a larger-than-usual crowd of journalists. Franklin wasn't the draw this time. The crowd had come to hear the Marsy's Law testimony from the increasingly impatient and irritated members of the victims' families. Franklin, wearing orange prison scrubs, maintained a seemingly bored and uninterested gaze throughout the two-hour proceedings.

Barbara Ware's stepmother, Diana, and Monique Alexander's father, Porter, had become the most vocal in the group of family members. It made sense that Diana would take the stand first.

Speaking forcefully, with just a trace of emotion in her voice, she laid out her feelings about the long delay.

"I am committed to attending every hearing I can and want to see justice done in this case," Diana told the court. "Some people ask why I try to attend every hearing when it is not required. But I want Mr. Franklin and the defense team to see that Barbara was loved by her family and friends, and her life counted . . . We will not give up on the justice system but are praying that a trial date will soon be set."

Barbara Ware's half sister Treva Anderson told the judge that the delays were like "a slap in the face to everyone who loved my sister, Barbara Ware. Barbara was a precious member of our family, and she left not only a daughter, but a large extended family behind. After all this time, we find out that she died at the hands of a coward. Now the state of California is letting this coward delay justice further . . . I would like to ask that the death penalty be removed as an option, if it will make this matter move along. If he dies in prison, it won't be justice, but it will give us some measure of closure. We are all getting older, and we would like to see justice served on this monster."

Porter Alexander, in a mix of anger and raw emotion, told Kennedy that he "lost the most dearest thing in my life" when his daughter Monique died. "My young, my baby, from somebody that thinks he is a cock of the walk, a man that thinks he can dictate, control life, who lives or who dies. He took a person from me. He took a limb from me. Every time I look, I look and I see that I am missing an arm or a leg. It is hard to understand when you lose somebody dear to you, as I lost my baby."

"Mr. Amster walks in, feeling like he has the right to just do how he please, talk to you any way he wants to talk, stands up and has fits," Porter went on, looking directly at Amster. "This is a murder case. This is a man that viciously took lives from somebody, and then we have to sit there and endure what he has to offer. I can't believe that this is going on."

"I am 74 years old. I have never had any problems with no man, no woman, because I give what they deserve; I give them respect and expect no less," he said. "Hopefully we can move this thing on forward, try to make closure of this because as God is my witness, I am going to live to see it. I have already been spoken to by my Father telling me that 'You will make it through.' And I will not have anything less than trying to see this man put where he is supposed to be."

With that, Porter made his way from the stand, and Henrietta Wright's daughter Rochell Johnson took his place. "Because of that man right there, my mom didn't have a chance to raise me," the young hairstylist told Kennedy. "And I didn't even know my mom because of this person right here. So in a sense I am still suffering, as if my mom's body is still lying in that alley, because he is not put where he needs to be put. And by me having to come here every three weeks or every two weeks and every other month to spend my money to come, still look at his face, I am still suffering . . . So I am here to try to help this case get moved forward so we can all get closure, because I don't have no closure. That happened when I was 4 years old; I am 33 years old. I want to be able to move forward and have some type of closure."

Black Coalition Fighting Back Serial Murders leader Margaret Prescod also told Kennedy that the families needed closure. "Janecia's son turned 13 this past Wednesday," she said. "He is going into his teenaged years. I am a mom, and I know how difficult those years are. I spoke to Laverne, Janecia's mother, just early this morning. And she told me about how difficult it is for her, for [Janecia's] son; he has to deal with it. They miss Janecia each and every day, just as Mary and Porter and Debra, Barbara—all of the family members who are here today."

Prescod also echoed some of the family members' thoughts that had the Grim Sleeper victims been white and not African American women with drug addictions, the trial would have moved along much faster.

"Now, we have said before that if these were young women who were young students at West Virginia or UCLA, blonde students, the whole world would know about this, and there would be justice in this case," she said. "But these are impoverished women, black women in South L.A., and it is about time that their lives are of equal value as anyone else's. And we want the court to take that into consideration."

One of the last to take the stand was survivor Enietra Washington, who agreed with Prescod that the delays and court dates for the trial being continuously pushed back were about the color of the victims' skin and not about justice.

"I am thinking the reason he is being dragged along is because we will eventually forget about it," she said angrily. "And it is not going to happen . . . None of us are going to ever forget anything. And had the situation been reversed and I been blonde-haired and blue-eyed, or a high-school student, blonde-haired and blue-eyed, or even a Latina, light-skinned, closer to you, it would have been over with."

However, Enietra saved most of her anger for the person who was responsible for all of them being in court that day: Lonnie Franklin. In her no-nonsense way, she laid into him.

"You knocked us out," she said, glaring at Franklin. "We passed out. You shot me and left me for dead. I don't know what happened to me. I know what I woke up to. But I know it is you."

Enietra reminded Franklin of the conversation they had that dreaded night in 1988. "You could sit there and ignore me all you want because you thought I was dead," she said. "But we had a conversation when I told you, if I died you had to take care of my children because I didn't know you from Adam or Eve. And if God had let me die, I would have come back and haunted you every day of your life. But instead, he let me live, so I still get to haunt you because I am still here."

Enietra told him that she believed he attacked her because she turned him down at first and wouldn't get into his car. "I think you just got mad because I told you no," she theorized. "You was too short for my stature because I don't like short men; I am sorry. I like them tall, dark, and bald. Okay? I am not going to lie. And you bothered me. I didn't bother you. You bothered me. You harassed me for a ride. I told you I was okay; I could walk by myself. I wasn't going that far. But no, then you want to harass me and talk about, 'That's what's wrong with you black women.' Like, you know, white women are only good enough for you. So this is what you do to us? This is what you do to us? The woman who carried you was a black woman. You a black man. How did you disrespect us so like that? And you want us to stand up for you? No. You deserve whatever you get. And then some. But God is going to take care of you in another different kind of way. I know this. I feel this."

Franklin, Enietra said, tried to make her feel guilty about initially turning down his offer for a ride. "And I knew when I said no he made me feel guilty about not allowing him to help a black woman home, you know? That's a mind game."

Enietra then told Kennedy she couldn't forgive Franklin for what he did to her. "I thought I forgave him, but I was wrong," she told the judge. "Lord, forgive me, but I was wrong. I thought I could forgive him, being in the Christian spirit. I can't, because you have done a whole lot more to some young kids who didn't even get a chance in life. You stole so many people's lives. Their lives. And then you want to sit here with a grin on your face and hold your head up like it is a high-standard thing? You go back to Satan where you belong."

At the end of the family statements, Franklin sat expressionless. During the hearing, he occasionally looked quickly toward a family member but never made direct eye contact. There was no remorse. There was no head hung in shame. Watching him, I wondered if he simply didn't have the ability to feel remorse. Maybe he just felt numb.

After all the family members who wanted to had their say, Silverman asked the judge to set a start date for the trial. The bottom line, she stressed, her eyes drifting toward the victims' families, was that "there is nothing for any of these people to look forward to, and there is nothing to work toward. All we hear is the same story over and over.

"And I know that it is maybe in your mind a moot point because we keep setting them, and it doesn't really have any significance," she added, "but maybe it will have some significance, at least for the family, and maybe at some point the court will decide that enough is enough and that you are going to have to force this case to trial before we lose any more of our witnesses, before any more of the mothers die, before we have to retest more evidence."

Kennedy had listened intently to the testimony and looked tired when she finally addressed the wide swath of frustrations and concerns the family members presented.

"I know there has been a lot of delays in this case," she said. "And one of the speakers early on mentioned something about the fact that this is a death-penalty trial, or the people are seeking the death penalty in this case and alluded to the notion that if it wasn't a death penalty case, it would go faster, or would it go faster. And I will tell you that the decision on whether to seek the death penalty in a matter is not the court's decision; that is the prosecution's decision. But I will say—and I have handled many death-penalty matters in this court—that death-penalty matters do take longer than other kinds of cases. And they take longer whether the defendant is, or the victims are, black, white, Hispanic, Asian, whatever. They take longer. And I apologize for that, but that is the truth."

That said, Kennedy then set a trial date for June 30, 2015. Even with the emotional barrage of family stories at the hearing, 800 Task Force Detective Dupree and the prosecution team were skeptical of the date. The defense, they were well aware, still hadn't tested the DNA and ballistics evidence. The families left the courtroom more hopeful, but their elation didn't last long. There were plenty more hurdles to overcome.

• • •

Silverman's, Rizzo's, and Dupree's skepticism about the appointed start date was borne out. The delays over DNA and other evidence testing dragged on as usual. June 30 came and went.

Another potentially delaying complication arose in November of 2015. Once again, it involved Pensanti. This time, the prosecution team pointed out that she was about to be suspended from practicing law because she was unable to produce proof that she passed the Multistate Professional Responsibility Exam, a requirement of the 2013 probation she was hit with by the California State Bar.

If she didn't show proof she had taken and passed the exam, Pensanti would be suspended as of November 16, 2015. Pensanti had made a request to delay the stay on the suspension, and that was pending state bar approval.

In a follow-up hearing on November 16, while the request to delay the suspension was still pending, along with an answer to the question of whether or not she had passed the exam, which she had written the week before, Amster asked the judge to replace her with another attorney. He didn't want to deal with the uncertainty.

"I have had a discussion with Mr. Franklin this morning, and he has stated that he would acquiesce to me and not ask for her to come back," said Amster. "I never predicted Miss Pensanti not to have a license."

"As of right now, as I see it, Miss Pensanti is no longer an attorney of record on this case," Amster told the judge and prosecutors. "I don't feel that in this magnitude of a case we can be held hostage by what's happening in Miss Pensanti's life."

A couple of weeks later, Amster informed the court that Claremont, California, Defense Attorney Dale Atherton would be his second chair. Amster had worked with Atherton on previous cases, liked his work ethic, and knew Atherton liked working with him, too.

With no more delays anticipated, a court date of February 16, 2016, was set for the start of the trial. The defense and prosecutors began picking a jury.

CHAPTER 29

THE TRIAL

DEPUTY DISTRICT ATTORNEY BETH Silverman began her opening statements in the long-delayed Grim Sleeper trial with a story. This story was about a serial killer who stalked the streets of South Central with abandon for more than two decades. She then set the scene of the mystery she was going to solve for the jury.

"The 1980s in South Central Los Angeles was an era that was marked by a lethal epidemic, and that was crack cocaine," Silverman told the twelve jurors and six alternates—some of whom weren't even born back then. "You're going to hear and learn that crack devoured those who succumbed to its seductively cheap price and powerful high, and also that it disproportionately affected low-income communities. It also left a legacy of destruction for families, for neighborhoods, for entire communities. Many people overdosed. Others lost their jobs, their homes, and their families.

"And even though all of this was true and that this drug was so deadly, it was also so addictive that some women were willing to risk everything in order to acquire more," she said, as a giant mug shot of Franklin was displayed from an overhead projector on a side wall above where Franklin was sitting. "Some gave into that stranglehold that this drug had over them and were willing to sell their bodies and their souls in order to gratify their dependency on this powerful drug."

Their addictions, said Silverman, made them easy prey for a serial killer. "And unfortunately what you're going to hear is that this addiction caused these women to be extremely vulnerable to someone who wanted to take advantage of this tragic situation, because he knew that they didn't worry about their safety, that they were only focused on where they could get more, and that they were very easy targets.

"And so this was the perfect opportunity for someone who preyed on women, someone who knew the streets and the dark alleys by heart, someone who lived there and was able to blend in, someone who knew where the drug-addicted women and perhaps prostitutes would congregate and who knew how to lure potential victims into the darkness or the isolation of a vehicle with the promise of crack. So it was the perfect place and time for a serial killer to roam the streets of Los Angeles, really without detection."

Silverman stood at the podium facing the jury and said in her matter-of-fact tone that although the women didn't know each other in life, they shared similarities in death.

"All of them were African American women, or girls; almost all of them were found in filthy alleyways, mostly in South Los Angeles. All of them were dumped like trash. Some of them were left to rot. Some of them were actually dumped into trash dumpsters, and that was Bernita Sparks and Janecia Peters."

It was the uniqueness of the killings that stood out, Silverman told the jury. All the shooting victims were shot in the same manner, except for Janecia Peters, who was shot in the back. No bullets were found at any of the crime scenes, nor was any identification. All the women were unidentified Jane Does when they were transported to the coroner.

The prosecution's case, she emphasized during her opening

statement, was built on DNA and ballistics evidence. "And, most importantly, what you're going to learn is that all of [the victims], every single one of them, was connected to the same serial killer either by DNA evidence or firearms evidence or both. And that serial killer, ladies and gentleman, is Lonnie Franklin."

Silverman told the jury that defense attorney Amster would focus his case on evidence that crime-scene analysts found, most specifically that some of the women had DNA profiles of unknown males on them.

"Given that some of the victims resorted to prostitution to feed their drug addiction, it's not surprising that in certain cases other male profiles were also found on various items in their sexual-assault kits," she said, addressing the issue head on.

Silverman, however, expressed no doubt about Franklin's guilt.

"You're going to learn that several of the murdered victims' cases are linked to one another by the same unique male DNA profile," she hammered into the minds of the jury.

Silverman's opening statement lasted the better part of the first day of the trial. She laid out each of the victim's cases in agonizing detail, describing how they met their horrible end, while photos were projected on the screen above Franklin: Debra Jackson's bloated corpse; Princess Berthomieux's nude body lying facedown in weeds; Henrietta Wright with a shirt stuffed in her bloodied mouth.

After years of delays, the Grim Sleeper trial was underway, and it would go on for almost three months. The prosecution would present more than forty witnesses, including DNA and ballistics experts, the county coroner, the patrol officers who first arrived at the crime scenes, the homicide detectives who originally investigated the murders, survivor Enietra Washington, and the doctor who pried the bullet out of Enietra's chest.

The search-team members who sifted through Franklin's house and garage after his 2010 arrest made great witnesses for the prosecution. The search proved to be the largest in LAPD history and included a command post, nicknamed "The Pit," set up outside Franklin's home. The large blue tent erected across the width of the front lawn allowed Robbery-Homicide detectives room to quickly examine and process the evidence taken from the house. A section of 81st Street, from Harvard Boulevard to Western Avenue, was blocked off to everyone but the immediate residents. No one entered or left without permission from the police.

The jury heard that Franklin's three-car garage was a nightmare for detectives to search. More than eight hundred pieces of evidence, including twenty cameras and fifteen phones capable of taking pictures and hundreds of sexually explicit photos of naked women,[26] were collected from the house and garage during the three-day search by 800 Task Force members, Robbery-Homicide detectives, criminalists, firearm experts, and photographers. Three of the five-member teams were assigned to search Franklin's garage. The other three teams of five were tasked with searching the home.

One of the first hurdles of the search was dealing with the more than twenty steering wheels outfitted with air bags that were discovered in Franklin's backyard. They were potential bombs waiting to explode if not handled correctly. The bomb squad was called in to blow them up. Each one was covered by a bombproof blanket and then detonated by an electrical charge. One of them flew up in the air and broke a neighbor's car window.

Franklin's garage, which was divided by walls into three areas, was set back behind the main house and stacked from floor to ceiling with car parts and speakers, boxes filled with Quaker State motor oil, soda pop, radio and electronic equipment, light bulbs, and tools. Car and bicycle parts hung from the ceiling. Once the investigators peeled away the clutter, the search got really interesting, and the most damning evidence was revealed.

Criminalist Genaro Arredondo told the jury that while he was searching the central garage, he noticed a section of damaged dry-

---

26. Some of these pictures are viewable at the LAPD website.

wall. When he stepped toward it to take a closer look, he noticed debris had fallen into the cavity between the walls. He pulled away the broken drywall and found on the ground a Polaroid photograph of a woman with her breast exposed. He didn't know at the time, but it was a picture of Enietra Washington. She was dressed in the same clothes she was wearing the night she was shot and left for dead. Her blue-and-cream peasant blouse was covered in blood.

Lt. Mike Oppelt testified that inside the door of a mini-fridge in the eastern garage detectives discovered an envelope with a photo of Janecia Peters with a smile on her face and her breast exposed. At the time, the search team had no idea that the woman in the photo was the last known victim of the Grim Sleeper.

Oppelt and his team also found a Kodak VHS cassette tape box with $10,000 inside and a gray lockbox containing $7,000 in cash. There were women's undergarments strewn about: a black bra, a camisole, and two pairs of thong panties were on the hood of a white Nissan pickup truck. A lingerie set was on the truck's dashboard.

There was a pair of pink panties on top of a red toolbox on the floor that was jammed with car parts, car doors vertically stacked against each other, tools, and junk.

Detective Sharlene Johnson testified that she found a Polaroid camera on top of a Toyota Corolla in the west garage during the search. Also discovered were boxes of .25 auto ammunition, copper-jacketed bullets—the same type of bullets used in the Grim Sleeper killings.

Inside the house, there was more damning evidence.

Robbery-Homicide Detective Tracey Benjamin testified that her team searched the dining room and that on the top of a wood china cabinet they found two LAPD field-officer notebooks with Miranda Rights printed on the inside flap. This suggested that Franklin may have disguised himself as a police officer when he attacked women. There were also several photographs of Franklin in his sanitation department uniform taken at various local landfills.

Criminalist Rafael Garcia testified that inside a bedroom dresser drawer strewn with cables and remote controls he found an F.I.E. Titan .25-caliber semiautomatic handgun, a loaded magazine with four live copper-jacketed bullets, and ten loose bullets inside a black case. It was proven to be the gun used to kill Janecia Peters.

Detective Luis "Sweet Lou" Rivera testified that he discovered the receipt for the murder weapon in a file cabinet in another bedroom. Rivera noted that the Western Surplus receipt, in Franklin's sister's name, was dated February 17 of 1982, three years before the Grim Sleeper murders began. The instruction manual was found with the receipt.

The gun-shop receipt was also meaningful because the company was located just down the street from 1707 West 85th Street, the address Franklin provided as his home address when he was working for the Department of Sanitation. The house belonged to his mother, Ruby.

A Jennings .22 long rifle pistol manufactured by Bryco Arms was discovered in the southeast bedroom closet, along with 136 live rounds of ammunition. The gun was on a shelf in a box with "Lonnie Franklin" written on the side. A Ruger .22 revolver as well as a Smith and Wesson .38 revolver and a Ruger .22 rifle were found in the Winnebago that was parked in the yard.

A Raven .25-caliber pistol manufactured by Phoenix Arms loaded with six rounds of live ammunition was discovered inside the pocket of an Army jacket hanging inside a hallway closet. A .380 pistol with a loaded magazine was found in the northwest bedroom on the floor of a closet, concealed under a pile of items. The serial number had been scraped off.

Jurors also heard that during the three-day search of Franklin's property, investigators found a cache of homemade pornographic videos. The prosecutors showed one of them to the jury. In the video, Franklin is engaging in sex with an unknown young black woman who appeared unaware that she was being recorded. The tape starts out with Franklin standing in a room with a camera in his hand. A few seconds later, the young woman emerges from the bathroom in a large purple baggy T-shirt. Franklin takes photographs of her as she takes her top off. He then puts down the camera and pulls his pants down. As the woman strokes his erect penis, Franklin leans in and begins to kiss her breasts. After he ejaculates, the young woman walks back into the bathroom. Franklin walks out of the view of the video camera as well. Seconds later, they both emerge, and it looks like Franklin has cash in his hand. He walks over to the video camera and turns it off.

The prosecution team wanted the jury to understand that this is how they suspected Franklin operated and how his victims likely ended up with saliva on their breasts.

When it came time to present the DNA evidence implicating Franklin, which was at the center of their case, prosecutor Marguerite Rizzo, the former scientist, took over from Silverman. Her witnesses included an expert mix of DNA analysts from the LAPD and the L.A. County Sheriff's Department, as well as forensic experts from outside labs. They testified that there were DNA profiles from other men found on some of the women. But none of those profiles were found on more than one. Franklin's human detritus, however, was found on seven of the victims, an all-but indisputable constant.

For example, Supria Rosner, a supervisor in the LAPD's DNA unit, testified that Franklin's DNA profile so perfectly matched the DNA profile developed from Barbara Ware's oral swab that the likelihood of finding another person other than Franklin who had the same match was one in 11 quintillion.

In the Bernita Sparks case, Rosner said the major male DNA profile found on Bernita's right nipple was Franklin's. In this test, she said, the likelihood of finding another person other than Franklin who had the same match was one in 81 quadrillion, or one million times the population of the planet Earth.

In another example, Angela Meyers, DNA analyst from the California Department of Justice's crime lab, testified about the DNA found on Mary Lowe's right nipple. Again, the major male profile matched Franklin, with the probability of finding another person other than Franklin who had the same match being one in 82 quadrillion African Americans.

Meyers also testified about her analysis of the DNA found on Valerie McCorvey's left nipple. The conclusion of that test was that the odds of finding another person other than Franklin who had the same match was one in 120 trillion in the African American population.

Cristina Gonzalez, a DNA analyst at the Los Angeles County Sheriff's crime lab, testified she tested the DNA found on Lachrica Jefferson's left nipple. Again, the major male profile matched Franklin, with the prospect of finding another individual other than Franklin who had the same match being one in 27.2 quintillion.

Gonzalez also did the DNA testing in the Princess Berthomieux case. The major male profile found on her right nipple matched Franklin; the statistical calculation came to one in 81 quadrillion. She also testified that Franklin was included as a possible contributor to the partial DNA profile developed from the right nipple sample.

The DNA found on the zip tie fastened around the plastic bag in which Janecia Peters was found was analyzed by Kelli Byrd, a forensic scientist at the time with the Orchid Cellmark lab. Byrd used touch DNA technology and found skin cells from both Peters and Franklin on the zip tie. The odds of finding another individual other than Franklin who had the same match, she said, were one in 81.43 quadrillion in the African American population.

The conclusion, the prosecution underscored for the jury, was the scientifically substantiated fact that it was only Franklin's unique profile that was repeated from victim to victim to victim.

Ballistic testing was also crucial to the prosecution's case, and the results were equally damning for the defense.

They brought in LAPD firearms examiners Daniel Rubin and Allison Manfreda and Los Angeles County Sheriff's Department firearms examiner Manuel Munoz to prove their point. The examiners did their own microscopic comparison of the bullets—all .25 calibers—independently. By identifying a unique signature on the bullets, they were able to determine that each of the bullets were fired from the same handgun used to kill the seven victims and wound Enietra Washington in the '80s

Rubin also testified that the .25-caliber pistol found inside the dresser drawer in Franklin's home was the same gun that was used to kill Janecia Peters. In order to come to that conclusion he said he test-fired the gun into a water tank and then compared those bullets with the bullet pulled out of Janecia and determined they had the same unique markings.

Aside from the DNA and the ballistics, the most compelling testimony by far came from Franklin's close friend, Ray Davis, who 800 Task Force Detective Dupree had noticed standing near Franklin's house the day in 2010 that the LAPD began its three-day search. Davis, who was a former security officer with the Los Angeles Unified School District, told the jury that Franklin regularly bragged about his sexual conquests. Davis said Franklin would regularly show him stacks of photos of women, many of them naked.

"Approximately how many pictures do you think the defendant would show you or has shown you over the years?" asked Silverman.

"I would say about seventy," answered Davis.

"Did you tell Detective Dupree that the defendant told you that they were pictures of prostitutes?" asked Silverman.

"Yeah, I told Dupree that some of the girls in the pictures was the girls that Lonnie had said that he had picked up off the street," he responded.

"And did the defendant ever show you any type of lingerie that he would keep and pass out to these women?" Silverman asked.

"Yes," said Davis.

"What kind of lingerie was it?"

"He had some, some bras and panties," he said. "They was in a bag."

"Did he ever show you movies, homemade porn?"

"Not homemade porns," said Davis. "He would show me porns that, he said, that these people in this porn live in the neighborhood."

"Did the defendant tell you that he would pick up girls around 1:30 in the morning who were walking the streets?"

"Most of the girls he say he picked up was walking the street, yes," said Davis.

"Did the defendant tell you what he would do with these girls that he would pick up off the street?" asked Silverman.

"Some he said he would have sex with them," said Davis. "Some of them, he was just—just to show somebody that he had a girl."

"Did he ever tell you that he had sex with the girls in his vans or in his camper?"

"Yes," said Davis.

Davis told the jury that he remembered that Franklin once owned a Ford Pinto.

"It was a dark-colored Pinto and it had the little, tomato stripes we called it, on it . . . Something like *Starsky and Hutch*, the car with the—you know, with the little—the stripes."

"Where would the stripes be, if you recall?" asked Silverman.

"The stripes was on the side, on the side of the vehicle," he said.

"Do you recall telling Detective Dupree that it was an orange Pinto with white stripes and custom wheels?" asked Silverman.

"Yeah," said Davis. "I remember that—the custom wheels and—yeah. That was in 2010."

"Do you recall when the defendant possessed this orange Pinto with the Baretta stripes?" asked Silverman.

"Well, I can tell you the first time I saw that was in the late '80s."

"When was the last time you saw that vehicle?"

"Maybe '89," he said.

It seemed that cars, like his "girls," moved in and out of Franklin's life. When he had no more use for a car, he took it to an auto dismantler for it to be crushed, Davis said.

Under cross-examination by Amster, Davis riveted the jury with a story about a chance meeting he had with Franklin and one of his "girls."

The year was 2006. Davis was driving by a friend's house when he saw Franklin's white van parked in the driveway. Franklin appeared, and he saw him walk to the back of the van. Davis backed up and stopped. He got out of the car, and when he went over to the van to speak to Franklin, he saw a girl in the back of the van sitting on a mattress.

Franklin wasn't pleased.

"Hey, what are you doing?" Franklin asked him.

"What are YOU doing?" Davis responded.

Franklin told him to leave, and he closed the door of the van. Davis didn't think much of it until a few years later when he started seeing reward billboards pop up that showed Grim Sleeper victims. He saw a smaller version of the billboard on a board one day when he was inside the 77th Street Division station. He thought one of the women looked familiar.

"And that's when I said, 'Look like I seen this girl somewhere before,'" Davis told the jury. That woman, Davis later told Dupree, was Janecia Peters. She was the woman he believed he saw in Franklin's van.

Amster asked Davis why he didn't call the police if he saw one of the Grim Sleeper victims with Franklin.

"And you remember that you saw this girl with Mr. Franklin, and you realized that the billboard is about trying to find the person who did harm to her; why didn't you call the police and say, 'I believe Mr. Franklin did harm to this girl?'" he asked.

"I don't know if Mr. Franklin did harm to the girl," Davis responded. "I just said that I had saw the girl with Mr. Franklin. And then when I saw the picture, I wasn't really still sure until I saw that picture blown up and saw a good picture of it and saw it up close; then I could recognize and say that I think this was the girl. But when I'm just looking at the girl on the billboard in that little picture, I couldn't recognize just for sure that that was the girl that I used to see anyway that was walking the street on Ninety-third or Ninety-fourth and Western all the time."

"So you saw this girl more than the time you saw her in the van with Mr. Franklin?" asked Amster.

"Yes," said Davis. "The girl was one of the street girls that walked on Western and Ninety-second that we passed and see her at different times."

"Do you ever remember seeing her after you saw her in the van with Mr. Franklin?" Amster asked.

"No," he responded.

CHAPTER 30
KEEPING VIGIL

IT TOOK SEVERAL WEEKS FOR THE torrent of testimony and details to be put into the record, a passage of time that brought unexpected consequences for some of the family members of the victims. Lachrica Jefferson's aunt Yvonne Bell, who suffered from heart issues, had to be hospitalized at one point. Diana Ware, who attended almost every hearing leading up to the trial, needed hernia surgery and missed much of what she had waited decades to see.

Others persevered, no matter the challenges.

Every morning, Porter and Mary Alexander and their son Donnell took a limousine to court and sat through the day's testimony in memory of Porter's Road Dog, his nickname for Monique. Porter couldn't drive anymore. Several eye surgeries to repair mini-strokes had taken their toll. Porter believed his strokes were due to the stress of the case. Mary, who had finally quit smoking after years of her daughter Anita imploring her to do so, was driven by the stress to start again.

Donnell was there to make sure his parents, by now in their mid 70s, were okay.

The death of the spunky teenaged Monique had catastrophic consequences for the Alexander family, particularly for Mary, who repeatedly suffered health problems ever since. But with each day in court, the fog that had surrounded Mary since Monique's death slowly started to lift. Donnell could see the change in his mother. "She is slowly starting to get her feisty attitude back," he told me one afternoon during a morning break. Mary had berated her middle son after he confronted a friend of Franklin's who turned up at the court one day. To Donnell that was a sign.

Donnell got into the habit of bringing a notebook to court to sketch the key moments playing out. Sketching was something he and Monique did growing up and he took comfort in it. His many drawings included portraits of his father, Judge Kennedy, and Franklin.

Every day at trial brought Porter one step closer to finding justice for Monique. From his perspective in the spectator's gallery, the trial was heading toward a guilty verdict. It wasn't about Franklin's guilt or innocence—that was obvious—but rather about whether or not Franklin would be sentenced to death or life without the possibility of parole. Porter had made it very clear what he considered justice.

"An eye for an eye," he told me.

Donnell said he would catch Franklin's sneaky glances at the breasts of the dead women in the pictures on the overhead projector. It irked Donnell. So did Franklin's lack of remorse and the way he kept his head bowed so he didn't have to look into the spectator gallery at the family members. Franklin was a coward, plain and simple, Donnell decided.

The gruesome crime-scene photos projected on the screen above Franklin were hard for family members to bear. The prosecution had developed a plan to signal the family members in the courtroom whenever a disturbing photo of a dead relative was going to be presented or talked about. If, for example, the conversation would return to an autopsy report of a dead relative, a signal would give the families a chance to clear the courtroom.

Once, Mary Alexander failed to notice the signal from Silverman to leave the courtroom and she saw a photo of her daughter's decomposed body flash across the screen. Mary cried in the hallway that day, and Donnell was there to softly remind her that she had to stay alert.

A different day, Donnell told me during a break about his suspicions that a neighborhood girl named Freda had fallen prey to the former mechanic.

The girl, who was a teen when she allegedly vanished without a trace in the early '70s, was dating a guy named Lonnie, Donnell recounted. Everyone in the neighborhood wondered if the boy named Lonnie grew up to be the adult sitting quietly at the defendant's table. A few days later, I met Donnell at his parents' house down the street from where a heart was carved in the pavement. There were three words inside the heart: "Freda love Lonnie."

Like Donnell, I started wondering if Freda was another victim of the Grim Sleeper.

The following day, I told Detective Dupree outside the courtroom about Freda, and I asked if he might be able to find out if she was ever reported missing. I gave him her first and last name and her address back then, and he agreed to look into it.

Donnell and I were standing in the hallway two days later when Dupree approached us with the news. Freda, he said, was alive and well, living in Apple Valley, California. And she had never heard of Lonnie Franklin.

Lachrica Jefferson's sister, Romy, would attend the trial periodically despite battling the flu and some chronic health problems. After Lachrica's death, Romy had a hard time coping. Her life had become a series of tragedies after her sister's death. She lost her husband to diabetes in the '90s and her mother, Wanda, to murder in 2006. Wanda, then 59, was strangled to death by her husband and found in the trunk of her car three weeks after she went missing. Although attending the trial was like "Crisha killed all over again," Romy wanted justice for her sister.

Samara Herard was also there to seek justice for her foster sister Princess. Samara last spoke to Princess in the fall of 2001, a few months before her March 9, 2002, murder. Princess informed her that her biological father wanted her back.

"Over my dead body," Samara remembered telling her. "I said if he tries to take you let me know what day in court. I almost threw up from the damage he did to her. You don't forget images like that."

Samara's father, David, was the one who had broken the news to her about Princess's death. But to spare her some pain, he told her Princess had died of a drug overdose. Samara didn't find out until years later that Princess was the victim of a serial killer.

"I questioned my faith," she told me. She wondered why God saved Princess from her birth father only to have her die at the hands of a serial killer. "What was the point? You saved her from that hell for this?"

Henrietta Wright's daughter Rochell Johnson was also a regular fixture in the courtroom, but for another reason. Rochell was just a toddler when her mother was murdered. She didn't remember her and knew very little about her mother's death. She was there to learn the details. Rochell grew up thinking that her aunt Ella Mae was her mother. It wasn't until she was nine that she was told the truth. "I remember being told she was raped and killed by three guys, and the next story I was told it was a police officer, and after that I stopped figuring it out," she told me.

Rochell said she ended up telling her school friends that her mother died of pneumonia.

Rochell had heard stories about her mother's crack addiction, but she held no lasting bitterness toward her for it. "I never was mad at my mom for the thing she did regarding me and not raising me," she said. "I didn't take it too hard. I took it that she was giving me a mother she couldn't be. Which was a good thing. If she had lived, I believe she would have changed eventually."

CHAPTER 31
AMSTER FOR THE DEFENSE

IT TOOK A MONTH FOR THE PROSECUTION to wind up its case, leaving it then up to Franklin's defense team to prove he was not guilty beyond a reasonable doubt. Attorney Seymour Amster gave his opening statements on March 21, 2016. He knew his best hope to get Franklin off was to hit back hard against the DNA evidence. Prosecutors had told jurors that Franklin's DNA on the victims was unassailable evidence of his guilt. Amster's goal was to cast doubt on the prosecution's case by underscoring as strongly as he could that the DNA of other men found on some victims raised the possibility that others may have done the killings.

For one example, he pointed out that DNA samplings from three contributors were found underneath the left-hand fingernails of Princess Berthomieux.

"And at least two of the contributors of that DNA found underneath her fingernails were male. And Lonnie Franklin was excluded as being a potential source of the contributor of the DNA, male DNA, found underneath her fingernails that could have been there to prevent her from being strangled," he said.

Likewise, Amster also proffered that analysts found a mixture of DNA profiles on Barbara Ware's vaginal swab, underwear, bra, and shirt. "You will hear that they found a mixture of DNA profiles from a minimum of two contributors," said Amster. "And one, the major DNA profile, was an unknown male, and it was suitable for comparison. Lonnie Franklin was excluded as being that major contributor of that sperm fraction."

Also, in the case of Bernita Sparks, Amster pointed out, unknown male DNA was found on her vaginal swab, external genital swab, vaginal aspirate sperm fraction, and anal swab sperm fraction. Lonnie Franklin was excluded as being the potential donor, he said.

DNA was not his only card, though. Amster turned his attention to Enietra Washington's testimony, bringing up that Enietra had told conflicting stories over the years about her encounter with Franklin.

To prove his point, he called his first witness, Enietra's friend Lynda Hoover, to the stand. On that fateful night of Enietra's attack, Lynda came home to find Enietra on her doorstep in a fetal position, bleeding. Lynda called an ambulance and spoke to her friend in the days after she was shot.

Lynda told the jury that, at first, Enietra told her one man was responsible for attacking her but later said two men were involved. "In the beginning she said 'he' and afterward she said 'they,'" Lynda testified. "She mentioned 'they' wouldn't let her out of the car."

On another front, on the last day of defense testimony, Amster told the jury that the method used by the police ballistics experts to examine bullets was "not proper science." To prove that point, he called materials scientist David LaMagna to the stand.

LaMagna testified that police used inferior microscopes, 2-D comparison microscopes, when they should have used higher-powered microscopes with 3-D mapping or electron microscopes when identifying a unique pattern on a bullet.

In her cross-examination, Silverman made a case that, despite Amster labeling him an expert witness, LaMagna was not an expert in tool-mark analysis or microscopy. When she asked him if he had tested the theories he'd testified to, he admitted he had not. That was because, he explained, it would have been too costly.

Silverman then introduced an expert rebuttal witness to dispute LaMagna's claims. James Hamby, director of the Indianapolis-Marion County Forensic Services Agency, testified that microscopic comparison using a comparison microscope was the standard technology utilized across the country and around the world for decades, and had withstood decades of peer review.

LaMagna's theories, Hamby said, were unsound.

With that, after more than a month of waging his defense counterattack, Amster rested his case

CHAPTER 32
CLOSING THE CASE

ON MONDAY, MAY 2, 2016, Silverman summarized the prosecution's evidence in her closing argument.

"Ten young women, all of them cruelly murdered by that man—the defendant, Lonnie Franklin," she told the jury while looking toward Franklin. Silverman implored the jury to "listen to what the evidence tells you. The evidence in this case is the voice of the victims who can no longer speak for themselves."

The victims, she said, were preyed on because of their vulnerabilities. Franklin, she said, lured them in with the promise of drugs, and, if they weren't submissive enough, they were shot and killed.

"These crimes were about power and control," Silverman told the jury. "Like Enietra Washington, who the defendant believed had dogged him, or disrespected him. The other victims also probably put up a fight. And like Detective Dupree explained to you, women who grew up in South Central, they were tough. They are tough; they have to be to survive.

"Why else does the defendant bring a loaded gun to look for women? And once he saw that he could get away with murder, literally, he just kept doing it . . . And as Detective Kilcoyne said to the defendant during that interview that you saw in July of 2010, science is the only thing that stopped the serial killer."

Silverman then talked about Franklin's likely motive. "It should be obvious," she said. "The defendant is a sexual predator."

She went on: "Sexual gratification was his clear motive here. His sperm was found in Barbara Ware's mouth. His DNA from his saliva, as we all saw in that sex videotape, was left on the breasts of seven victims. Seven victims had his saliva on their breasts."

Silverman reiterated the testimony of the defendant's friend, Ray Davis, to accentuate her point about Franklin's near-constant pursuit of sexual gratification. Davis, she said, had testified that Franklin "was always talking about sex. Always talking about women; that he had pet names for women based on the appearance of their breasts."

Silverman then summed up the prosecution's case. "From the evidence it's clear that the defendant got pleasure from killing these young women, as that is how they all wound up, with the exception of Enietra Washington, where the defendant was unsuccessful. And it's also obvious from viewing the crime scenes that the defendant desperately wanted to degrade his victims, to degrade these women by dumping their dead bodies, as I said, like trash, as you have seen from the crime-scene photos. He got off on that, too, and that's why he did it over and over again. It gave him gratification."

Silverman then told the jury that it was time for Franklin to pay for his crimes. "Most of these victims have been dead for over twenty years," she concluded. "It's time. It's time that justice was served in this case."

Silverman thanked the jury and walked back to her seat next to Marguerite Rizzo and Detective Daryn Dupree.

• • •

The stage was now Amster's. He knew the outcome rested in large part on his closing argument. Of course he would start out by hitting back at every point he could, but his arsenal had more to it than that. He planned to top off his case with the launch of a secret weapon—a heretofore undisclosed tale that would put the blame for the killings on an unnamed mystery man. Someone, obviously, other than Lonnie Franklin.

Amster stood in front of the jury, cleared his throat, and told them, albeit at times through a convoluted maze of language and logic, that the case against his client was largely circumstantial. Franklin's DNA, he pointed out, was not the only DNA found on the victims.

"What about this unknown DNA from people?" Amster pressed. "Could that mean they could have done it? You must find that all the unknown DNA is unreasonable for those individuals to have been the actual killer to find Lonnie Franklin guilty."

Amster told the jury that the prosecution team was misleading them, trying to point out patterns that were not necessarily there.

"The government wants to see patterns here over a long period of time, saying that because this body was found in the alley, or that body was found in the alley . . . they are trying to find patterns." But, he emphasized, "There is an absence of information for these patterns."

He then had a brief allegory for them, one he hoped would make crystal clear where he was going. "You know, there's a story of a rancher who wanted all of his neighbors to feel he was a great marksman. So he went to his barn and he took out his gun and he fired several bullets against the barn. And so there were bullet holes in multiple places on his barn. And then he went with his bullet holes on his barn to draw bull's-eyes around the bullet holes. Now maybe he was a good marksman; maybe he wasn't. But the bullets were there first, and then he drew the circles. And then he called his neighbors out and said, 'Look at my barn.' Didn't give them all the facts. Didn't tell them what came first; they didn't ask questions. And they said, 'Wow, he's a great marksman.' Now maybe he is a great marksman; maybe he's not. But without a proper inquiry, we really don't know. And that is the problem with the pattern. If you don't have all the information, if you don't make all the proper inquiries, you don't know, is it a true pattern or is it an illusion?"

They should know, he told the jury, that they don't have all the information in the case. Don't be like one of those rancher's neighbors, he said. "Just because you see bull's-eyes . . . is he truly a good marksman, or is this an illusion that is not what we think it is?"

He then laid out some examples of the illusions that the prosecutors would have them believe.

"The defendant is a sanitation engineer," he said. "He works with a garbage truck; therefore, he knows where all the dumpsters are. Well, wait a second. He worked from around 1985 . . . He knew where all the routes are and where the dumpsters are, and yet he is leaving bodies in alleys, not in dumpsters for them to be collected by the routes of the sanitation trucks? You can't say you got a pattern but exclude parts of the pattern.

"So if you are working as a sanitation engineer and you know the routes, and you want to get rid of the bodies, well it's easy just to put that body in a dumpster, wait, time it right for the garbage truck to come by, or your own, put it in the garbage truck and take it to the dump and that's the end of it. No. This is an illusion. Does it mean he didn't do it? No. But it doesn't mean he did it either. It is just part of the pattern that really doesn't exist."

The same, he said, held true for the DNA evidence. "The pattern of the defendant's DNA being on these victims for a period of time; again, it's an illusion. What other girls did he have his DNA on?

"You see, they want to bring up the fact that the defendant is into sex. We will concede that point right now. You don't have that number of pictures, a videotape, always talking about sex and not being obsessed with sex. Okay? He is obsessed with sex. And, unfortunately, there were a lot of women out there that made the opportunity for him to have sex. I'm not saying it's moral. Morality is not the judgment here.

"What happened between him and his wife is between him and

his wife. And it doesn't make him a murderer. So we saw this nice video of him having sex with a woman. But did we see any violence attached to it? Did we see that she was being forced to do anything? No. She even, I think, seemed to be smiling about it. What does that prove to us? It's the illusion. Yes, he is having sex. His DNA was probably on more women out there than we'll ever know. I don't know if that's right; I don't know if that's wrong. Certainly not a way that many of us would live our lives. But what does that tell us? What does that give us? It's the illusion of trying to say it's a pattern when it might not be."

Next, Amster turned his focus on Ray Davis, whose testimony cast a dark shadow on his friend Lonnie Franklin.

"What did Ray Davis tell us? Nothing," Amster told the jury. "He said that he saw Lonnie with lots of girls. Well, if Lonnie was trying to murder these girls, why would he be open about it and letting people see him with these girls? Okay? They were his girls. Ray Davis never called the police. Why? Because he never saw anything wrong with the girls and Lonnie. Never saw any violence. Never saw anything wrong. You don't think a lot of people in the neighborhood didn't see him with girls? Why didn't they call the police? Because they never saw anything wrong. These were Lonnie's girls. Right or wrong, they were Lonnie's girls."

Amster switched course again and took another whack at the DNA evidence, which he told the jury was built around "inferior technology and science." The testing used was "not up to the standard" used in private industry. The prosecution, he charged, was "trying to prove something is true to eliminate the randomness of nature into something exact, to eliminate the reasonable doubt when it cannot be done."

It was late in the day and the jury was sent home. Amster hadn't yet pulled out his secret weapon, his alternate-killer theory that he hoped would decimate the DA's case. That would have to wait until the following morning.

When court reconvened the next day, Amster set right into

weaving the tale. His tactic caught everyone in the courtroom by surprise, except perhaps his co-counsel and the defendant.

Amster told the jury about a mystery man with an "attitude" who Enietra said made contact with her outside the liquor store and then wanted to stop at his uncle's house to pick up some money.

Amster pointed out to the jury that Franklin didn't need any money. Police found more than $10,000 in his garage.

"Why would the defendant, Lonnie Franklin, need to go to his uncle's house for money? He had money. But would a nephew know to go to his uncle's house for money?

"We have in this case a mystery man," Amster said. "And so it might be stated, what do you mean, 'uncle'? There were many question marks about Enietra's testimony. Enietra did state different things at different times. But what she never changed in her testimony was the suspect who picked her up in that Pinto was going to his uncle's house. That maintained from the beginning to the end. And was going to his uncle's house for money. And what did she tell us about this mystery man?"

Amster told the jury that Enietra also used the term "youngster" when she described her attacker.

"We have Lonnie's driver's license," said Amster. "Lonnie's driver's license shows that his date of birth is August 30, 1952. That means on the date of the incident with Miss Washington, Mr. Franklin would have been 36 years of age. At no time did Miss Washington describe the individual who picked her up as being in his mid- to late-30s. She gave us a range of early 20s to early 30s. That is what she stated. So now we have a nephew and we have an uncle. Who is who, is our question."

Amster then tried to further his "nephew" theory by mentioning that Enietra saw school books in her attacker's car. "Miss Washington stated there were books in the car. School books . . . Economic books or math books are not books that an elementary-school child or a middle-school child would utilize. Economics is something a high-school individual would utilize, but even more importantly probably a community-college-age individual would utilize, one that is befitting of a nephew and not of an uncle who has children."

At this point Amster was just getting started explaining his alternate-killer theory, putting almost everything the jury had heard over weeks and weeks through the "mystery man" filter. He next reminded the jury how Enietra had described her attacker to the police sketch artist as someone with pockmarks.

"Mr. Franklin never had pockmarks," said Amster. "This is a youngster. This is not the uncle. This is the nephew that could have been found at the right time. This is an individual who had access to the entire house."

"So what do we know about the suspect?" asked Amster. "We know he is pockmarked; we know he has an attitude. What do you covet? You covet what you see every single day but you cannot get."

Amster was on a roll, an increasingly turbulent roll that very well might determine if his client would live or die or go free.

"We have a mystery man with a mystery gun," he continued. "Because all of the bullets associated with the Enietra Washington bullet removed from her from surgery are from the same gun, according to the government . . . No DNA of Lonnie Franklin was testified to being found on Enietra Washington.

"So the mystery man with the mystery gun with the mystery DNA saw his uncle picking up girls every day. He coveted them, but he was unable to get them either because of pockmarks or attitude, and [he] brought harm to them, his uncle Lonnie's girls.

"He stalked them. He knew where they were. He knew where they could be, and he did it. Now maybe Lonnie Franklin knows who this person is. Maybe Lonnie Franklin could have come forward. Yes, maybe his soul is corrupt. Maybe he has got a lot to answer for. But it's not a crime, and it's not murder."

Amster then addressed the Polaroid pictures discovered at Franklin's house.

"And a Polaroid was taken of Enietra Washington, a Polaroid

that the person in the car with her had possession of, and that Polaroid was found at the residence. But we know that the nephew was on the grounds at that residence. How often, how much access he had, we do not know."

Again, Amster asked the jury to question the truth and veracity of the evidence. "Each and every murder that occurred in this case could have been done by the mystery man with the mystery gun with the mystery DNA," Amster hammered. "Or, if he was there with Enietra Washington and he had access, then he knew who Lonnie's girlfriends were, or Lonnie's girls were. And he could have followed them and stalked them and coveted them but could never get them, probably never could have sex with them. Because that's what he was looking for; that's what he wanted. And he was frustrated and upset because he had an attitude and he was pockmarked. We cannot eliminate that there were two people there; we just have to determine which one is the uncle and which one is the nephew."

He then put the final screws into his mystery-man alternate-killer theory, telling the jury that Franklin's neighborhood friend of thirty years, Paul Williams Jr., testified that Franklin never had pockmarks. And yet, pockmarks are part of the description Enietra gave police.

"The pockmarks exist, and it's uncontradicted," he continued. "So if the nephew had access to a Pinto, to Enietra Washington, to Lonnie's girls, to the Polaroid, does he not have access to the Titan F.I.E.? To the final gun that is used to kill Janecia Peters? Of course he does. He has access to everything. He exists from the beginning to the end."

Having, he hoped, created a whole new way for the jury to look at the facts in this case, Amster then came back once again to the DNA evidence. Specifically, the unknown male DNA found on some of the victims.

For example, "On Bernita Sparks, we have another unknown male number one found on a vaginal swab sperm fraction, the same unknown male found on the external genital swab sperm fraction; the same unknown male on a DNA profile found on a vaginal aspirate epithelial fraction; the same unknown male found on the vaginal aspirate sperm fraction; the same unknown male found on the anal swab sperm fraction. And each of these, Lonnie Franklin is excluded as the source. And it goes on for the same unknown male found on the inner crotch sperm fraction and the same unknown male found on the swabbing of jeans. But yet the government puts forth that only Lonnie Franklin can be the actual killer; that this unknown male could not have been the one who did the foul deed, even though the evidence is pretty clear of recent sexual intercourse with Bernita Sparks."

Amster then added that unknown male DNA was found in Princess Berthomieux's vaginal swabs as well as fingernail clippings. "Princess Berthomieux died as a result of strangulation," Amster said. "And what did the coroner tell us that usually a person who is being strangled is going to do? They are going to try to fight off their assailant using their hands, using their fingernails. And what do we have? We have DNA underneath the fingernails that not only does not match Lonnie Franklin; it excludes him."

Amster told the jury that technicians had found DNA profiles from a minimum of five male contributors on a right-nipple swab as well as both the left-hand and right-hand fingernail scrapings of Valerie McCorvey.

"What we know that cannot be argued is that there's more than one male underneath the fingernail scrapings," said Amster. "And we know Valerie McCorvey was strangled."

Amster posed the question: "And we are to believe that Lonnie Franklin is the only possible slayer, the only actual killer, where we have no DNA there to be harvested to say it comes from Lonnie Franklin? And we know there were five [DNA contributors], at least. But yet you are to find, beyond a reasonable doubt, it could only have been Lonnie when the most critical piece of evidence is not some saliva left on the nipple; it's what's underneath the fingernails."

Amster then revisited his criticism of the ballistics testing, telling the jury once again that the science used was "outdated" and that they should reject its findings.

Summing up, Amster told the jury that the lack of evidence in the case compels the jury to find Franklin not guilty.

"There have been times in this country where individuals have been asked to make tough decisions on individuals not well-liked by society," he said, readying a final tale to leave with the jurors. "One of the times it occurred was before the formation of this country during the Boston Massacre, a time when Redcoats who were not liked opened up and fired upon colonials in Massachusetts. And they were tried, these British soldiers, for murder. And a jury of American colonists sat on that jury and made a decision on the culpability of those British soldiers that so many of their fellow countrymen wanted to be found guilty to have a reason for the American Revolution. But those jurors, understanding the importance of justice and fairness, made a very tough decision that the British soldiers were not responsible for the act of murder and set them free. Do any of us know the names of those jurors? No. They have melted into history because they chose not to be known. But they knew that what is most important is to look at the facts, come to an honest decision, and do what is right. Because any decision not based upon the laws, any decision that is persuaded by pressure remains a cancer among us and will grow and will not serve us well. We must believe in our system; we must stand by our system, and we must make our decisions based upon the law. And that, I know, each of you will do."

• • •

Silverman got her chance next, during the state's rebuttal, to hit back at Amster's mystery-man surprise and other counterpunches.

She told the jury that Amster would have raised the theory of the mystery man earlier in the trial if there were evidence to support the claim.

"You have to base your decision on the evidence," said Silverman. "The theory of the defense is basically the equivalent to the skies opening up, a spaceship descending and murdering all these women . . . They have the same evidence of that as they do of some mystery nephew who we have never heard of and don't even know if he exists.

"They're just making things up," Silverman said of the defense's closing argument. "It is an attempt to distort, to distract, to manipulate. They are just trying to distract you."

If the purported nephew was the killer, then why was Enietra's photo found at Franklin's house, Silverman asked.

"Why doesn't the imaginary nephew have it at his imaginary home?" she continued. "If there is some mystery man out there, then where is his DNA and why didn't we pick it up on victim after victim after victim? Wouldn't we find his DNA on some of the victims? The only DNA profile that repeats itself again and again and again is the defendant's.

"The evidence in this case is staggering," Silverman stressed, and she ended her summation much like she did her closing. "It is time to bring justice to these women. It is time."

CHAPTER 33
WHAT SAY THE JURY?

FOLLOWING THE CLOSE OF SILVERMAN'S summation on Tuesday afternoon, May 3, 2016, the jury began its deliberations.

The jury was still deliberating the next day, so I went into the office—I was now a senior crime writer at *People* magazine. Most of the victims' families left the courthouse too, but the Alexanders chose to wait a good portion of Tuesday and Wednesday in the hallway outside courtroom 109.

I was in my office on Thursday, May 5, when I got a call from a public-information officer with the Los Angeles Superior Court that the jury reached a verdict. It would be read in Kennedy's courtroom at one thirty that afternoon.

Feeling incredibly nervous, I raced for my car. I wasn't worried about my car getting there—Maude Jr. had long gone to the scrap yard—it was L.A.'s notorious gridlock that had me on edge. There was fifteen miles of congested freeway between the *People* magazine offices on Wilshire Boulevard in Brentwood and the criminal courts building downtown. I had invested so much of my heart, soul, and mind in this case for almost ten years, and I had no intention of being late for the verdict.

I arrived downtown at 1:15 P.M., found a parking space about three blocks from the courthouse, and ran the rest of the way there. I was out of breath when I got off the elevator on the ninth floor.

I wasn't the only one who rushed. Margaret Prescod, the founder of the Black Coalition Fighting Back Serial Murders, fought crosstown traffic to get there on time; Dennis Kilcoyne made the fifty-mile drive from his home near Santa Clarita in fifty minutes. About twenty family members of the ten victims were standing together in a designated cordoned-off section for family members near the front door of Kennedy's courtroom when I arrived. They were talking quietly among themselves as members of the press milled about in the hallway.

My eyes immediately found Mary Alexander and her son Donnell. Both were confident the verdict would go their way, but their eyes betrayed the weariness of years waiting for justice and months of long days at the courthouse during the trial.

The doors of courtroom 109 opened at exactly 1:30 P.M., and the families were led inside, followed by Silverman and Rizzo, Dupree and Kilcoyne, and then the media.

All eyes were on Franklin when the bailiffs led him into the courtroom from the holding cell. He took his regular seat and fixed his eyes on his usual invisible spot on the wall next to Kennedy. The only difference in his demeanor on this day was that his right leg appeared to twitch uncontrollably every minute or so.

Franklin's lead defense attorney, Seymour Amster, was notably absent. His co-counsel, Dale Atherton, stood at Franklin's side.

Amster later told me he couldn't make it because he had to help a friend who was having issues with the Department of Motor Vehicles.

The jury was led inside the courtroom moments after Franklin was seated. The room buzzed with chatter. When the bailiff called for order, everyone halted mid-word and then seemed to take a collective deep breath. The judge handed a folded paper with the verdict written on it to the court clerk, who stood and read each charge, followed by the jury's verdict.

One after the other, ten times in all.

Ten times guilty.

Debra Jackson, Henrietta Wright, Barbara Ware, Bernita Sparks, Mary Lowe, Lachrica Jefferson, Monique Alexander, Princess Berthomieux, Valerie McCorvey, and Janecia Peters finally got the justice they deserved.

The jurors also found Franklin guilty of the attempted murder of Enietra Washington.

While the crimes and verdicts were read out loud for each victim, Franklin's usual smug face remained unchanged. Even as he was led away, he looked no different than he had throughout the trial.

As each of the verdicts were read, I glanced over at the corresponding family members. I saw tears streaming down the face of Henrietta's daughter Rochell Johnson. I heard Mary Alexander, seated behind me, whisper to Porter, "God is good," when Franklin was found guilty of killing Monique. I saw Donnell and Darin hide their faces, overcome by raw emotion. And I watched as Princess's foster sister Samara Herard quietly sobbed.

Tears poured down my face, too.

I glanced at Kilcoyne, who was seated behind the prosecution table. The former tough-as-nails cop was visibly moved by the outcome. He looked at me and winked. It had been a long process for him, too.

The faces of 800 Task Force Detective Daryn Dupree and prosecutors Beth Silverman and Marguerite Rizzo portrayed a mix of satisfaction and relief.

As reporters ran from the courtroom to file their stories and the families quietly wept for joy, I sat glued to my seat in the front row. This decade-long journey, in which I had spent most of my free time working on or thinking about the case, had come to an end.

My thoughts went to my parents, who had passed away. My mum, Mary, died in December of 2010, five months after Franklin was arrested. My father, Joe, passed away in May of 2015, less than one year before the trial. They had become as obsessed as I was with the case and were proud of my determination to try to help the victims get their justice and to see this saga through to its end.

When I finally walked out of the courtroom about ten minutes later, I came across a happy, joyous scene in the hallway. Detectives were hugging members of the victims' families, prosecutors were hugging detectives, and the grieving families were soon hugging me. This long journey was finally over. The verdict was what they hoped for, and, at that moment, everyone was on the same side.

Donnell Alexander walked toward me, his face wet with tears, and pulled me into his arms. He thanked me for knocking on his door almost a decade earlier and writing about a series of murders that so many people had overlooked.

"Thank you," he said between sobs. "You cared."

CHAPTER 34

LIFE OR DEATH

THE PENALTY PHASE OF THE GRIM Sleeper trial began one week after Lonnie Franklin Jr. was convicted of ten murders and one attempted murder. The same jury that had convicted him now had to decide whether to recommend death or life in prison without the possibility of parole.

Over the next month, the prosecution presented evidence they had found soon after Franklin's arrest that linked him to the murders of an additional four women during his savage Grim Sleeper spree. Concerned that adding these four murders to their case would push back the start of the trial and delay justice for the victims' families, the prosecution decided not to include them in the proceedings. As it turned out, the trial was held up anyway for close to six years.

Three of these four murders were discovered when the 800 Task Force was searching through more than three hundred unsolved homicide cases and missing-person reports dating back to 1976, the year that Franklin returned to L.A. from Germany. The fourth murder came from evidence found in the post-arrest search of his garage.

The lives and deaths of these women were almost replicas of the ten murders Franklin was found guilty of committing. All four women were young, black, and drug-addicted.

Taking these additional homicides into account, it would appear that Franklin's first murder took place on January 15, 1984. Sharon Alicia Dismuke, 21, was killed a year and a half before Debra Jackson, who was previously thought to be Franklin's first victim.

Sharon was discovered on the floor beside the toilet in the men's bathroom of an abandoned gas station on the corner of Martin Luther King Jr. Boulevard and South San Pedro Street in South Central after an anonymous telephone report of a dead body at the location. She had been covered with a piece of old carpet. A filthy white rag was stuffed in her mouth. Her bare heels were coated in grease from being dragged from the parking lot of the gas station to the grimy bathroom.

The coroner, Lakshmanan Sathyavagiswaran, testified during the post-verdict penalty phase that Sharon had been shot twice at close range in the left side of her chest. One of the .25-caliber copper-jacketed bullets went through her left upper arm before it entered her chest. She also suffered a blow to the right temple.

Deputy District Attorney Beth Silverman again called to the stand LAPD firearms examiner Daniel Rubin, who testified that the same Titan .25-caliber semiautomatic used to kill Janecia Peters in 2007 was used in the murder of Sharon Dismuke twenty-three years earlier.

Sharon's sister Tina Saunders took the stand and told the jury how the death of her sister destroyed her mother.

"My mom—when my sister died, it also killed my mother," she said. "My mom did therapy for years. Years. Well into my adulthood. And—I was 15 years old. I felt like I lost my mom and my sister. She was there physically, but mentally, she didn't have much to give."

Sharon was strong-willed, smart, and very protective, said Tina, and she recounted a childhood story to explain her point.

"I caught myself having a little boyfriend," Tina told the jury. "I guess I was about 14. And we were playing around, and he got a little too rough and left a mark on my leg. And she came over to the house and saw it and asked me what happened. And after I told her, she went and knocked on his door and chewed him out really good. And he came over and apologized, told me my sister was crazy. But, yeah, she made sure he didn't do that again."

But drugs, the scourge of South Central in the '80s, eventually took over Sharon's life.

"I knew that she was struggling, but I know that she wanted to do better," said Tina. "I don't think she knew how. I don't think anybody knew how to help her."

Sharon wanted to make sure her little sister didn't go down that same road. "She was trying to help me with some homework, and she was a little off," she recalled. "I guess she had taken something and was on something. But she couldn't help me the way that she wanted to. And I just remember her grabbing me by my shirt and pulling me to her and just telling me, 'Don't ever do drugs, or I'll kill you.' You know. She just wanted better for me."

Deputy District Attorney Marguerite Rizzo, who was handling many of the witness impact statements for the prosecution, asked Tina if she remembered her last conversation with her sister.

"One of the last was—my sisters that are in between, both of them were pregnant at the same time. And I just remember her being so excited. And she said she can't wait for those babies to be born. And she never got to see it."

Four years later, on August 15, 1988, police discovered the body of Inez Warren, 28, lying in an alley in the 10300 block of Western Avenue. An anonymous tipster, who made a call from a public phone, told police he had watched "some guys drop off a girl in the alley."

Detective John Skaggs, then a patrol officer with the LAPD's Seventy-seventh Division Station, testified that Inez was alive when he arrived at the scene. She had been shot once in the left side of her chest and suffered blunt-force trauma to the head. But she was "breathing and moaning a bit," he told the jury. She died at Martin Luther King Jr. Community Hospital.

The bullet that killed Inez went right through her and was never found, but the size of the wound was consistent with that of a .25-caliber gunshot. Inez was murdered three weeks before Monique Alexander was found dead in an alley on September 11, 1988.

The body of the third victim that prosecutors linked to Franklin was never found. However, prosecutors and the 800 Task Force were certain that Rolenia Morris, a 31-year-old mother of two young children, died by Franklin's hands. Rolenia had vanished under mysterious circumstances on September 5, 2005. She lived nine blocks from Franklin's house. Her Nevada driver's license was found on the back shelf of Franklin's garage during the three-day search of his home. In addition, two of her photos were found in an envelope in the mini-fridge in his garage, along with the photo of Janecia Peters and the school identification card of 18-year-old Ayellah Marshall, who disappeared without a trace in February of 2005. (Although prosecutors believed Franklin killed Ayellah, her body was never found, and the evidence linking him to the crime was insufficient.)

The fourth murdered woman that the jury didn't hear about during the trial but were hearing about during the death-penalty phase was Georgia Mae Thomas, discovered along a dirt sidewalk in a warehouse district on East 57th Street on December 28, 2000.

Her sister Vivian Williams told the jury that she was heartbroken and still in shock when she had to identify her 43-year-old sister's body and plan her funeral.

"It was hard," Vivian told the jury. "But it was my responsibility as the oldest sibling. We didn't have parents. Her father lives in Arkansas, and we didn't have a mother."

The jury learned that Georgia Mae's body had been cleaned and re-dressed after she was shot twice in the left side of her chest. When her body was found, her white bra was partially unhooked in the back, and her Guess jeans were unzipped. Blood on her bra had been cleaned up, as was the blood around the two bullet wounds.

She wasn't wearing any underpants. One of her brown socks was on inside out. She had on one brown shoe. The other shoe was found a few blocks away.

Her case had gone cold until Franklin's arrest, when the police, searching behind a false wall in Franklin's central garage, found the .25-caliber pistol used to kill her.

Jeff Deacon, an LAPD fingerprint specialist, testified that he matched a fingerprint on the gun magazine to Franklin's left thumb.

Vivian Williams was still on the stand when Silverman dropped a bombshell with her next line of questioning.

"Now, years ago, did you ever take your sister to visit a friend who lived on Eighty-first Street?" asked Silverman.

"Yes," said Vivian.

"Do you remember what the house looked like?" asked Silverman.

"I used to tease her and tell her it looked like a cookie house," said Vivian, who was implying that the house she dropped her sister off at was Franklin's mint-green bungalow, although police found no proof of that.

"How many times, approximately, do you think you took your sister and dropped her off at her friend's on Eighty-first Street just off of Western?"

"Maybe eight, ten times," said Vivian.

"And when you dropped her off there, did you ever see her friend?" asked Silverman.

"Yes," said Vivian.

"And where did you see her friend?" asked Silverman.

"At the gate," said Vivian. "Her friend would open the gate to let her in because I would never leave until I saw her and I saw somebody let her in."

"And was the friend a female or a male?" asked Silverman.

"It was a man," said Vivian. "A black man."

"And did your sister ever tell you her friend's name?" asked Silverman.

"Lonnie," said Vivian.

• • •

The penalty portion of the Grim Sleeper case was chugging along, but on May 26 there was an eruption of bluster and grandstanding in the courtroom over the next witness called to testify. Ingrid W., who more than forty years earlier at age 17 was raped in Germany by Franklin and other U.S. Army soldiers, had come to L.A. to tell her story. Her presence triggered an extended bombastic and at times caustic exchange between Amster, Silverman, and the judge.

Amster was adamant that Ingrid W., whose last name was withheld to protect her identity, should not be allowed to testify. His stance was based on what he described as a longstanding policy by the German government to not allow its citizens, because of the horrors of the Holocaust, to testify in support of the death penalty in a trial outside of Germany.

Silverman disagreed, saying that Amster was off base in his judicial references and, citing her own family's Holocaust experiences, said his comments were offensive. She accused him of insulting Ingrid W. by making his charges in her presence. Amster, citing his Jewish heritage, expressed his own outrage in response.

Judge Kennedy ruled that Ingrid W. could testify. But no sooner had she begun her testimony than Amster stopped the proceedings to ask the judge, at a private conference at her bench, to admonish Ingrid W.'s husband, who he said was "Trying to stare me down."

Kennedy, exasperated, told him she would do no such thing, and, finally, Ingrid W. was allowed to tell her story.

"Can you tell us what impact, if any, that experience, the kidnapping and the gang rape, what impact that had or has had on your life," Silverman asked Ingrid.

"I'm still afraid to this day when it gets dark," said Ingrid, who testified through a German translator. "I do not go outside by myself when it's dark. If I am home alone, I turn on the lights in the entire house and . . . we got a large dog. And my entire family, my daughter and my grandchildren, suffer from it because I pass this fear on to them."

"How has this impacted the way that you deal with your own daughter and your grandchildren?" asked Silverman.

"They are taken by car everywhere," said Ingrid. "They are taken to school, picked up again. The big [granddaughter] is now 19, and she is still being driven to school, being picked up. And it was the same with my own daughter."

"And is that because of your fears from what happened to you?" asked Silverman.

"Yes. Because I did tell my daughter about it, and she got afraid," said Ingrid. "And she naturally feels that way about her children."

"You said you got a big dog?" Silverman asked.

"Yes. I do not feel secure without a dog when I'm home alone," said Ingrid.

"What kind of dog did you get?" asked Silverman.

"A Newfoundland," Ingrid told her.

"So not a big dog; a gigantic dog?"

"Yes," replied Ingrid.

After less than thirty minutes on the stand, recounting the still-painful details of her assault, Ingrid went back to her seat without ever looking at Franklin.

• • •

During Silverman's closing argument in the penalty phase of the trial on Thursday, June 2, she posed the question to the courtroom: Does Lonnie David Franklin Jr. deserve mercy?

Fourteen women are dead at his hands, she told the jury.

"So the question becomes, does he deserve mercy? Because again, I suspect this is the argument you're going to hear [from the defense] because they don't have anything else," she said. "What mercy did he show to all of his victims?"

Silverman continued. "When you think about a case like this, the one takeaway I would think would be that there are some crimes that are so horrendous, that are so beyond the pale, it's almost like a bad movie, a horror movie," she said. "They are so horrendous, these crimes, that they literally define the person who commits them. That's this case.

"So this is the question. Are you going to seek justice for the victims? Or are you going to grant mercy to their killer? Because again, the definition of mercy in my mind is withholding punishment, even when justice demands it. So this is a fork in the road for you. You can either give mercy to him, the serial killer, or you can impose justice. But you can't do both. You have to make a choice."

Silverman then talked about the callousness of the murders. "They were so calculated and they were so demeaning, the way that these women ended up," she said about the victims. "Half of them naked, unclothed. All of them in these filthy alleys. One of them is a 15-year-old girl. And he left her naked in an alley in bushes. One of them is an 18-year-old girl. And he left her in a filthy alley to decompose. There is nothing, nothing that's more abhorrent or unconscionable than the murder of innocent, unsuspecting, vulnerable victims, especially young girls. And we know from listening to the victim-impact evidence that each of these victims were robbed of their futures, and society was also robbed of whatever contributions they may have made, be it large or small, to this world. They were robbed of those opportunities. It wasn't enough that he murdered these victims; he had to degrade them, even in death. Because of him, their lives had no apparent value."

Silverman went on. "Now the defendant wants life. And he wants life as a reward, a reward for his crimes. Don't reward him. Life without parole, as I said, is a gift, and he doesn't deserve it . . . And you're thinking about it in terms of how you would feel, how someone with a conscience would feel if you sat in a cell all day long for the rest of your life and all you had to do was think about all the horrible things you have done. And you are right; in that circumstance, maybe it would be worse. The difference is, he doesn't have a conscience. So if you think he's going to sit around in his cell feeling guilty about the lives he destroyed, think again."

"This isn't a case where a defense attorney can stand up and say, 'You know what? My client led an exemplary life. He did so many great things except for this one terrible thing.' His entire life has been about violence perpetrated against women."

Silverman then asked the jury to step into the shoes of Franklin's victims.

"What's it like to die afraid and alone and in pain? And struggle to survive? And we heard about that from the coroners. When their chest cavities were filling up with blood and they are gasping for air? Imagine what they must have endured in those last moments of their lives and thinking about what their hopes must have been, you know, what were they thinking about as their lives were fading away? What were the last emotions that they experienced? Likely, as I said, panic and fear. Pain . . . The defendant chose to end their lives. He acted as the judge. He acted as the jury. He acted as their executioner . . . For all of this, he deserves to pay the ultimate penalty."

• • •

Amster was caught in a conundrum. During the trial, he had received word from the judge that the jury had found him intimidating. Now, at this crucial point for his client, he very much wanted to be the one to make the case to the jury that Franklin deserved to get life, not death. This is where he thrived. But he knew the most eloquent of arguments would not work if the jury wasn't really listening to him. So he spoke with co-counsel Dale Atherton about taking over the task.

"My first thought was it is in the best interest of the client," Amster told me. "And I felt it was time for the jury to hear from another voice. We didn't make the decision right away, but I felt it was the right decision."

Atherton gave the closing argument on Friday, June 3. It was a plea to the jurors to spare Franklin's life from the death penalty.

"Every case must be decided on its own individual merits, not some profile created by the prosecution," he told them. "I don't want you to listen to me. I want you to open up your heart and your mind to me for just a moment . . . I want you to give me a fair opportunity to persuade you to vote for life. And then it is up to you."

Atherton asked them to give him their attention for an hour or so to try to persuade them. "In this case, you have two choices: life or death. In my argument, I think it could be best summed up in a poem that I learned as a young man. And it goes like this:

> *The road stretched east and the road stretched west.*
> *The young lad knew not which road was best.*
> *So he took the road, which let him down,*
> *and he lost the race and the victor's crown*
> *because there was no one there to show him the better way.*
> *Another day at this selfsame place, a young man with high hopes stood.*
> *He, too, set for the manly race; he, too, seeking things that were good.*
> *But there was someone there whom the roads did know.*
> *He showed that young lad which way to go.*
> *Now the young lad walks the highways fair*
> *because someone stood at the crossroads there*
> *to show him the better way.'*

Then, Atherton told the jurors, "I want you to know that if you vote for death, that's fine. That's up to you. It's a fair and just verdict. But my point to you today is that there is a better way."

Atherton then spent the next forty minutes attempting to discredit the prosecution's case. He told the jury that Franklin wasn't the only person with exclusive access to his garage. There was "no evidence that he was the only one who was in there," he said. And he said there was also no evidence linking Franklin to the photo of Enietra found on the garage wall.

"Strange place for a trophy picture," said Atherton. "How did it get there? Who put it there? Were there fingerprints on it? Or was there any forensic evidence linking it to Lonnie? Lonnie is the only person in the whole world that could have put that picture there?"

Atherton asked the jury to consider that Enietra's attacker was not Franklin. "Maybe it's a family member," he said. "Maybe it's a friend. What does that mean? That means that all of these homicides, all of these homicides right here in this unknown gun group, are in serious trouble. Serious doubt. Because they can't put the gun in his hand."

Atherton asked the jury what happened to the gun that was used to kill Monique Alexander, Henrietta Wright, Debra Jackson, Bernita Sparks, Barbara Ware, Lachrica Jefferson, and Mary Lowe.

"He keeps all of his guns," he said, referring to his client. "He has receipts for them. Why wouldn't he keep this one? Why is this one missing? Why is it the mystery gun?"

Atherton asked the jury, "Where is the absolute proof that only Lonnie Franklin had access to those guns, the only person in the whole world who had access to those guns? Where is the absolute proof that Lonnie Franklin himself shot each of the victims in this case? Where is the proof? There is zero evidence presented how these murders happened, when they happened, how many people were there or who the shooter was. Before you vote for death, is it too much to ask that there is at least one credible witness that can testify that that man over there shot that woman? Just one."

Atherton then waded into the DNA evidence. "Count three. Barbara Ware. DNA consistent with Lonnie found on an oral swab sperm fraction. I believe that was in the mouth. On the vaginal aspirate we have three unknown males. Lonnie is excluded in the vaginal aspirate. You will see this theme occur over and over again. Except for Barbara Ware with the sperm fraction in the mouth, every victim has his DNA; when his DNA shows up, it's on the breast. Never vaginal. Never vaginal.

"So who are those three guys? Who are they? Did they have sexual contact with Miss Ware before Lonnie Franklin, after Lonnie Franklin, or at the same time? We don't know. There's lingering doubt."

After going through the DNA found on Bernita Sparks, Princess Berthomieux, and Valerie McCorvey, Atherton posed the question: "Before you vote for the death penalty, wouldn't you like to know who all of these people are and what role did they play, if any, in this case?"

"Each of these young ladies were engaged in activities that put them in danger at a dangerous time and at dangerous places," Atherton said. "Anybody that they ran into could have done things like this."

And then he told a story.

"And now I want to talk to you a little bit about the scientific evidence that you heard in this case. Charles H. Duell was the commissioner of the U.S. Patent Office in 1899, over one hundred years ago. Mr. Duell's most famous attributed utterance is that quote 'Everything that can be invented has been invented.' In 1899, the man leading the patent office said that's it. Anything that could possibly be invented has already been invented. We will see no more inventions. I wonder what he would think now if he were to see our day. See computers, phones, put a man on the moon. Space shuttle and tablets and laptops and all the new technology. Amazing advancements. Science and medicine and everywhere. He would be shocked. My point is, science is always advancing. Science is always getting better, and that includes DNA . . . What if we get to a point where the DNA in science is now so advanced, we can identify all of those unknown males? We can identify them.

"And what if we do that and we find another suspect emerges equal to Lonnie Franklin? And you hear about this. You return a verdict of death, and five years, ten years, fifteen years from now you hear the news that another suspect has been identified because the science got good enough to identify them. How will you feel if that happens?"

"Death is absolute," said Atherton. "If you made a mistake, you cannot fix it. It's absolute."

Atherton then attacked the prosecution's ballistic testing methods. "They eyeball it," he said. "They look at it with their eyeballs and say, 'I know it when I see it.' They don't count. They don't measure; they just eyeball it."

Atherton ended his closing argument citing a 2011 newspaper article that told the story of a Minnesota mother who made a choice to show mercy to the 16-year-old who killed her son in 1993. At first she had only hatred for him, but then, with the help of a support group, she decided to visit the young man in prison to see if there was any way she could forgive him.

Ultimately, the article noted, they became close friends. When [after seventeen years] he was released from prison eighteen months early, the mother introduced him to her landlord, and he moved into the building, and they share a porch. She said she had a selfish motive. "Unforgiveness is like a cancer," she said. "It will eat you from the inside."

"It is not about the other person," she said. "Me forgiving him does not diminish what he has done. Yes, he murdered my son. But the forgiveness is for me."

Atherton then connected that tale to his.

"The government in this case doesn't want mercy," he said. "It wants retribution. Payback. It wants revenge. They claim that Lonnie hated and killed, and now you have to hate and kill.

"Revenge, in all its impotent fury, has never healed a broken heart. But mercy heals everything it touches. A death verdict will delay the healing process. It puts another event on the calendar, something for the families to have to notice and keep track of, another reminder that there is no final closure. Every time they think of the approaching execution date, it will be like opening their wounds afresh. We ask you to choose life and bring this case to a close."

Atherton then concluded his plea for mercy with an echo back to the poem he cited earlier. "Death is fine," he said. "It's a just verdict if you want. You are not murderers. I just want you to know there's a better way, and the better way is life."

The court then adjourned for the weekend.

On Monday, June 6, 2016, the jury recommended death for Lonnie Franklin Jr.

CHAPTER 35

JUSTICE DESERVED

COURTROOM 109 WAS AGAIN FILLED with familiar faces on Wednesday, August 10, 2016. Family members had returned to hear Judge Kathleen Kennedy officially deliver the death sentence to Lonnie Franklin Jr., who was back in his orange jail outfit sitting quietly next to his defense team.

But before Kennedy would sentence Franklin, the members of the victims' families had one final opportunity to address the court with their own victim-impact statements. Seventeen of the mothers, fathers, brothers, sisters, and nieces whose families were devastated by what Lonnie Franklin did were prepared to tell Franklin what they thought of him.

Most of them were religious and felt a need to forgive Franklin despite the pain he inflicted on their lives.

Laverne Peters, the mother of Janecia Peters, spoke first. Dressed elegantly, as usual, Laverne looked toward Franklin when she approached the lectern next to the jury, but when she spoke she looked straight at the judge in front of her.

"Janecia Peters was found murdered January 1, 2007," she said.

"And it has been a long, hard, difficult journey. But we continue to stand strong. I know that she would have wanted us to stay strong, and we are strong. The defendant took my daughter, murdered her, put her in a plastic bag, a trash bag like she was trash, and put her in the dumpster. Well, my hope is that he spend the rest of his glory days in his jail cell, which will become his plastic bag. I am so thankful to the homeless persons who were salvaging for recyclables, and I was lucky enough that my daughter was found. And thank you."

When Rochell Johnson, Henrietta Wright's daughter, addressed Franklin, she referenced the comments made during his police interview when he called her mother butt ugly. Rochell wasn't at court the day the jury heard Franklin's crude comments about her mother, but she later heard Silverman make reference to them. The words, she felt, were much better suited to describe Franklin's impact on the community.

"I would like to say what he did to this community, that's what you call butt ugly," said the pretty hairdresser, who closely resembles her mother. "And actions that he took over and over and over again, he has made the rest of his life butt ugly. And I would like to say once again, thank you to everybody for putting this puzzle together to paint a picture of evil, and that's who he is. Thank you."

Henrietta Wright's niece Irene Ephriam, who regularly sat through the trial proceedings with her cousin Rochell, told the judge that she feels a measure of peace knowing that Franklin will never be on the streets again.

"You know, he sat there. He doesn't care. You know, he never once looked back. Just—he is in a dark place, you know? And like I said, it gives me peace to know that he can't hurt anybody no more; that he is where he need to be. And maybe him and Charles Manson can share stories, because they are both two sick individuals."

"This has been a very, very long, long process," Princess's foster sister Samara Herard said at the podium. "She was 15 years old. Princess was 15. And we are just a year short of her whole lifespan to get to this point from when she died—fourteen years. She deserved to live, as did all of the different victims. And we are all going to be short a puzzle piece. Every one of us is missing something, not just here but all the extended families . . . But you move on every day. You keep going, and you keep it going. And you keep things together as best you can. And you put a smile on your face. And you're grateful that no one else will have to go through, at least by his hands, what we were all subjected to."

Enietra Washington, who had last been in court to testify during the trial, looked straight at Franklin from the lectern and didn't hold back. "I really think you are truly a piece of evil," she told Franklin, who didn't meet her gaze. "The hurting part about it is that you did it to your own," she said. "I have fear of a man that's supposed to take care of me, protect me. You took that away. You make me look at people differently, and I shouldn't.

"You're a Satan representative," Enietra continued. "I really am so hurt by this whole thing because I don't have no closure because I'm still living. It's a good thing. I mean, praise God. I thank him every day for it. But how can you live in a world that you have fear in? How can you just go places—and I try. But how do I know I'm not going to see another you?"

With her head held high, Enietra returned to her seat.

Listening intently from the spectator's gallery to Enietra's victim-impact statement was the one woman in the courtroom who could relate to how she was feeling. Laura Moore, a 52-year-old black woman wearing a red dress with the word *love* printed on the fabric, was waiting her turn to speak.

Laura contacted the police after she saw a news report about Franklin's 2010 arrest. She told police a now-familiar story. She got into a car with Franklin, and he allegedly shot her in the chest, too. She fell out of the car, and he left her there to die. But she didn't. A bystander called the police, and she remembered vividly that when the paramedics were saving her life, she saw Franklin drive slowly by, looking at her. Her case was not included with the others because there was no bullet or other evidence found to trace back to Franklin.

"Laura, would you like to speak now?" Silverman asked after Enietra moved away from the lectern.

Laura nodded her head and made her way past the rows of family members to stand by the lectern and let out a lifetime of anguish.

"My name is Laura Moore," she told the jury. "And Franklin shot me on May 5, 1984 [according to police, she was shot on May 29, 1985]. I was at a bus stop at 108th getting off from work. And he came passing by, passing by, telling me I shouldn't be on Figueroa because of the prostitutes.

"And I told him I'm getting off from work. I'm not worried about that; I am waiting on a bus. He kept passing by and said, 'The bus is not going to come. And I don't want, you being young, [you] being out here for no bad guys to pick you up.' I said, 'Thank you very much, but I'm going to be okay.'"

After a couple of other comments, she recounted, she returned to waiting for the bus. "It took a while for the bus to come. So he came back and he asked—he say, 'The bus is not here. Let me take you where you have to go.' I had to go on 111th [Street]. And I searched his car before I got in. I didn't find a weapon or anything. I told him I'd give him ten dollars. I was 21. I searched his car. I didn't find no weapon or anything . . . I got in."

After he briefly stopped at an auto shop across the street, he "made a right and made another right and went through an alley and proceeded. And he shot me six times and started laughing at me.

"I said, 'Why are you doing that? I'm going to die.' And he said, 'No, you not.'

"I just prayed," she told the jury. "I hold my head down and got the handle of the car and crawled in the middle of the streets to the other side of Hoover [Street] and just laid there. A man was watering the grass, and they called the ambulance. When they was cutting my clothes off, trying to save my life, I seen him pass by, looking right at it. I just want to ask him, why? Why? Why?" she said, glancing at Franklin for the first time. "I didn't do anything to him. I don't know him or anything. And I just want to know why? Really, why?"

Echoing Enietra's words, Laura went on, "I trust no one today. No one. Because a person can do that and go home and eat like nothing ever happened. And that's what he was doing."

Laura told the judge that she has come to find out that some of her friends knew him. "I am just finding this out," she said. "And during school time, when he was going to school, no girls liked him . . . He was weird."

In closing, Laura asked him again why he shot her. "And I just would like to talk to him and ask him, why? Why? That's all. Thanks."

For close to six years, Donnell Alexander had made his way to the courthouse to seek justice for his sister, Monique, and all throughout he maintained his decorum. He had never addressed Franklin, and this was a moment he had been waiting for for more than two decades.

"Growing up, getting that news that my sister wouldn't be coming home no longer, I wasn't able to make that funeral," he said. "So a lot of times in life I started to go to the dark side because I didn't know then what was what. I mean, my father always taught us to do the right thing, to try and treat everyone right. Now here it is, my baby sister. One minute you turn your head and she is gone. We don't have any answers. For twenty-five years we wondered, you know, who did it? Where is she? What happened? Now, come to find out that we have a man that's out there; that he found it upon himself to take the lives of grandmothers, aunties, sisters. We don't understand that.

"We try to find in ourselves, even now, not to hate anyone," he continued. "You know. This is what I have to deal with, to try to balance, you know, saying where do I want to go in the next life? Will I see my sister again? And this is something I have to continue to talk about, to reflect and to make sure that I don't get this spirit of hate in me because of what he done to our family."

Donnell said he hoped the victims' families could find the strength to move ahead from the hate.

"We can't do anything about the past," he said. "But we did have a jury that sat there and thought about everything that he done to each one of them victims. And we appreciate the time and the effort that you put in that . . . And we believe in this system, and we know it works."

Donnell left his last words for Franklin. "And for Lonnie, this is the last time that you hurt a black mother or sister or child or anything like that. And I just thank you guys for hearing us. Thank you."

Donnell's mother, Mary, went next and asked Franklin to look at her.

"I would like for Mr. Franklin to turn around and look—face me," she said.

Franklin actually looked over his shoulder at her.

"I'd like to know, why?" she said. "What did Alicia Monique do to you? I would like to know that. I know she was such a—she was just a loving person. Wouldn't hurt anyone. And I would like to know why you did it."

Franklin looked directly at her. "I didn't do it," he said.

"I know she didn't do anything to hurt you," continued Mary, dismissing Franklin's utterance. "I'm sure of that, and I know I'm supposed to forgive, to love everyone and to forgive. And I am still battling that. I asked God to help me in forgiving you. But it's hard. Right now I don't see that forgiveness because you did so much wrong. Not only my daughter; all of these others. And I used to say all the time, 'I really don't think everybody has a heart and conscience.' But my husband would tell me, 'Oh, yeah they do.' I say, 'No, they can't, to do the things that they do in this world.' No conscience, you know, to harm other people, in, like, just throwing a piece of paper in the trash.

"It is horrible," she said, pausing to stare at him. "It is hard. And I would like to say I love my daughter. I miss her very much. I know I'll never get over it because I just, I just think about her all the time. I wake up in the night thinking about missing her. Sometimes, the sad times, I cry. Sometimes happy things that I remember. And it's just sad. But I thank God that I lived to see this day, because I know some of the parents didn't make it. And I'm praying for their family. And I want to thank you all."

Diana Ware, who along with the Alexanders had in many ways become the voice of the victims, hobbled, slightly bent over, to the podium next.

"When Mr. Franklin killed her, he extinguished the promise and potential of a 23-year-old single mother who had begun to turn her life around," she said, angrily. "He brutally murdered her, a beloved mother, daughter, baby sister, niece, cousin, and friend. A hole has been left in our family that has never been filled.

"We won't get closure, but through the grace of God, we get peace, a devastating pain in the heart of her father who passed away in 2002, never knowing that she was the victim of a serial killer.

"Not only our family was affected, but all of these people . . . probably half of the ones are not here today. They were loved. And they will be missed. They weren't trash, like you did most of them."

And like Mary Alexander, she asked, "I'd like to know why you did it. What was in your mind?"

Franklin didn't bother to look her way.

"I hope you have remorse, but I pray to God that I can—I do forgive you because I have to forgive you because the Lord says to forgive you. But I can't forget. And it's hard for me, and I pray every day to make it easier.

"Barbara had left a young child. She doesn't even remember her mother. It has been devastating. She died a terrible death, a violent visitation upon her person, a sexual assault. A shot through the heart. And then he discarded her like trash."

Diana told the judge that she believed that Barbara had known her killer.

"I think she had seen him around," she said, voicing out loud what she long suspected. "And she thought she was safe, but he was a wolf in sheep's clothing."

Then, addressing the jury, she said: "We, the family of Barbara, we thank the jury for the ultimate penalty that you gave him for taking her life, for stealing her tomorrows. There will be no wedding, no other children. There's an empty seat at our table at Thanksgiving. No presents to give or receive at Christmas. No cookouts at Labor Day or July 4. No family reunions. No birthday parties. No more memories made. But she'll always be in our heart."

And then, looking toward Franklin one last time, she said: "And I pray for your soul, Mr. Franklin, because you will meet our Savior one day, and you will have to answer to him. Thank you."

The next family member to speak was Vivian Williams, the sister of Georgia Mae Thomas.

"Lonnie, would you look this way, please?" asked Vivian. "I know you remember me."

"I have never seen her before in my life," said Franklin, glancing briefly toward Vivian.

"I remember waving at you," said Vivian.

"I ain't never saw you before," Franklin insisted.

"I used to wave at you," Vivian said.

"You never waved at me," said Franklin. "You a boldface liar."

"You knew her," said Vivian, unfazed. "I forgive you for killing her. I do. I forgive you because my Bible tells me that that's what I have to do. And I pray that you ask God to forgive you because that's what you need to do because you have done some horrible things.

"And you walked into this room and looked at us and looked straight ahead as though you thought you were God," she continued. "You sat here all prideful because you have done some horrible things. You have taken something that you couldn't give back. You have caused so much pain to so many people. Now you sit there and you act as though we owe you something. But you know what? All of us sat here today and we feel sorry for you in our own way, even though we hurt, because you've taken something from us.

"Every August 30 is my sister's birthday. And you know what? I'll think about you, too, because I'll remember it's your birthday also. I will. And because of the Jesus in me, I'll feel sorry for your family because they can't celebrate with you. I can't celebrate with my sister, and neither will your family be able to actually celebrate with you.

"You may be mean and hard on the outside, but on the inside I know that you are broken and you are hurting, just like all of us. So instead of the hardness, you may as well let us know you want us to pray for you, too. You don't have to ask us; when we pray, we'll ask God to help you because we know that you stand in the need of prayer. We know that you really need to be delivered."

And that was the last word from the victims' families, the brutalized collateral damage from Lonnie Franklin's Grim Sleeper rampage.

CHAPTER 36
SAN QUENTIN

IT WAS NOW JUDGE KATHLEEN Kennedy's turn to address Franklin, and she got right to the point.

"All right, Lonnie Franklin, the time has come.

"All of the family members that have wanted to speak have had a chance, and I spent a lot of time thinking about you and your case and all of the evidence that was heard," she told Franklin.

"And I've asked myself, as I'm sure many of the people in this audience have asked themselves, and I have heard expressed today, is why? Why did all of this happen? Why did you do all of these things?

"All of these women were defenseless. They were not a threat to you in any way, shape, or form. And after thinking about it and pondering it and going over it in my mind, I have come to this conclusion: that it doesn't matter why. There could never be a justification for what you've done. Because what you've done is not justifiable under the laws of God or the laws of man.

"And so it doesn't matter why, although I'm curious and I'm sure books will be written and maybe psychiatrists or psychologists will examine this and come up with some kind of a theory to explain it.

"I mean, it's obvious that you have a deep-seated hatred for women that started long ago. I mean, the first crime that we heard about was the rape of the woman from Germany that occurred in 1974. So this hatred of women is long and deep-seated. Why? I don't know.

"And I want it to be clear that even though all of these crimes that you have committed are horrible, and, as I said, without any kind of justification, the sentence that I'm about to impose is not a sentence of vengeance.

"I believe that a society has the right to make the determination that when someone has committed crimes that are as horrible as these crimes are, that society can say that person, as a punishment and as a protection for others, does not deserve to continue to live.

"And I can't think of anyone that I have encountered, in all my many years in the criminal-justice system, that has committed the kind of monstrous and the number of monstrous crimes that you have. These murders of these young women were horrible. And the attempted murder of Miss Washington, all horrible, and the effect of which all of these people have been suffering and will continue to suffer. But, hopefully, as many of them said, they feel they are going to receive some peace.

"And I hope that you are able to leave here with some peace today. But it's not vengeance; it's justice, Mr. Franklin.

"And so, Lonnie Franklin Jr.," Kennedy said, picking up a piece of paper to read, "For the first-degree murder of Debra Jackson as alleged in count one and the special circumstance of multiple murder, it is the judgment and sentence of this court that you shall suffer the death penalty.

"For the first-degree special-circumstance murder of Henrietta Wright as alleged in count two, it is the judgment and sentence of this court that you shall suffer the death penalty.

"For the first-degree and special-circumstance murder of Barbara

Ware as alleged in count three, it is the judgment and sentence of this court that you shall suffer the death penalty.

"For the first-degree special-circumstance murder of Bernita Sparks as alleged in count four, it is the judgment and sentence of this court that you shall suffer the death penalty.

"For the first-degree special-circumstance murder of Mary Lowe as alleged in count five, it is the judgment and sentence of this court that you shall suffer the death penalty.

"For the first-degree special-circumstance murder of Lachrica Jefferson as alleged in count six, it is the judgment and sentence of this court that you shall suffer the death penalty.

"For the first-degree special-circumstance murder of Alicia Alexander as alleged in count seven, it is the judgment and sentence of this court that you shall suffer the death penalty.

"For the first-degree special-circumstance murder of Princess Berthomieux as alleged in count nine, it is the judgment and sentence of this court that you shall suffer the death penalty.

"For the first-degree special-circumstance murder of Valerie McCorvey as alleged in count ten, it is the sentence of this court that you shall suffer the death penalty.

"And for the first-degree special-circumstance murder of Janecia Peters as alleged in count eleven, it is the judgment and sentence of this court that you shall suffer the death penalty."

On top of these death sentences, Franklin also received a life term for the attempted murder of Enietra Washington, count 8.

Kennedy next told Franklin that he would be delivered within the coming ten days from the custody of the L.A. County Sheriff's Department that handles the jails in Los Angeles to the warden of the maximum-security state penitentiary at San Quentin.

"All right, the defendant is remanded at this time," said Kennedy. "And thank all of you."

And with that, the case of Lonnie Franklin Jr., which dated back more than thirty years, was over. It was a good day for Los Angeles.

• • •

It was a good day for me, too, but an emotionally draining day at the same time. This case didn't go back thirty years for me, but it had consumed me for the last ten years—a major chunk of my life. I had seen senseless murder up close and witnessed how it ravaged families. I watched how the acts of one sick man shaped the lives of those left to live in his wake. When he ended these women's lives, he set off a chain reaction that had devastating consequences. He irrevocably changed their loved ones forever, leaving human shells where vibrant beings once existed.

So, on this day when Lonnie Franklin Jr. met justice, I felt a weight lift; the hold that this dark, sad story had on me for so long finally let up. My only regret—one I am sure I share with the victims' family members—is never finding out what drove Franklin to commit such heinous crimes.

• • •

On August 17, 2016, Lonnie Franklin Jr., 64, was admitted to San Quentin's death row, an alley that for him has only one way out.

ACKNOWLEDGMENTS

This book could not have been written without the help of the victims' families and friends who lived through the nightmare of losing someone close to them. I am extremely grateful to them for sharing their stories. They include Diana Ware; the Alexander family; Romy Lampkins; Laverne Peters; Samara Herard; Jermaine Jackson; Lucinda Nobles; Rochell Johnson, Alice Brown, Irvin Forrest; and Irene Ephriam.

I also want to extend my deep appreciation to LAPD detectives Rich Haro, Cliff Shepard, Paul Coulter, Dennis Kilcoyne and Daryn Dupree. Your dedication to the case was inspiring.

Special thanks to prosecutors Marguerite Rizzo, Beth Silverman and defense attorneys Seymour Amster and Louisa Pensanti for sharing their valuable time with me.

And with gratitude to Enietra Washington, a strong woman who opened up to me and re-lived painful details from the most traumatic episode of her life.

To Jeff Weingrad and my dear friend Gale Holland for their editorial acumen and Brenda Shelton, Monica Clark and Sabrina Ford for their research and fact-checking prowess. Thanks to my sister Amanda and my friends Alexis Keefe, Sandy Cohen and Deborah Vankin for their support and stopping me from jumping off a cliff.

Most of all, I want to thank my good friend and extremely talented editor Kate Robertson for her help and guidance throughout this journey. Her contribution was indispensable. I could not have started or finished this book without her.